This book is dedicated
to the memory of
Christine Mary Morson
who died on
15 February, 2000

A FORCE
REMEMBERED

The Illustrated History of the Norwich City Police 1836-1967

A FORCE REMEMBERED

The Illustrated History of the Norwich City Police 1836-1967

Maurice Morson

The Breedon Books
Publishing Company
Derby

First published in Great Britain by
The Breedon Books Publishing Company Limited
Breedon House, 44 Friar Gate, Derby, DE1 1DA.
2000

by the same author:

A City's Finest
The Lost Years

ISBN 1 85983 190 7

Printed and bound by Butler & Tanner Ltd., Selwood Printing Works, Caxton
Road, Frome, Somerset.

Colour separations and jacket printing by
GreenShires Group Ltd, Leicester.

Contents

Foreword

THE years 1967-68 brought to an end the long and proud history of most small City and Borough Police Forces. Amalgamation of forces trumpeted on the back of efficiency paved the way for the 1974 Reorganisation and even now calls for a regional police reminds the reader that change is the only constant.

Thirty-two years on Norwich City Police is not forgotten. Its spirit is restless and new legislation – The Crime and Disorder Act – reminds the Constabulary that their strength lies in their community. So poignant a signal that once again police are reorganising command structures to complement the old order.

But Norwich City Police never lost its identity. Despite being consumed into a larger Constabulary and divisional boundaries being drawn to encompass the larger conurbation of Norwich, architects of change failed to acknowledge the power of History and the seductive pull identity has on a proud body of men and women. Such pride is well founded and *A Force Remembered* will provide a real reference for nostalgia and service pride. To those who love the City and the Constabulary and those with an insatiable appetite for local history this work is essential reading. The author masterfully brings to life the challenging world of policing. The context provided gives a vivid picture of the times and perhaps challenges those who cry romantically for policing to return to the way it was 'when I was a boy' – to think again.

Maurice Morson has opened our eyes. We are grateful.

Kenneth R.Williams.
Chief Constable of Norfolk, 1999.

Author's Notes and Acknowledgements

The photographs and pictures within this book are copyright or source credited where the information is known. Any fresh information received will be duly acknowledged and will be referenced in the archives of the Norfolk Constabulary, eventually, hopefully, to form the basis for a police museum in a new police headquarters.

Photographs and illustrations are captioned with information that has been obtained from records and through interviews, but in some cases details are incomplete and in others what has been ascertained remains doubtful or contradictory. Where the photograph remains important it is used and any doubts or contradictions are passed on to the reader. Some officers are identified by magnifying their collar number but this is fallible when the exact date of the photograph is unknown and accordingly some are left to the safety of anonymity.

This is a book written by one person and constructed by many.

Alan Brown, former member of the Norwich City Police and collector of memorabilia and fine photographs, pursued the objective of an illustrated history of the force with an enthusiasm that will be familiar to his colleagues, past and present. It is fair to say that this book would not have happened without his persistence. I am grateful for the idea, the persistence, and the time he so enthusiastically gave to researching the project.

The book would not have been written in such depth and detail without the dedication and application of John (Cecil) Mason, another former member of the Norwich City Police, now archivist to the Norfolk Constabulary. His database of information, tenacious research and time consuming detective work provided a vital platform of knowledge that kept the project on course. I am grateful for his major contribution.

I acknowledge the powers of recall, the willingness to help and the time given by the 'old brigade', the Norwich police officers of a very long yesteryear. Ernie Croxson and George Piercy were tireless and unfailing in their study of specimen chapters and scrutiny of photographs, fielding questions and withstanding probing visits with equanimity. In thanking them I also record my gratitude to Stan Abbott, Bob Bunting, Philip Hemmings, Willie Hobson, Tom Jones and Don and Audrey Martin who studied photographs and proffered information concerning times long ago, all of which proved vital.

My thanks go in no less measure to all retired officers and spouses who assisted: Andy Anderson, Vic Austin, Beryl Baker, Roger Brighton, Dudley Brook, Barry Catchpole, Eric Bussey, Daphne Cullington, Peter Ever-est, John Fletcher (now sadly deceased), Neville Garnham, Terry George, Margaret Goffin (also now sadly deceased), Jack and Joan Green, Ken Grist, Mike Henry, Cliff Jessop, Johnnie Johnson, Basil Kybird, Stan and Brenda Limmer, Terry Moore, Dick Pitt, Gordon Rooney, Cyril Scott, Don Seager, John Southgate, Ken Statham and Jean Stimpson (Duffy).

Some deceased Norwich City officers left legacies of stories, photographs and documents and I am grateful to their relatives for volunteering and allowing these to be used. History has been well served by the understanding and co-operation of Graham Burton, Geoffrey Christie, Christopher Ewing, Christine Fisk, Rachel Fleming, Joyce Fletcher and daughter Louise, Rita Fowler, Peter Harris, Bernard and Herbert Harrison, Barbara Huntingdon, Marjorie Marten, Patricia Monteath, Violet North, Eric Page, Duncan and Jenny Pigg, Monica Reid, Alan Rix, Margaret Salt and Joan Watts.

To the Chief Constable of the Norfolk Constabulary, Mr Kenneth Williams, go my thanks for the freedom of the police archives and the facilities provided to delve into the depths of the past. In this context my special thanks go to Ian Munday of the force photographic department who unstintingly gave of his time to copy old photographs.

I am grateful to Chief Superintendent Roger Sandall for his assistance at Bethel Street Police Station and to Derek James, the Features Editor of Norwich's own newspaper, the *Eastern Evening News*, who researched and circulated information, and retrieved photographs that otherwise would not have been found.

Many helped in varying ways, from many different standpoints, through information, pictures, documents and articles. I am pleased to acknowledge the help given by Capricorn Cameras, the Crome Gallery, Norfolk Fire Service, Norfolk Reference Library, Norfolk Public Record Office, Norwich Castle Museum, Norwich Cathedral Library, Norwich City Council Cemeteries' Office, Royal Norfolk Regimental Museum, John Brister, Trevor Clarke, Sergeant Kevin Clark, Richard Clements, Mr R.M.Cork, Mike Dixon, Detective Sergeant John Eglen, Peter French, Inspector Jimmy James, Stella Jordan, Maurice Kent, Harry King, Constable Mel Lacey, Judith Maxted, Peter Murray, Peter Pilgrim, Constance Roe and Anthony Williamson.

And an in-house thank you to Christine Morson for her interest and support and to Neil Morson for his valuable time and computer expertise.

To all those who took an interest, advised or helped in any way, whether named or not, I am grateful. Every piece of assistance was appreciated.

Introduction

THIS is a story of professionalism from humble beginnings, respect engendered from historic adversity. The police of today are born of difficult and troubled times and so it was with Norwich, a fine city progressively developing a fine police force that was eventually to lose its identity in the name of progress. The pioneering yesteryear, when the force began, and the day nearly 132 years later when it finished as a city entity, is a story of wide differences but a common purpose that continues to this present day.

A complete authoritative record of all who served in the Norwich City Police does not exist, though the present police archives come very near. Neither is there a chronological and definitive list of events, episodes and incidents. This history of the force is, therefore, not encyclopaedic but a reflection, mirroring the force as accurately as possible from its beginning to its end. It is built from official minutes, memoranda and reports, unofficial notes, press reports, various articles and documents, family mementoes, memories – personal and written, and, above all, photographs – many photographs. From this treasure trove of pictorial history came the opportunity, recognised and voiced by several persons, to prospect, discover and deliver the past. A picture speaks a thousand words.

Today, training and teamwork dominate policing. Officers at Carrow Road football ground control a crowd of 20,000 (at best), aided by CCTV and radio. At night, the overstated Riot Squad tours sensitive city areas to put down public disturbances, which are usually minor confrontations arising from drunkenness.

Nevertheless, they are prepared. They use vans specially equipped to repel a crowd assault. In addition, beat patrol cars and fast response cars are equipped with radios, sirens and illuminated signs, firearms in some cases. Officers are equipped with shields, batons, gas canisters, visors, body armour and, of course, radios. They are part of a large, well-trained police force: the Norfolk Constabulary, a divisional component of which applies itself to the city of Norwich and, if necessary, calls reinforcements or specialists from its environs in the county of Norfolk. And before?

Until 31 December 1967, the police force was special and specific to the city of Norwich. They also kept order, maintained the Queen's (or King's) peace and the law, and had done so with the inadequate tools of the different ages, dealing with, at times, an unappreciative society and people racked by poverty, war and civil unrest. They walked in isolation, relying on a stick and whistle, graduating to horses and cycles, then motor vehicles, summoned by the occasion, the complainant or a crowd, then a telephone beckoning light, gradually developing a rapport with the city they served. The city police evolved through more than a century of invention and fast moving change to become well staffed, well equipped and well respected. It was the foundation of what can be seen today. Its history has not previously been written. It deserves to be. What is seen today was born of yesterday.

If I have seen further it is by standing on the shoulders of giants.
Isaac Newton

(ECN)

CHAPTER ONE
The New Police
A beginning and troubled progress

In 1820, the 'owners and occupiers' of the city of Norwich met in the Guildhall to state that crime was rife and honest men were at their wit's end. If they made a decision of purpose at that meeting then it has escaped record or notice, and honest men seemingly remained at their wit's end, for several years.

It began for Norwich in January 1836 with the firmly stated intention to appoint a body of trained, efficient and disciplined men to professionally police the city. The Municipal Corporations Act of 1835 pointed the way.

A Council was elected and in turn spawned a Watch Committee. They met, 12 members, chaired by the Mayor, and agreed the creation of a police force. The sequence of notable January dates is recorded as, confirmation of intention 4/5th, appointment 18th and swearing-in 22nd.

It is a matter of record through the *Norfolk Chronicle* that 'on Tuesday last (1 March) the new police commenced duty under Superintendent Wright'. It was not seen as an event of great importance, being accorded a passing mention only.

The early days, and years, were difficult. Some of the newly-appointed Constables fell short of the disciplined efficiency required (one having been appointed failed to make the starting date), and many of the founder members laid foundations in public houses. A predilection to strong drink was to curse the force for many years.

The new policemen were required to be of an age between 25 and 50 years, a minimum height of 5ft 6ins and in good health. The starting number was 18, supplemented by 32 night watchmen, an organisation already operating within the city walls. In 1839 the police were increased to 24.

A John Moll is listed in the original 18 and there is a record of a John Moll, aged 33 years, 'having not succeeded in business', being, in 1833, 'extremely desirous' of joining the Metropolitan Police. His reference from 'J.J.Gurney, Banker, Norwich' describes him as 'strong and healthy in body and bears the character of an honest and industrious man'. John Moll was later to appear in Norwich City Police disciplinary records for drunkenness; not a career block because in 1848 he was an Inspector. That was, however, the end. He was dismissed the service suffering from heart disease and given a gratuity of 6s in appreciation of long service and good conduct.

There were reserves, six supernumeraries, to be taken up as and when vacancies occurred, which was frequently. The Watch Committee resolved on 8 September 1837 that 'the committee shall fill all vacancies which may hereafter occur in the police force from the most capable and deserving of the supernumeraries'. The problem was they could not always agree who among the supernumeraries fitted that description and rotated candidates in the post of Constable over a period of weeks before making a selection.

Pay for the new Constables was 15s (75p) per week with 1s (5p) stopped for clothing, despite the fact they had to provide their own trousers, which had to be ankle strapped and of a uniform matching colour. (In 1847 the 1s stoppage for clothing was suspended for three months because of the 'high cost of foodstuffs'.) Three Sergeants got an extra 2s 6d per week from 1837.

The new police were issued with a dark blue swallow-tailed coat, a leather top hat, greatcoat, cape, belt, lanthorn, truncheon, rattle and handcuffs. Notebooks were issued in 1838, whistles in 1860. Both lasted the duration of the force, whistles more in an ornamental capacity.

So equipped, and not altogether welcomed, they went forth to battle against the forces of lawlessness and disorder, of which there were many examples. Crime, drunkenness, violence, vagrancy, and other miscellaneous threats to the peace abounded. Constables on patrol were sometimes physically attacked because they 'interfered' and sometimes, simply because they were Constables. Verbal abuse was hurled, along with more substantial items, hats were tipped off – thrown in the river on one occasion with the intention that the two dispossessed Constables should follow them, and generally there was less than a rapturous welcome for the new order.

Eleven years after inception the Watch Committee recorded a note of public recognition and appreciation of the force, and dissatisfaction. Mr Girling of Earlham Road complained of the absence of the police (a cry not unfamiliar to police forces in 1999). In November 1847 the response to this complaint was exceptional, certain to be unmatched by today's police force. The Watch Committee ordered that the beat Constable passing Mr Girling's house should ring his doorbell.

The new police, and their problems, should be seen in the context of the period in which they began. The populace was generally poor and uneducated, not that the police were very different, and it was a time of industrial decline in the city when ale was cheap and freely available, vagrancy was rife and disturbances and riots were not uncommon. It was the age in which Charles Dickens lived, sanitation, public lighting and made up roads were minimal or non-existent, and a coach journey to London was a day's exhausting experience. Hanging and transportation were among punishments meted out by the courts, treadmills were in use, a court heard a complaint of witchcraft in all seriousness and an inquest ruled that a four month-old baby had died of starvation.

Public hangings were still carried out at Norwich Castle, watched by an exulting noisy crowd, many travelling from afar for the spectacle, on foot or by horse and carriage, families seeking a special day out in the city and determined not to miss the main event.

They thronged the castle area infused with anticipation fostered and surreally overlaid by the solemn tolling of the bell of St Peter Mancroft. Here the new police force gained its crowd control experience.

The size and jollity of these morbid crowds did not escape the attention of the authorities, possibly reported upon by the police, and steps were taken to reduce the attendance. What was to be the last public hanging in Norwich, in 1867, was unusually set at eight o'clock in the morning to deter the number of spectators, a plan that did not work. This execution was described in the public notice that followed as taking place in front of 'a large assembled concourse'. For the benefit of those who could not be there the notice also described in detail the trembling prisoner's passage to the scaffold and his final waiting moments. And the black flag was still hoisted above the castle after the trapdoor had clattered open. Such were the times.

Hangings became private affairs, later transferred to the newly-built prison at Mousehold where the press still witnessed the execution, and still reported in great and gruesome detail. Following the execution of George Watt on 12 July 1898 for the shooting of his wife at Sprowston, a press report said, 'A small body of police on duty outside the prison walls could distinctly hear the drop and the sound of it had hardly died away when one of the officers (Constable Peacock) fainted away into the arms of his comrades standing near'.

The first criminal statistics, from 25 December 1837 to 25 December 1838, show that the police dealt with 69 felonies, 56 assaults, 113 disorderly persons and 5 cases of uttering false coins.

Fees were paid for some extra duties, which included arrests, and this must have inevitably led to a predatory instinct among those with a financial eye. A sliding scale of class distinction prevailed. A vagrant or disorderly person only counted 1s while a felon committed for trial was worth 5s, 3s 6d if not committed. Searches where goods (presumably stolen) were found paid 5s, 3s if goods were not found. On the downside was a scale of fines for being late on parade: ten minutes equalled 6d, half an hour was 1s and one hour warranted suspension until the next Watch Committee meeting. The early policeman was not short of incentives.

In January 1838 Sergeant Peck presented to the

Watch Committee a 'petition signed by him', 'on behalf of all the force', thanking them for the gratuity granted. This possibly says something about the literacy of the force as well as their gratitude for the generous award of 2s 6d to each police and watch member 'for coronation duties'.

The uniformed night watchmen also received fees for extra duties, though at a lower rate, and one can only surmise at the degree of competitiveness that might have existed.

In May 1838 all the watchmen were ordered before the Watch Committee and instructed not to act as policemen when off duty, 'until called upon'. They must then produce staves and make themselves known to Constables to prevent mistakes. A record cannot be found of an incident that might have inspired this order, possibly lost in embarrassment. Visions of flailing truncheons in a civil war of mistaken identities!

In 1852 the watchmen were officially incorporated into the regular force though they had effectively been integrated before then. There is a record of the Superintendent of the Night Watch being required to do duty in the 'station house' in the absence of the Superintendent of the Police and, in September 1839, '2 Superintendents and 30 Constables' were on duty for Festival week – '40 on the night of the ball'. Constables William Sharpe and Isaac Rudman were suspended for being drunk at the Festival.

Superintendent Wright gave notice that he would leave on 24 December 1839, following which a committee was formed to make the police 'more efficient at less cost'. Nothing more is known of this committee.

A Constable, according to rules of 1840, 'must be cautious but act with coolness, firmness and promptitude. He must always have perfect command of temper, never suffering himself to be irritated or moved by ill language or threats.' To the very end the word 'promptitude' was much loved by those who made rules and regulations.

Promptitude and other attributes continued to be rivalled by indiscipline and inefficiency. Drunkenness was a reoccurring theme. One Constable was dismissed for 'being found working his beat with his arm round the waist of a woman' and another was 'severely dealt with' for 'singing on duty'. Another Constable

was dismissed for 'sitting down on doorsteps while on duty'. The offence of Constable Edmund Hazell was more intriguing. He was 'allowed to resign' because he had permitted 'a female servant to enter her master's house by ladder at night'.

Constable Lacey was suspended for 14 days for publicly insulting Sergeant Peck and Constable Godfrey Weston, who appears to have committed no specific offence, was 'cautioned to improve himself in intelligence'.

Constable Lovett was suspended for one week in 1840 for being drunk at the end of his tour of duty, but the Watch Committee noted 'under extenuating circumstances'. We will never know what they were.

Pity the poor Constables who signed their pay book in the wrong place and were fined 1s. The offence was absolute, the penalty mandatory, and some officers offended with misplaced signatures more than once.

The saddest case was that of Constable Quantrill who joined the Night Watch in 1836 and was dismissed in 1843 because of the bad character of his two sons. In consequence of his own good behaviour he was granted a gratuity of £1.

Constable Samuel Watts, appointed on 25 January 1836 to replace the appointee who had failed to make the starting date, managed 11 disciplinary convictions which saw him reprimanded, suspended, admonished, discharged and re-appointed, and eventually discharged again in 1843 never to be taken back. One of his misdeeds was taking a prisoner to jail via a public house.

In 1858 Constable Noller handcuffed and took his prisoner directly to the police station, and wished he hadn't. The Constable was fined 30s and suspended for seven days for being drunk. It is not known what happened to the prisoner.

Constable Bailey was dismissed for a breach of the peace and fighting in public while Constable Smith was reprimanded for 'lack of courage in apprehension of a prisoner'. Tough times!

Some Constables were in a trade or business, some had political affiliations, and there is reason to suppose that one or more had a criminal conviction. Scrounging, favouring and touting for 'Christmas boxes' and fees were noted. This appeared not to upset

Watch Committee. The record shows that in December 1837 they declined to interfere in police matters 'in respect of them soliciting for offerings'. Further strange thinking of the time was revealed in their edict: 'a policeman is to attend the collector of the Cattle Market. Any attempt to take fees or gratuities will result in dismissal on second offence.' Punishment for the first offence was not decreed.

On the occasion of the force inspection at St Andrew's Hall on 27 October 1848 the Watch Committee expressed satisfaction with the efficiency and discipline of the entire force and ordered that each man receive a pint of beer. This generous, and reckless, gesture appears at odds with their statements of displeasure a short time later, in January 1849, when they issued numerous reprimands and threats to dismiss officers who were required to 'improve themselves', 'to be more alert' and 'improve their intelligence'.

Superintendent Dunne, who became chief officer in 1851 was concerned about what he called 'disreputable and disgraceful practices'.

There is some evidence that those charged with providing a police force, and equipping it with uniforms, tried to reduce the initial cost and unwisely supplied clothing that looked the part but failed to resist the weather. The new force paraded under the gaze of the press but it rained heavily and the shrinkage of uniforms that followed was excessive, so much so that, according to the press report, 'the police had difficulty in appearing decent'.

In 1847 the force petitioned to be supplied with boots and an extra pair of thick 'trowsers' for night duty. 41 pairs of boots were obtained at a cost of £20 10s. In this same year George Womack tended to supply 41 pairs of 'white duck trousers'.

Thinness of material was not apparently the problem of the time, more an uncomfortable heavy cloth. One member of the force grumbled that his trousers stood up by themselves.

An 1845 order required the cloth for Inspector's uniforms to be of a superior quality.

At the quarterly inspection of the police force at St Andrew's Hall in August 1853, reported in the *Norwich Chronicle*, 'the Watch Committee discovered that the greatcoats and capes of half the men in the force were in a wretched condition, not fit to be worn

by day'. The strength of the force was then given as '61 Constables and 12 officers'.

After this inspection Mr Bignold (Watch Committee) addressed the men, pointing out the 'necessity of sobriety and attention to their duties'. The press went further. They concluded, 'There is a well grounded impression existing among the inhabitants that the class of men who have lately joined the force, although of good character are not possessed of those attributes and qualifications, shrewdness, activity and intelligence, so indispensably necessary for a police officer employed in a densely populated city like Norwich'. Reporting that 50 men had left the force since January 1852 (some discharged) the press advised improvements in 'pay and other establishments'.

In 1855 the swallow-tailed long coat, described as

Police Constable c.1850. (Force archives)

unsightly, gave way to a frock coat and in 1879 the uniform was modified again, the frock coat and ankle-strapped trousers giving way to a short coat and what today would be more easily known as trousers. Most significant of all was the introduction of the famous helmet in 1871. This headgear in succeeding years was to be variously adorned with badges, spikes, chains and combs, with varying degrees of polishing and blackening required, and was ingeniously to serve as a useful receptacle for many officers. Confirmed incidences of its carrying and hiding ability include a bottle of ale and a bread roll.

In 1879 permission was granted for greatcoats to be left off during the three months commonly deputed as summer.

Uniforms proved troublesome to the end of the century. In the 1890s the force practised physical discrimination by appointing only applicants who fitted the uniforms available.

The 1890s formed part of a period of open dissatisfaction over conditions and facts of service (see fol-

lowing chapter), and inadequate uniforms had their place. Letters to the local press and Police Review, under pseudonyms, referred to 'very inferior material wet through after a shower of half an hour's duration'. New cloth capes were apparently of better material and were worn at the 1894 annual inspection, but then forbidden to be worn again by order of the Chief Constable; not until the next inspection in the opinion of one letter writer.

Not all the pseudonyms of letter writers disguised serving policemen. An 1895 letter to the Eastern Daily Press was signed 'One in the Trade' and bemoaned the lack of quality in issued police boots, saying, 'Nothing is so piteous as to see officers walking as though they had hard uncooked peas in their boots'.

Boots were briefly supplied as part of the uniform but for most of the force's history they had to be supplied by the officer, assisted by an allowance that remained inadequate at all times. Help was offered in 1919 when the Chief Clerk's office issued a memorandum advising all beat Constables that the force was in

The Guildhall c.1840.

possession of a quantity of disused tyres suitable for repairing boots.

A lower room at the eastern end of Guildhall was the first police station. In succeeding years a growing force with growing responsibilities was at varying times to additionally use a number of premises in the city. Various buildings in Pope's Head Yard, Lower Goat Lane, St Giles' Street, Bethel Street, St Peter's Street, Gentleman's Walk and Pottergate are documented.

This era of geographical piecemeal policing continued well into the next century, even after the Bethel Street Police Station came into use in 1938. Yards and rooms in buildings in Bethel Street, Lady Lane and the top of Hay Hill were improvised for lectures and storage of vehicles and property, until they were pulled down to begin a new library and car park – pulled down in turn after a disastrous fire in 1994.

Nineteenth-century records reveal specialist policing with Constables permanently appointed to the markets, railway, Corn Exchange and Carrow Works.

In 1861 a flint-faced extension was built on the south side of the Guildhall to accommodate the Town Clerk's offices, the Chief Constable's office, a waiting room and two cells. Later, an internal re-organisation caused the Chief Constable to move elsewhere in the Guildhall but to this day the words 'Norwich Chief Constable' can be seen carved in the stone surround facing London Street and Gentleman's Walk. In 1999 it overlooks a parade of taxis, and sometimes a collection of languishing itinerants.

Records show that rooms in Pope's Head Yard (off St Peter's Street) were used as cells during the 1861 alterations to the Guildhall. These records do not confirm other reports that restoration work on the Guildhall caused the police to temporarily move into public houses on the Market Place, places not unfamiliar to them.

Superintendent Wright, the first chief officer of the Norwich City Police, was but a brief appointment. Superintendent Yarrington replaced him in 1839, creating some historical confusion because there were two Yarringtons, William and his son, Peter. William was Superintendent of the Night Watch and he apparently used his position to secure a post for his son in the new police force, following which the son was appointed Superintendent. According to 1840 records the Superintendent of Police was paid £20 per quarter year and the Superintendent of Watch £13 per quarter year.

The Yarringtons were to be well tested. On 16 June 1848, 11 prisoners in the City Gaol at St Giles completed a sentence of 21 days imposed for disorderly conduct and were released. As inmates of the workhouse situated at St Andrews they had objected to the workhouse rule that separated them from their wives and families and had protested, and been imprisoned. Their imprisonment was not, however, the end of the matter. Upon release they remained unhappy and roamed the city generating support and sympathy, becoming part of a mob of 200-300 persons. They solicited money by thrusting collecting boxes into faces, later drinking the proceeds in Pockthorpe public houses.

At 7pm they went to the workhouse and were admitted, provided with supper and allowed to be with their wives, themselves showing some indignation as reports of their husbands' progress had filtered through.

At 9pm the Master of the Workhouse requested they retire separately and the previous dispute flared again. The men refused. The Mayor, George Coleman, already on notice because of the earlier rowdy progress of the men, was called in with Magistrates, Mr Bolingbroke and Captain Money. They went to the workhouse with a detachment of 40 police under Superintendent Peter Yarrington. A noisy, swelling crowd gathered outside the building.

The men were largely steadfast in their refusal to be separated, but one did agree and another was in any case to be moved with his wife to another establishment. The remaining nine were seemingly unconcerned at being given in charge to the police and the Mayor was later to say that they conveyed the attitude of expectation of rescue from the noisy crowd outside.

The police sought to move their prisoners to the City Gaol as soon as possible. The crowd, now estimated as in excess of 2,000, with hundreds more reported to be congregating in nearby streets, greeted their appearance with groans, hoots and jeers, while cheering any sign from the prisoners.

The police took the route of St Andrew's Broad

Street, Post Office Street and St Giles' Street, moving the prisoners by forming a square around them and moving off at 'double quick march time', the 'mob flying in all directions before them', according to the press.

Stones rained upon the fast-stepping police column, some striking the prisoners, and the missiles were accompanied by an incessant and terrific yelling, particularly from women seen with aprons bulging with stones: 'for the purpose of handing them to the men', noted the press.

The Mayor had ordered the gates of the City Gaol to be opened to receive the prisoners and escort on the run and, under a continual bombardment of noise and stones, the column pressed on. They made it without losing a prisoner; in fact they gained one. The Mayor arrested a stone thrower on the way.

The crowd remained outside the gaol, not inclined to disperse, still noisy and aggressive. They greeted the reappearance of the police with a volley of stones. A second volley followed and several Constables received injuries; at least four police hats were beaten in. The Mayor ordered the police to clear the streets and on a word of command, Inspector Peck is reported to have given the order 'right about face – quick march – go for them', the police formed a line three deep and went forward at 'full speed', truncheons drawn, driving the crowd before them.

The police dispersed the crowd in St Giles but were then stoned from the rear, at which point Constable Callow was struck on the head and helped into a nearby shop. The police wheeled and charged the stone throwers into Unthank Road then about-faced and fought infuriated pockets of stone and bottle throwers back along St Giles and into the Market Place, doubling back to clear Bethel Street.

As bleeding and injured police returned to the Guildhall, ordering abusive persons outside to leave, a Magistrate, Mr T.Springfield, appeared and, surprisingly, asked what was the matter with the police. He was told and Constable Stamp showed him his battered hat. Springfield replied, in the hearing of Captain Money and those shouting outside, that the police should not to be so officious and if bad laws were made they must take the consequences. Those shouting outside seemed pleased. Constable Stamp

reported the Magistrate's remark, supported by Captain Money.

The police casualty list included Constable Barnard with spinal injuries and Constables Day, Harman, Ecclestone and Callow with head wounds. Constable William Callow, the father of five children, died seven days later.

Some Councillors thought the police were drunk and a local journal thought that injuries received by the prisoners came from police truncheons rather than stones from the crowd. These assertions, and Mr Springfield's remark, were given an airing at the inquest upon Constable Callow, commenced at the Goldbeater's Arms in Bethel Street and adjourned to the Guildhall.

Superintendents William and Peter Yarrington gave evidence of the number of night watch and day Constables employed on the date in question, their refreshment and general disposition. The night watch was on duty for 12 hours and the day Constables 14 hours. In the morning their refreshment included two pints of porter per man. Men recalled in the afternoon were given a pint of beer and 4d worth of meat and bread. The Coroner was told that stand-by periods were occupied by drilling the men.

The Mayor gave evidence that the police were 'fair and determined and merely did their duty'. Captain Money said of the police he had 'never seen men behave better in his life' and a barrister witness, upon whose evidence the Coroner set great store, said the police acted with 'great forbearance'.

The Coroner adjourned the inquest again in order that those who believed the police had acted improperly could come forward. None came and at the resumed hearing the Coroner sent for Mr Springfield but he could not be found.

The jury found that William Callow had died from an infected head wound, possibly accelerated by the fact he had not been in good health previously, and recorded, 'wilful murder by person or persons unknown'. They added that they wished to record their unanimous approbation of the conduct of the police, believing that they acted with the greatest forbearance.

Those who had precipitated the disturbance, the recalcitrant nine from the workhouse, were variously dealt with. Ringleaders Jonathan Moore, William

Norwich City gaol – scene of events leading to the murder of a Norwich policeman.　　　(A.Brown)

Johnson, Robert Duffield and John Banham were given sentences of imprisonment with hard labour. The remaining five were discharged back to the workhouse under promises of good behaviour. The stone thrower captured by the Mayor, a William Wood, was fined £2.

Two other arrests were made from related fractious incidents. Constable Ecclestone tried to move Henry Bradbury on Gentleman's Walk and received a blow to the head for his trouble. Bradbury was fined £3.

The case of 'Mr. Williams of Heigham' was more complicated, occurring after the main event. He had berated police officers making enquiries in St Giles' Street upon the condition of Constable Callow, persistently calling them 'cowardly rascals', only desisting when Constable Thompson struck him in the mouth and then arrested him, facts not disputed by the Constable. Williams took his supporters to the court and told his story to the accompaniment of cries of 'shame, shame' from the public gallery. The Magistrate, Mr Hudson, ruled, 'If he (Williams) used that language the policeman served him perfectly right'. He then fined him £3.

Superintendent Yarrington, the police one, distinguished himself in 1849 by organising a police reception for a gang of notorious London pickpockets, incongruously known as 'The Swell Mob', travelling via the new railway to visit Norwich. One report says their intended visit coincided with the large crowd that was expected to welcome Jenny Lind and another report relates their visit to the even larger crowd expected at the public hanging at Norwich Castle of James Rush. Both reports are essentially correct. Jenny Lind was visiting and singing at St Andrew's Hall and James Rush was being hanged at Norwich Castle.

Norwich City Police had more than a passing interest in Rush, the convicted murderer of the Norwich Recorder Isaac Jermy and his son at Stanfield Hall, Wymondham. Constable John Mortar had effected the arrest of Rush shortly after news of the murders had been telegraphed from Wymondham.

The new railway brought the Swell Mob and the new telegraph brought the warning, and the new police did something about it. Again diverse reports: one recording that London detectives transferred the mob to the 'up train' at Attleborough but missed some who carried on to Norwich, another report merely indicating that the mob arrived at Thorpe Station. Possibly both reports are right. What is not in dispute is that the villains, so identified, were met at the railway station by Norwich police officers. From there reports diverge again with the mob being held in custody until the crowd, wherever, had dispersed or, in another version, they were promptly sent back whence they had come, in handcuffs. Again it is suggested the essential facts are correct and only the timing is left to conflicting historical record. Over a century and half later such forceful and effective action might attract comment from libertarian groups. It could be recorded as an early example of crime prevention.

The Swell Mob meet the city police, an artist's impression.
(T.George)

Superintendent Yarrington gave way to Superintendent Dunne in 1851, an officer who roundly condemned the discipline and efficiency of the force and engaged in some determined reform before resigning in 1852, then being reinstated and resigning again in 1853, saying that he had been 'so much obstructed by those who ought to have assisted in the discharge of his duties'. He further incurred the Watch Committee's displeasure by taking his official coat with him. They demanded it back for his successor, Superintendent English, and presumably got it.

Superintendent Dunne's reforming zeal included an opinion that the city force should be amalgamated with the county force, formed in 1839. He really was a man ahead of his time. He was later knighted and

Constable Amos Blake who joined the Norwich Police Force in 1861 and retired in 1891. (Norfolk Reference Library)

became Chief Constable of Cumberland and Westmorland.

Superintendent Stephen English was the last of the Superintendents as chief officer (1853-1859). He actually called himself Chief Constable and this caused bad feeling with the Chief Constable of Norfolk, George Black, who disputed Norwich's right to the title, believing it to be the prerogative of the county force. (The title of Chief Constable was actually in use before the police were formed, applied to a Mr Hobart who held a senior position in the organisation of ward Constables and was one of the advocates of a new professional police force.)

In support of his belief, Chief Constable Black made scathing remarks about Superintendent English and followed them up by issuing handbills condemning the Superintendent's previous career. He also wrote to the Norwich Watch Committee, several times, concluding one of his letters, 'Under all circumstances, I have no hesitation in saying that to permit the Superintendent of the Norwich police to hold the title of Chief Constable is an insult to every county police force in England'. Superintendent English sued the Chief Constable of Norfolk for defamation. The court case that followed would have been manna to the media of the present day. The Chief Constable's counsel set out to discredit Superintendent English and he was not short of ammunition.

Superintendent English, cross examined in court, admitted knowing a Mrs Ferraby, a public house licensee in Hertfordshire, but denied offering to show her 'French prints' and 'taking liberties' with her. Evidence was then given that the Superintendent had been dismissed from the Hertfordshire force 'having taken improper liberties' with Mrs Ferraby. It also transpired that the Superintendent had earlier been required to resign from the Essex force over a letter containing forceful language, written and sent by him to his tailor in reply to a request for settlement of an outstanding debt.

His service with the Newport Borough Police was not put before the court, certainly not the fact that he been before the Watch Committee of that force accused of borrowing money from beer house keepers, receiving bribes and allowing spirits to be drunk on unlicensed premises, among other things. He had

resigned and then been described in the committee minutes as a 'sober, intelligent and active officer'.

Superintendent English was questioned concerning a complaint made against him in the Norwich force, instigated by a Sergeant Smith. The Superintendent was reported to have advised a publican, a Mrs Brown, on the subject of after hours drinking. She said his advice was, 'When someone knocks say, "Wait till I get a key", then get someone to clear the glasses away, open your bible, and look religious'. Without admitting or denying the offence the Superintendent told the court the Watch Committee had dealt with the complaint and he had been admonished; but the Town Clerk was unable to confirm this statement and today the minutes do not reveal any such record. It is believed that he had merely been told to be aware of the ill-will of Sergeant Smith.

Superintendent English won his case against the Chief Constable of Norfolk and was awarded £50 damages. A subscription to defray the Chief Constable's legal costs was led by the Earl of Leicester and the *Norwich Mercury* commented, 'The public will be pleased to see that the county has thus determined to mark its sense, both of the action and verdict so contrary to evidence'.

By 1887 the strength of the Norwich City Police had grown to 111. In 1889 Joseph Betts aimed to reduce that number, with a revolver.

Betts lived in Northumberland Street and came to notice in 1883 when he sent threatening letters to the Bishop of Norwich and Mr J.J.Colman. The Bishop declined to proceed with charges, a decision described by the Judge as acting in 'a handsome and generous manner', while the Colman case, in which Betts threatened to murder Mr Colman unless he proportionately distributed his 'last year's balance' among his workmen, went ahead. Betts was sentenced to 12 months imprisonment. He was also ordered to keep the peace.

At 6.30am on 21 February 1889 Betts confronted Constable 45 James Southgate in Northumberland Street as the officer proceeded home off night duty. After mumbling something about false charges by the police Betts drew and fired a revolver, the bullet passing through the Constable's greatcoat between arm and body, wounding him on the inside of the arm. The Constable saw Betts preparing to fire again and withdrew, quickly, shortly to return with Constables Clarke and Holland. They found Betts in his house in Northumberland Street, threatening to shoot anyone who came near him.

The Magistrates granted a warrant of arrest and at noon Inspector Guiett and other officers went to the house to execute it. Betts refused them admittance.

The Inspector obtained a ladder and placed it against Betts' bedroom window. He had one foot on the bottom rung when Betts appeared at the window and fired the revolver at him. The bullet struck the peak of the Inspector's cap and deviated across his forehead, tearing the flesh but causing no substantial injury. The Inspector was conveyed to the police station for his wound to be dressed.

Officers entered the house and found the bedroom door barricaded with furniture, though Constable Airey and Sergeant Hall managed to push it open six inches. Betts fired through the aperture just as Hall was peering through, the bullet passing unpleasantly close to the officer.

No further attempt was made on the door. Police occupied all but the bedroom and the impasse continued.

At 2.45pm the Chief Constable, Robert Hitchman, arrived in a hansom cab accompanied by Constable Mickleburgh. He made his way through the watching crowd, which extended across the road (today the public would not get within two streets of such an incident), and stood at the front of and within a few yards of the house, but next to a high wall. Betts appeared at the window, laughing, pointing the revolver at the Chief Constable who stepped smartly behind the wall. Betts continued to point the revolver and seemed to enjoy the recoiling response of the crowd.

Officers present in or around the house were named as Inspector Scarff, Sergeants Williams, Watson and Hardy, Acting Sergeant Mills, Detective Constable Rushmer and Constable Varley. The Eastern Daily Press reporter at the forefront of the crowd (again, today, he would have been two streets away and told to await an official statement), described the police as a 'display of power not sufficient to overawe Betts in his impregnable position'.

The reporter, Mr F.J.Hook, suddenly found himself

This photograph of the Norwich force was taken between 1880 and 1888, during a rare period when numbers were worn on the tunic lapel. The Chief Constable, Robert Hitchman, is seated between the top-hatted men who are most likely HM Inspector of Constabulary and the Chairman of the Watch Committee. Note Constable Henry Hook, fifth from right in the front row, joined in 1880 and killed in 1892 in the line of duty – described in next chapter. Sixth from left at the back is Constable 22 Charles Elliott High, later to be Head of CID and also to die in service – see next chapter and chapter seven.

(Force archives)

removed from the crowd, invited to join the police in the house, and then offered a starring role in future events. Detective Rushmer had 'parleyed' with Betts (today the role of trained negotiator), and learned that he was willing to give himself up to a solicitor. History records that the police could not find a solicitor, and

An 1896 picture of the swimming section members of the force. They have been named as, back row, left to right: Constables Ward, Giles, Piercy, Sissen, Horner and Golden. Middle row: Constables Capon, Smith, Hardey, Freestone, Bloomfield, Small, Holland, Williamson and Ridley. Seated: Constables Woods, Rollett, Brown, Sergeants Martin, Hardy and Snell, Constables Wentford, Brown, Wailey and Watts. Reclining: Constables Sayer, Woods, Beeston and Harrison. Some of these names appear in later chapters. (Force archives)

also unashamedly records that they created one; Mr Hook was persuaded to a change of profession, Inspector Scarff genially assuring him that Betts would not shoot him because he was a stranger.

Hook was introduced through the bedroom door as Mr Sadd, solicitor, and then, on Betts' instructions taken outside and presented to the bedroom window.

Betts asked Hook to step forward so that he could look at him and the quavering Hook, later to write an interesting article, recalled that Betts had looked at Southgate and Guiett only long enough to take aim. But, after a brief exchange, in which Hook nervously assured Betts he would be taken care off, Betts agreed to come down and the ladder was raised to the window. It was noted that at this point Detective Rushmer advised Betts in a fatherly voice to be careful not to cut himself on the broken glass.

Betts climbed down the ladder and disappeared under a mound of suddenly appearing police, ringed by a cheering crowd. The siege was over. The Chief Constable took the prisoner to the police station in his hansom cab.

Betts' actions earned him 15 years penal servitude. He was later transferred to a mental institution.

With the approach of the new century came promise. One commentator spoke of 'tremendous improvement' in the force and attributed much of this to the more 'rigorous weeding out of unsuitable recruits'.

Crowds no longer assembled to watch somebody put to death, but life was still harsh for many, and accepted as such. In 1890 a 12-year-old boy was sentenced to six strokes of the birch for stealing cocoa valued at 2d.

Norwich Magistrates erred towards leniency and crime prevention when Mary Pearce, a prostitute, was hauled before them. She was ordered to catch the first train to Yarmouth. Problem shifted.

1897 and over 60 years of progress from the pioneer to the established police. A Constable strides in front of Municipal Buildings decorated to celebrate another 60 years: Queen Victoria's Diamond Jubilee. The 'on duty' striped armband was later discontinued.

(ECN)

CHAPTER TWO

Fires, Riots and Hard Times

The emergence of a fire brigade and the incidence of public disorder and police discontent

A policeman's lot is not a happy one.
W.S.Gilbert

FIRES and riots formed a significant part of a policeman's lot in the concluding part of the 19th century and, to a lessening degree, on into the 20th. This period also marked some unhappiness within the force.

The police responsibility for fire fighting was an early one. On 25 January 1836, with the newly-appointed police waiting to begin duties, the Watch Committee noted 'a conference to be held upon the appointment of firemen', but implementation did not immediately follow. Not until November 1846 were a Sergeant and five Constables appointed as police firemen: 'to be Constables in the daytime, to sleep near station house where fire engine kept and answer night calls'. The Sergeant lasted 16 months before being dismissed for being drunk on duty and two other founder members managed two years before they were dismissed for inefficiency.

The efforts of the police firemen were not always appreciated. In April 1847 a deputation of people living in St John Maddermarket complained of the way the fire brigade dealt with a recent fire in the parish and the Watch Committee responded by approving the action of the firemen, awarding Constables Allen and Callow (to die the following year) 20s each and Fairhead and Day 10s each. This response was tempered the following month by a special committee ordering that 'the Town Clerk be requested to investigate as to fires which have lately happened in the city. In future the usual rewards will be given at the discre-

tion of the committee not merely with reference to the arrival of an engine'. Fees were paid for the arrival of police firemen at fires (not specifically for putting them out). The Chief Constable was also paid for attending.

In 1852, 26 Constables were appointed to fire brigade duties under Inspector Robert Thompson who was to deal solely with fire service matters. Inspector William Curtis replaced him in 1855, covering police and fire duties.

In 1853 the Watch Committee ordered that an iron shed be erected on the south side of the Guildhall to house the fire escape, at a cost not to exceed £10.

In 1857, the Chief Constable hired a house in St Benedict's Street from a Mr Collins for use as a police section house and identified the building by displaying a board 'City Police Section House No 1' (there wasn't a No 2). This house became living quarters for single police firemen who were required to live there for a minimum of three years and to remain single for that period. (Even in the middle of the 20th century a police officer required his Chief Constable's permission to get married. And the proposed bride was vetted!)

Receiving word of a fire in sufficient time to extinguish it was a problem in an age of unsophisticated communication. And the citizens of Norwich were not immediately aware of the extent of their new public service. Fires were usually dealt with by private brigades belonging to insurance companies such as Norwich Union, or factories such as Carrow Works, and if the fire was not within their remit then it fell to the efforts of the military or citizenry. With the event of the new fire brigade handbills were printed to inform the public that fires should immediately be reported to the Guildhall Police Station.

Summoning sufficient fire fighting Constables was achieved by firing a rocket from outside the Guildhall, from a pipe set in the pavement, a practice that later received some scrutiny after a descending rocket plunged through the roof of a printing shop on Gentleman's Walk and set it alight. The discussion that followed favoured the use of an exploding 'mortar shell'. (Some of these shells were discovered in the Guildhall as late as 1930 and a Constable took one home and blew his November the fifth bonfire to pieces.)

Signal rockets were not the prerogative of the police, as this excerpt from 'Police General Regulations, Instructions and Orders' of 1894 shows: 'In the case of a fire occurring at Messrs Colmans a Report Rocket will be sent up followed by a green one. Inspector on duty at the Police Station will answer by discharging a rocket'.

A Watch Committee note of September 1885 reveals another divergence of opinion over the ability of police firemen. Councillor Bignold spoke of the 'good and efficient way' the fire brigade behaved in a fire at St Swithins. A committee member did not agree, why is not recorded. A special meeting was called and held one week later, at which it was agreed that the 'Chief Constable had done a good job as a fire-man' and a notice to this effect was to be put in the local newspaper. Additionally, the firemen at the St Swithins' fire were awarded 5s each.

Norwich had many fires and public disturbances of varying degrees of severity during the time of its own police force and not all can be recounted, but some of these conflagrations and confrontations are histori-cally important, representative of the people, police and the age in which they occurred. They are matters for history, and the reader.

Disaffection and opposition to authority often came from the impoverished and unemployed, one related to the other; and strong drink, political ambi-tion and purely anti-social views had a part to play. They made for hard times all round, especially tough

for policemen who were always available to be insulted and attacked, more so when the malcontents could expel their anger and frustration anonymously in a crowd, for the police were not generally a much loved body of men.

On the night of 14 March 1886 there was a public disturbance; and the public were not involved! Sergeant William Johnson and Constable Edward Fellowes of the Norwich police were the antagonists, contriving to dent whatever image of the force existed at the time.

Sergeant Johnson paraded the night shift and thought Constable Fellowes was drunk and said so to Inspector Clements. Fellowes then became excited and called the Sergeant a 'mucky scamp', following which the Inspector took him to one side until the remaining men were marched out. Inspector Scarff and Sergeant Meale joined Inspector Clements and it was decided that Fellowes was not drunk and was fit for duty. He was sent out onto his beat. Sergeant Johnson went out on supervisory patrol.

Shortly after midnight a bloodstained Sergeant Johnson returned to the station, quickly followed by an even bloodier Constable Fellowes suffering from a severe head wound, which he said had been caused by the Sergeant's truncheon.

Fellowes said to Johnson, 'You mucky scoundrel, to strike a man with that thing'.

Johnson replied, 'I would strike any man that would strike me first'. He admitted to Inspector Clements striking the Constable with his truncheon.

Fellowes said, 'I shall not charge him', but the Chief Constable, contacted by Inspector Clements, thought differently. He ordered that Sergeant Johnson be arrested and charged with wounding.

Constable Fellowes had served in the force for 14 years and Sergeant Johnson for 16 years without pre-vious ill-feeling.

Doctor Mills, the police surgeon, examined Fellowes and Johnson and reported injuries to both consistent with blows from a blunt instrument. The main wound to Fellowes' head was found to be quite serious, coming near to fracturing the skull and described by the surgeon as potentially life threatening and near to brain damage.

Fellowes recovered after a period of sick leave and

on 6 April gave evidence at Norwich Quarter Sessions. He stoutly resisted the suggestion that he was drunk when he paraded for night duty but agreed that he had imbibed a little whisky during the day.

He said that his beat had been in the Cathedral Close and he had met Sergeant Johnson near the Deanery and had said to him, 'You are a fine fellow to say I am drunk'. What followed, and was not essentially disputed, was that Johnson rushed Fellowes and Fellowes hit him with an ash stick that he had procured from the porter at the Close gate – he said he always carried it on the Close beat. Johnson drew his truncheon and struck back with blows to the Constable's head, which he said were in self-defence.

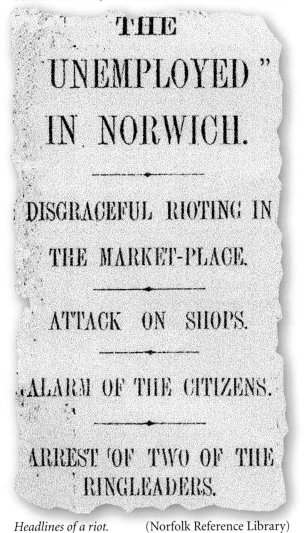

THE

" UNEMPLOYED "

IN NORWICH.

DISGRACEFUL RIOTING IN

THE MARKET-PLACE.

ATTACK ON SHOPS.

ALARM OF THE CITIZENS.

ARREST OF TWO OF THE

RINGLEADERS.

Headlines of a riot.   (Norfolk Reference Library)

Johnson told the court he thought he was acting in the interests of the force and the public.

The jury quickly came to the conclusion that there was no hope of them agreeing upon a verdict. They were discharged.

On 30 June Sergeant Johnson was again arraigned at Norwich Quarter Sessions. This time the jury found him guilty, but recommended mercy. The Judge spoke of the pain of the jury in reaching their verdict and his own duty. He said self-defence was entitled and one blow only might have brought a verdict of not guilty. He sentenced Sergeant Johnson to six months hard labour.

Crowd threats and violence, noisily moving and escalating, were a frightening experience to a sober, reasoned and unwilling witness, the degree of fear depending upon distance and perception. But the unwilling citizen could depart. The policeman could not flee the scene and a crowd was not always benevolent or indifferent to a police presence.

The Norwich riot of 1888 was by implication and intent far reaching; insurrection and revolution were not beyond the aims of the ringleaders.

On Friday, 14 January 1888, a meeting took place at Hay Hill of the unemployed, inspired by handbills prepared and issued by socialists. These handbills served to warn the police of possible trouble and Detective Sergeant Robert Barlow mingled with the crowd while other officers kept a watchful eye.

Charles Mowbray, a political agitator known to the Metropolitan Police, elected himself as chairman and told the crowd he meant to talk of sedition. He then launched into a condemnation of capitalists, press and police, advocating that it was no crime to take what nature required, making special mention of the hunger of the unemployed and the bread shops in the city. When a member of the crowd challenged Mowbray's views another man leapt forward, calling himself 'comrade' and strongly supporting everything Mowbray had said. 'Comrade' Frederick Henderson declared that he was related to Robert Kett and therefore had rebel blood in his veins.

Mowbray and Henderson roused the crowd and it was agreed that a deputation be sent to the Mayor to ask him 'to take steps to mitigate the present distress'. Three bricklayers, named Waterfield, Brightwell and

Minter, were selected along with comrade Henderson. Mowbray remained at the Hay Hill meeting.

The Mayor was engaged with the Watch Committee in the Guildhall and did not immediately receive the deputation, a fact relayed to Mowbray who then led the crowd to the Guildhall. The police, now well aware of the way things were going, prevented Mowbray entering the Guildhall. At this point Mowbray was suspicious of Detective Sergeant Barlow. He challenged him and asked if he was with the meeting. Barlow said he was, which was true.

Mowbray made a speech, in fact several speeches, from the Guildhall steps, and urged to crowd to yell to let the Mayor know they were there. They obliged but he said they were not loud enough and repeatedly called for them to yell. They repeatedly obliged. Mowbray then called for them to surround the Guildhall and hold the Mayor hostage and although there was much scuffling and movement, and Gaol Hill and Guildhall Hill were now effectively barred to traffic – the crowd seizing horse's heads to turn them away, this proposal came to nought. Instead, Mowbray shouted for them to stand firm and take the law into their own hands if they were attacked by the police or, as he put it, 'if the employed classes come among you grinning'. He claimed the police were hemming in the crowd with taxi-cabs and gave the Mayor ten minutes to answer the stalled deputation.

The Mayor saw the deputation and offered to form a committee to look into their grievances. This satisfied all except Henderson who appeared on the Guildhall steps and sang a song called 'The Starving Poor', the upshot of which was the crowd moving off to attack shops on the Walk, most of which had by now prudently placed shutters over their windows.

Lacon's Bank suffered a broken window, as did a number of shops. A ham emerged from a shop and sailed over the crowd to quickly disappear and never to be recovered, something that caused momentary merriment among learned counsel at the subsequent court proceedings: pigs might fly! A full-scale riot was now under way.

The police waded into the crowd with truncheons raised, except for Sergeant Martins who lost his truncheon when it was torn from his trousers by clutching hands that ripped his trousers in the process.

Mowbray was seen brandishing this truncheon aloft and was later to tell the court that he had taken it to prevent mischief being done.

Mowbray was arrested and, through the liberal use of truncheons, held against a rescue attempt. Henderson was arrested when he unwisely led the rescue attempt. Two others arrested were Harry Hall, later to say that he had picked up a stick and could remember nothing else because someone hit him on the head with another stick, and Henry Hurrell who said someone threw a stone and he picked it up and threw it back but unfortunately it hit a policeman.

With the disappearance of the vociferous ringleaders the riot petered out and the crowd went home. The four arrested men faced charges of unlawful assembly, disturbing the peace, assault and damage.

The press and the court were fulsome in their praise of the police. The press said, before the trial, 'The police behaved with praiseworthy coolness'. Mr Blofeld, prosecuting counsel, said, in opening the case at Norwich Assize, that the police had saved Norwich from a great calamity. He said that he applauded their promptitude.

Evidence was given by Inspector Mason, Detective Sergeant Barlow, Sergeant's Martins and Bix, Constables Beeston, Varley, Cheeseborough, Beckwith, Sands and Slaughter.

In his summing-up Judge Grantham compared the actions of the Norwich City Police with their counterparts in London during recent disturbances in the capital. He told the jury they 'could make such comparison between the way in which the police of Norwich were managed and behaved and of the conduct and management of other police on a memorable occasion'. The courtroom resounded to applause. The Judge had more to say. He thought it was his duty to express his commendation of the way in which the police had comported themselves for they had stepped in at the right moment and quelled what might have been a very serious disturbance. (All this before the jury's verdict.)

The jury deliberated for five minutes and found the prisoners guilty on all charges. Henderson was stopped from making a speech to the court. Mowbray received nine months hard labour, Henderson four months hard labour (he later became a city councillor), Hall hard labour for a month and Hurrell was

Constable William Beeston, pictured with his wife, gave evidence in the 1888 riot case. He was born in 1860 and joined the force in 1880, retiring in 1909. He was reported to be an exceptionally smart officer, so much so that Chief Constable Hitchman 'determined that he would be useful as a special department man without uniform'. Constable Beeston had a successful CID career and one of his cases appears later in this book. For 25 years of his police service he was macebearer to the City Corporation, holding the position of senior macebearer when he retired from the force. He was a member of the First Police Reserve during World War One. William Beeston died in 1930. A member of the public learning of his death wrote to the press recalling him as 'one of the most popular officers who ever donned a uniform'. (D. & J.Pigg)

Telephone 29.

NORWICH CITY POLICE.

Photo and description of

ROBERT LARGE,

alias "Seymour," an ex-convict and notorious poacher, wanted on warrant in this City, charged with assault on Police on 13th August, 1904.

Aged 37 years, height 6 feet 1 inch, swarthy complexion, dark brown hair, brown moustache, brown eyes, proportionate build, stoops slightly, long, swinging gait; a native of Gt. Witchingham, Norfolk. Marks :—scar middle forehead, left side neck, scar front left thumb, palm of hand, back little finger, top joint left little finger contracted, scar inside and 2 outside front right wrist, scar right of back and front left shin, mole left shoulder.

Dressed usually in light brown coat and vest, cord trousers, cap, and heavy lace boots.

May be found associating with poachers and thieves, or at low Public-houses.

Please cause every possible enquiry to be made for this man, and if found, arrest and wire me, when an officer shall be sent for him, or any information obtained kindly communicate to

E. F. WINCH,

Chief Constable.

The Guildhall, Norwich,
24th August, 1904.

Robert Large wanted in 1904, and quite often before that.
(Force archives)

found associating with poachers and thieves, or at low public houses'. In August 1888 he could be found in the newly-built Norwich Prison where he was serving three months for poaching, that is until he escaped accompanied by Robert Annison who was serving 12 months hard labour for 'fowl stealing'. Annison was captured at Martham by Constable Clipperton of the county force and taken to Acle Police Station where, according to the press, he received a 'cordial welcome'

sentenced to one week's imprisonment. So ended the uprising that was snuffed out by police monitoring, judgement and action.

Robert Large was a man who typified the criminality and policing of the age he lived in. The Norwich City Police 'wanted' notice of 1904 said that he 'may be from Superintendent Basham. But Large, described by the press as 'the notorious poacher', remained free for six more days, until he was arrested at his father's house at Lenwade, after a struggle.

Officers took him to the police station at Lenwade where, the press reported, 'a hostile crowd had assembled, nearly all the village turning out to show their indignation at the arrest'. The police braved a jeering and jostling crowd to get Large from the police station to the railway station and they 'steamed out of the station to the hooting of onlookers'.

Somehow the communications of the day were ahead of Large's train. It was met at Norwich City Station by people showering abuse upon the police and pouring words of encouragement into the ear of Large. The guarding officers managed to get Large into a cab, which the mob then threatened to overturn. The vehicle got away amid scenes of great hostility.

Large admitted that he had organised and attempted to lead a mass break-out from Norwich Prison but only Annison had chosen to accompany him. He disdainfully referred to the reluctance of his fellow prisoners with the comment, 'You might as well as tried to make them all of one height as all of one mind'.

The press praised the Chief Constables of the county and city 'for the energy and tact they displayed in the search for Large and his comrade'.

In July 1889 Constable Brown arrested Herbert Beckett for being drunk and disorderly in St Stephen's Street. Beckett became very upset and attracted a crowd. He was rescued from the Constable by a soldier, recaptured by the Constable, and then lost to the less than public-spirited crowd.

The persistent Constable got his man back and received a number of blows from him, following which the crowd became very excited. Three other Constables arrived and so began a running battle to the police station as the crowd sought to re-rescue Beckett and the Constables strove to hang on to him. The reluctant, struggling prisoner was eventually dragged into the Guildhall. He was fined 5s or five days imprisonment for being drunk and disorderly and 10s or seven days imprisonment for assault on police.

Crowd trouble came with a fire in 1890. The fire occurred at H.Cole's furnishing premises at St Giles' Gates and a crowd quickly gathered and set the mood by greeting the arriving police with hoots and jeers. A press report attributed this attitude to the dilatory response of the police after the 'alarm bombs were exploded', disputed by the Chief Constable who reported a police attendance within minutes of the 'bombs' exploding.

Other problems manifested. The Chief Constable reported that 'a most disorderly crowd most seriously obstructed the fire brigade by pulling, stamping and kinking the hose'.

Within the turmoil of heat, noise, and the feverish excitement generated by a jeering and interfering crowd, civilians, soldiers and police fought the fire – and, incredibly, each other. The Chief Constable claimed that police firemen were frustrated by over-helpful soldiers and struggled with them over possession of the hoses, a tug of war episode that could only have added to the excitement. Then a civilian named Townshend caused more excitement by falling 20ft and severely injuring himself.

The fire destroyed the interior of the premises.

In September 1892 police firemen went to a large fire in the three-storey building of confectionery manufacturers R.A.Cooper, situated at the corner of Queen Street and Upper King Street. The fire had taken a firm hold before it was discovered and was spreading quickly, flames shooting to a height from which they could be seen in all parts of the city, according to the press.

The Chief Constable, Robert Hitchman, seeing the 'vast crowd' at the scene, telegraphed for assistance and a 'goodly number of Hussars and Infantrymen were soon on the spot', reported the press. One report says that other premises in Queen Street and Upper King Street were threatened and at one time 400 men were fighting the fire. The heat was such that buildings on the far side of Upper King Street were blistered.

An hour into fighting the fire the front portion of the building collapsed, narrowly missing the firefighters, and as more water was propelled into the gutted building, intent upon saving the Compasses public house in Upper King Street, a huge chimney stack was seen to be tottering, then falling across Queen Street with a resounding crash.

The press reported, 'To the dismay of the spectators it was seen that one of the most active of the firemen, Police Constable Henry Hook, who had exerted himself to the utmost in the most dangerous positions, was knocked down by the heavy brickwork and it was at once apparent that he had sustained most serious injury'.

Constable Hook was extricated from the rubble and placed in an ambulance where he reportedly said, 'I'm done for'. At the Norfolk and Norwich Hospital his injuries were found to be severe and included a broken back.

The Chief Constable and the Mayor visited Henry

Constable Henry Hook. (See also photograph in chapter one.)
(Norfolk Reference Library)

The grave of Henry Hook and his wife at Earlham Cemetery – photographed in 1999. Beneath hands clasped over a police helmet, truncheon and fire axe is the inscription:'The late Constable Henry Hook who was fatally injured at a fire in Queen Street in the city Sep 5th 1892 aged 35 years. Bequeathed in the blood of Christ. Erected by 2 Inspectors, 10 Sergeants, 90 Constables, 8 ex-members of the Norwich City Police'.
(Author)

Hook in hospital, as did Mary Ensor who had, by her own account, 'striven to win his soul' for nearly 11 years. This lady ran bible classes for police officers every Monday evening.

The injured Constable died four days after receiving his injuries and Mary Ensor published a small book called *God Hath Spoken*, dedicated to him and the Norwich police, describing the Constable as 'a man

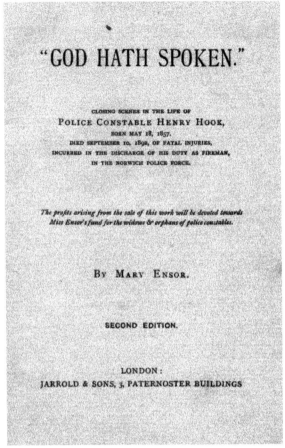

"GOD HATH SPOKEN."

CLOSING SCENES IN THE LIFE OF
POLICE CONSTABLE HENRY HOOK,
BORN MAY 18, 1857.
DIED SEPTEMBER 10, 1892, OF FATAL INJURIES,
INCURRED IN THE DISCHARGE OF HIS DUTY AS FIREMAN,
IN THE NORWICH POLICE FORCE.

The profits arising from the sale of this work will be devoted towards Miss Ensor's fund for the widows & orphans of police constables.

BY MARY ENSOR.

SECOND EDITION.

LONDON:
JARROLD & SONS, 3, PATERNOSTER BUILDINGS

'God Hath Spoken'. The book of tribute by Mary Ensor. Other tributes referred to Constable Hook's record in the force, which included rescuing a drowning boy at Pockthorpe and 'emerging victorious' from a 'severe struggle with soldiers' in Bank Plain. The Mayor instigated a fund for the welfare of the Constable's wife and five children. (Force archives)

of powerful build – with a bright and genial countenance who will long be remembered for his kindly character and generous treatment'. In the book she records that in hospital he 'had great pleasure in joining with Mrs Ripley of Earlham Hall in singing Rock of Ages'. Mary Ensor described his funeral in detail and published his photograph taken on his deathbed.

A new age of invention and progress saw the lessening of deprivation and hardship for many and the beginning of great social and technological change for all. Life would gradually get better. But the Norwich police in 1893 did not see a better future. On 28 March they submitted a petition of discontent to the Watch Committee. The signatories were an Inspector, 11 Sergeants and 91 Constables.

The petition called for, and is quoted exactly: '(1) the abolition of the age limit of 55 years for pensions (2) an increase of pay to all ranks (3) one day's leave of absence per month in place of one day in six weeks (4) discontinuance of Saturday night special duty (5) complaint that the men are out on Fridays to receive pay, and occasionally in attendance before Magistrates and (6) complaint that the men are required to attend on Mondays for drill'.

The Watch Committee requested a detailed return from the petitioners on the matters recorded, and ordered a report from the Chief Constable, Robert Hitchman

The petitioners, unable to submit a comprehensive record of their court appearances, special duties, times they had attended for pay when off duty and other related matters, waited unhappily for the Watch Committee to consider the Chief Constable's response. He listed their pay and allowances.

A Constable on appointment was paid £1 1s per week, rising to £1 8s after ten years service. After 26 years all ranks received an extra allowance of 1s per week. (In later years long service pay was allied to good conduct and not infrequently refused by the Watch Committee.)

Detectives received £1 17s 6d per week, Sergeants £1 9s 2d rising to £1 12s 8d and Inspectors were paid £95 per annum rising to £115. Extra duty was paid according to the scale of pay but in the previous year had only been paid on the two occasions when the whole force had been employed: the General Election and the fire at Cooper's premises in Queen Street. Police firemen received 5s for attending a fire in the city and 7s 6d for attending a fire in the county, and 1s per day was paid for attending Quarter Sessions or Assizes. The Chief Constable reported that hot coffee was served free at night all the year round at a cost to the force of £70 per annum and uniforms were free.

The Chief Constable's report was lengthy and not favourable to the petitioners. He wrote, 'The Norwich Police Force is recruited mainly from the labouring classes', detailing the average earnings of city and county labourers, and following up with tradesmen such as bricklayers, carpenters, and 'post officer letter-carriers'. Apparently a city labourer earned 12s 10d per week and a carpenter £1 6s 3d per week. The comparisons did not support the petitioners' case, but they had not seen themselves as general labourers or carpenters.

Two concessions were granted. The Chief Constable agreed to arrange for the men to obtain their pay without special attendance at the police station (which will be news to officers up to the late 1950s) and also he would grant a time-off allowance for night duty men attending court.

The Watch Committee moved to reject the remainder of the petition but a Mr Stevens said that the request for a day off each month was reasonable and a small matter to grant. His proposal to grant this request was defeated by 23 votes to 9.

The Secretary of Norwich and District Trades Council, Mr G.Cleverley, wrote to the press complaining of the 'one-sided report' of the Chief Constable saying, 'It contains indications that our Chief Constable and his men are not working as harmoniously as I think such a position demands'. Mr Cleverley went on to support the request for extra pay and said, 'The lamentable accident at the Queen Street fire is proof that 5s is not an exorbitant reward for such gallant services as are rendered, and at such terrible risks to life and limb'.

Another correspondent took a different view. He was gratified to 'learn how well the State and the City look after the civil force of the Empire'. He went on, 'What with pay and pensions the police live in clover. May they long enjoy their present happy lot'. The petition was doomed, even without this rejoicing correspondent, and the men got nothing more than the Chief Constable's concessions; and there is some doubt over their implementation.

Undaunted by rebuff and failure the rank and file of the force persisted with their grievances during what was undoubtedly a prolonged period of discontent, further worsening a 'them and us' relationship. A Watch Committee order that no member of the force was entitled to make representation to the Watch Committee was badly received and publicised in anonymous letters to the press and Police Review, still bitterly spoken of several years into the new century.

But persistence and enduring discontent paid off to

Robert Hitchman, the first undisputed Chief Constable, serving for a record 38 years in that post (1859-97). Despite petitions, deputations and Watch Committee wrangling over his suitability at the end of his service, he was, according to a handed down personal account, known within the force without acrimony as 'the old man', further described as a 'gentleman'. He died the year following his retirement.

(Force archives)

some extent. The Police Review reported in February 1896 that the Norwich Watch Committee had acceded to a petition from the members of the force asking for 'one day's leave of absence in every 28 days in place of one in 42'. It appears that the petition had a delayed fuse.

In May 1896 the Council openly disapproved and negated a Watch Committee resolution that detailed special night supervisory duties for Superintendent Mason and Inspector Scarff. The resolution was clearly a political ploy and cosmetic policing exercise to appease, or at least answer, a deputation of local tradesmen concerned at city centre burglaries (described in more detail in chapter five). Councillors went on to make 'strong remarks reflecting upon the management of the force'. The retirement of the Chief Constable was suggested, pointing out that he was over 70 years of age. There was talk of relieving him of his duties. (He retired the following year.)

In September 1896 the press reported upon 'the Pockthorpe riot'. This area of the city was squalid, poor, underprivileged and a potential source for disturbance, indeed there had been reports of localised disorder at the beginning of the century, before the new police was in being, and by all accounts its inhabitants remained poor, disaffected and inclined to disorder for many years. The ignition point in this particular case occurred when Constables Watts and Freestone arrested Arthur Pye. A crowd formed, including two of Pye's brothers, and threatened the Constables with violence if the prisoner was not released.

The Constables took their prisoner into Dun Cow Yard and held the crowd at bay with their truncheons before breaking out under a hail of stones and shouted threats. Near the Barrack Gate the crowd attacked and wrestled with the officers but reinforcements arrived in the shape of other officers and soldiers from the barracks. Four men were arrested from the crowd, three of whom were later sentenced to periods of hard labour. The Watch Committee report of this riot says that Constables Watts, Freestone, Woods and Plummer were assaulted, truncheons were drawn and military assistance was sought.

Police regulations of 1894, stated, 'It is better at all times to refrain from using violence as it irritates the public who may be called upon to assist the police'. Constables battling with the crowd in the Pockthorpe riot would not have agreed with the 'all times'.

The 1894 regulations addressed other issues and pointed to the extremes of police work. They required the beat Constable to 'remove orange peel from the pavement' and 'on Sunday caution all persons crying fish in the streets'.

Mr Mann, described as a 'cycle agent', surprised the police in October 1896. He went to the assistance of a Constable struggling with a prisoner in Magdalen Road. He helped to convey the prisoner to the police station but in the continuing struggle lost a gold ring. Mr Mann was later invited to the police station and presented with a new gold ring (paid for by subscription, collection or otherwise is not recorded). Superintendent Mason made the presentation and expressed his pleasure, and surprise, at what he called 'prompt and ready assistance from the public', adding, 'people were more inclined to frustrate and hinder the efforts of the police'. Mr Mann said he had only done his duty.

Edwin Winch replaced Robert Hitchman as Chief Constable in 1897 and went bankrupt in 1899. His public examination reported liabilities of £955 18s 9d and a deficiency of £750 5s. He told of living beyond his means and moneylenders charging 20 per cent interest. He offered his creditors 10s in the pound and this was accepted by all except one.

A new fire station was due to open in September 1898 in Pottergate, an area of congested buildings and narrow streets that included Dove Street.

Just before 4am on Monday, 1 August 1898, Mr and Mrs Booth of London Street walked into Dove Street and hesitated, sniffing a smell of burning upon the still night air. Their attention was then drawn to hot tar running down the gutters of Hurns' shop, a maker and retailer of rope, sail and wagon covers. The alarm was raised but it was too late. Tongues of flame pierced the blackness and what the press described as 'the great fire of Norwich' lit up the night sky.

The Guildhall Police Station was very close but that would not save Hurns. The shop was an old building fronting Dove Street, adjoining Chamberlins' cloth warehouse and surrounded by other stores and shops, including its second shop in Pottergate to which it was connected at the rear. This was an area of abutting walls, pocket-sized yards and narrow thoroughfares.

Hurns was full of inflammable material such as rope, canvas and tar and it was quickly lost, enveloped in flames before any concerted fire fighting attack could be mounted. Now it was a fight to save other

Aftermath of the great fire: looking into Pottergate from the Dove Street junction. The new fire station was to be situated on the left side of the street just beyond the line of destruction. (Norfolk Reference Library)

premises and, as events unfolded, the whole block of buildings.

The fire raged for more than five hours and between 7am and 7.30am was reported to be at its height. The Chief Constable, Edwin Winch, was in charge of the police fire brigade and, as police firemen failed to hold the advancing flames, the brigades of Carrow Works and the Anchor Brewery arrived to the accompaniment of loud cheers from a watching crowd. The absence of any wind was the only advantage enjoyed by the firefighters.

A press report refers to the 'greatest number of firemen ever seen at a Norwich fire' and Guildhall Hill 'paved with hose'. People living in buildings affected by what rapidly became a roaring furnace 'bolted with their belongings into the Guildhall', according to the press.

The fire consumed stores adjoining Hurns, spreading to their Pottergate shop and the Edinburgh Inn at the corner of Dove Street and Pottergate. It tore through Chamberlins' warehouse and into their main shop. Then a new, previously unforeseen, horror became possible. The public subscription library, containing many rare books, including the bequeathed and much-prized Norton antiquarian collection, was in danger by its proximity to Chamberlains.

At 6.45am the library was still intact, but then a jet of flame was seen in the north-east corner of the main hall, on the side close to Chamberlins' warehouse. Mr Quinton, secretary to the library institution, pleaded with firemen to get ladders to enable hose to be carried on to the portico and then onto the roof. Library ladders, used for bookshelves, were too short; but so were the brigade ladders. There was no time to find longer ladders. The fire festooned along the library galleries and tongues of flame burst out of the room devoted to the Norton Collection. The library was soon beyond saving. Such salvage as was later reported was described as 'pitifully small'.

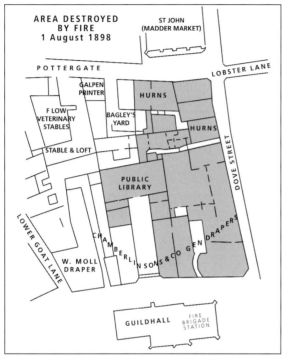

The area of destruction. (B.Veriod)

The final chapter in this disaster was the concerted attempt of four brigades (Harmer's factory brigade had joined the fight – Steward and Patteson's brewery sent their brigade as a fifth but by then it was all over), to stop the fire spreading to Lower Goat Lane, the Guildhall and other property outside the already devastated area. In this objective the firemen were successful, the flames dying into a smoke laden, steaming and waterlogged scene of charred, collapsed buildings. The front of Chamberlins' remained, as did the frame of the Edinburgh Inn (though this collapsed four days later injuring a number of people), while the library stood roofless and charred with the irreparable loss of contents so close to the hearts and minds of so many Norwich citizens. In a tragic irony of history, on the same date 96 years later, a new library, once again opposite a fire station, was also lost with treasured contents.

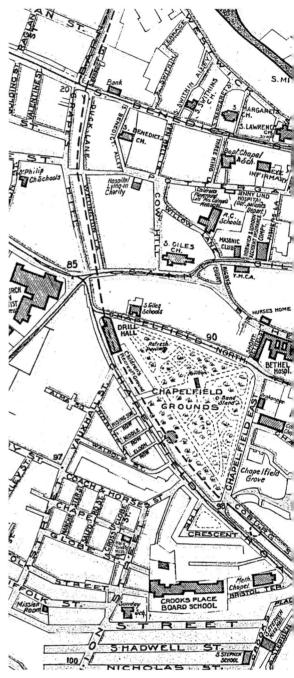

The city of Norwich 1899. (G.Piercy)

The perception and promise in the fading century of an improved and improving police force was gradually realised in the new century, though drunkenness on duty was never entirely absent, the pay book was

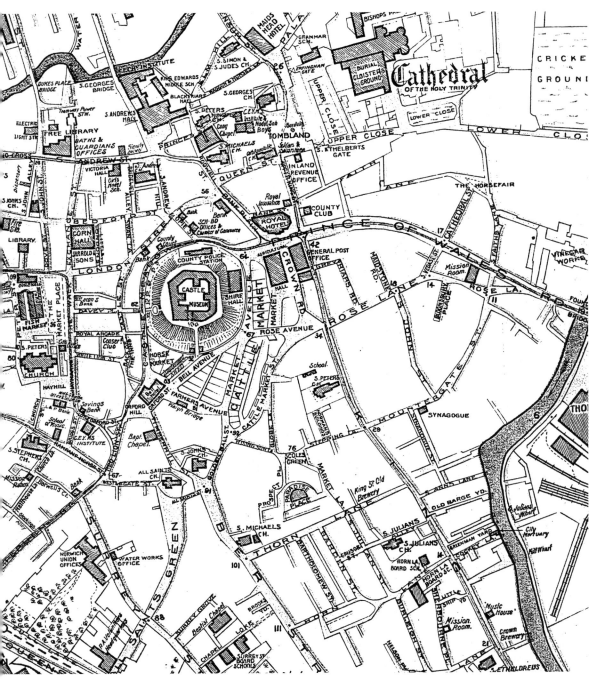

still signed in the wrong place and late for duty remained a common and persistent offence. (One officer, retiring in 1907, was fined on 40 occasions in a 21-year career for being late on duty.)

Drunk off duty was an offence that came to notice; a Sergeant so found was reduced in rank and a Constable found inebriated in the Section House, and consequently unfit for a fire call out, was dismissed. Also dismissed was the sober Constable who was 30 minutes late reporting off duty. What detained him is not recorded.

Not until 1908 would the incidence of disciplinary

offences move from a gradual reduction to a more swift and marked decline.

The quality of life improved. Chief Inspector Robert Barlow retired in 1902 after 32 years service. He spoke of Norwich of the 1870s being 'infested with several houses of a low and immoral character' and went on to praise the new century Norwich and its police force pointing out that crime was effectively reduced and 'there have been a great many improvements in the city since I have been here'.

Inspector George Seaman, who joined the force in 1888 from the Metropolitan Police, spoke at his retirement in 1915 of improved public relations, saying, 'Matters have altered now very much for the better' adding, 'one can now go about Norwich without being molested and one hears little of the foul language that was so rampant in the past'.

The 20th century saw improved communications, of a sort. A bugle announced a fire on Mousehold on 25 July 1904. An unofficial bugle! Sounded by a juvenile! At about 11am on that day a group of boys noticed a fire had started in the furze and bracken. One of the boys 'had a bugle with him' and, 'knowing the military fire call', sounded the alarm, heard at Britannia Barracks. One hundred and fifty men of the 3rd and 4th Norfolks turned out, followed by numerous civilians and the city police firemen. A strong wind fanned the flames and approximately 30 acres of the heath were destroyed. No detail is available of the bugle boy or any appreciation for him.

Another 20th-century occasion of a serious fire was devoid of the summoning urgency of rockets, bugles or the like. On 18 August 1916, the building of Roys of Wroxham caught fire (history later repeated) and the 'parish authorities' sent for the Norwich Fire Brigade, which promptly refused to attend. Wroxham was not a protected parish, that is a parish within reasonable distance of the Norwich City Police area and electing to pay a yearly fee for a fire service. The insurers, Norwich Union, were informed that the fire was assuming 'serious proportions' and they urgently contacted the Norwich Chief Constable, Edwin Winch, offering to pay the cost of the brigade attendance. Having received this assurance the Chief Constable and brigade attended and extinguished the fire.

The issue of the police dispensing as well as receiv-

ing violence received an airing in the Magistrates' Court in January 1919. A fracas occurred at the Agricultural Hall where a funfair was being held inside and outside the building. Involved were redundant, belligerent soldiers and hostile civilians, and ultimately and inevitably, the police.

> 'Oh, it's Tommy this, an' Tommy that, an
>   'Tommy, go away';
> But it's 'Thank you, Mister Atkins', when the
>   band begins to play.
> Rudyard Kipling 1890.

The disturbance swelled and moved to the Market Place where Special Constables were called in to assist the regular force. Windows were broken in the Guildhall. The Chief Constable later reported to the Watch Committee that he anticipated further trouble and was authorised to give notice of call-out to the First Police Reserve. The military were banned from using the Agricultural Hall.

Private Arthur Tickner of the Bedfordshire Regiment appeared before Norwich Magistrates to answer for his part in the disorder. He was charged with assaulting Constable James Wilby who told the court that police officers were being 'pushed about' and were forced from the Agricultural Hall into London Street by soldiers and civilians. He said that at the corner of London Street Tickner was swinging his belt in the air, inciting the crowd to attack the police, shouting, 'Come on, let's kill them all'. He was seen to kick and hit Constable Wilby with the swinging belt, actions that ceased when the Constable struck him on the head with his truncheon. Tickner was later arrested outside the Guildhall, a geographical advantage that quickly removed him from sight.

Tickner denied the offence and told the Magistrates he had been ill-treated by the police though, in answer to the Chief Constable, John Henry Dain, he agreed he had been well treated in the police station. The Chief Constable told the Magistrates that he did not encourage his men to use their truncheons unless 'absolutely unavoidable' and pointed out that 'one of my Sergeants has been severely injured by a brick which cut his head'. The Chief Constable thought that a cut on the prisoner's head had been caused by a bottle or brick and in a mitigating statement for Tickner (one that today would give rise to an inquiry), he said, 'This lad, however, has been severely punished with the truncheon'.

The Chairman of the Magistrates said he was bound to support the police and the prisoner had caused serious rioting in the city. He took note of his excitement and the fact he was wearing His Majesty's uniform and observed that if the prisoner had been a civilian he would have had no option but to send him to prison. He fined him £1.

Physical punishment was often summary, salutary and informal, also unlawful. What euphemistically may be called direct and positive policing faded with an enlightened age, though some examples of injudicious acts of violence are still recalled by givers and receivers. They were mostly directed at juvenile crime and nuisance, called by proponents 'a clip round the lug'ole', recalled with satisfaction by now aged deliverers and remembered, strangely, with some pride by no longer youthful receivers who claim it 'did them good', or at the very least 'no harm'. In 1913 there appeared some tacit recognition of this summary 'justice'. The Watch Committee approved the issue of canes for beat Constables to deal with the problem of 'nuisance by boys'. If they were ever used it has escaped historical record.

The most outstanding example of on the spot physical remonstration by a uniformed officer, not involving a juvenile or rioting protester, and not exactly a 'clip round the lug'ole' case, occurred well into the 20th century and concerned a well-known Norwich rogue who went under the sobriquet of 'Fagin'. That Fagin was disposed to argue and oppose any form of police counselling was equally well-known, and anticipated by the Constable who taxed him with his behaviour one night in Stump Cross. Fagin immediately engaged in a verbal altercation with the Constable, which heightened when he found himself with his head firmly stuck between the iron railings of St Saviour's Church. The Constable, who had put him there while making his point, and not meant for him to become stuck, became fearful of his career when the Fire Brigade and duty Inspector turned out. An unhappy Fagin was eventually prised free. He retired from the scene to consider the unorthodox ways of the police without further com-

Heading into trouble. (T.George)

plaint, not formally anyway. There were others who complained of ill-treatment by the police, and with less justification.

The Market Place, often the fulcrum for public statement and protest, had a history of riotous assembly before a police force existed, when bonfires were made and a bullock roasted by noisy crowds pursuing aims of politics, religion and general jollification. In 1812 the bonfire consisted of the fish stalls and the revellers were incarcerated in the Bridewell.

With the Market Place and Guildhall a homing centre for protest and demonstration the surrounding streets naturally bore the brunt of splinter actions. In December 1920, only a few days before Christmas, a large crowd gathered outside the Guildhall where the Lord Mayor was chairing a committee on the subject of the unemployed. The crowd was restless, shouting and visibly aggressive. More than once an emissary from the committee in session went outside to ask them to be quiet, without noticeable result. A 'strong force of police' was present, watching, waiting.

The crowd was described as full of 'young fellows' (translated by modern idiom into 'yobs') and there was some doubt whether they represented the gen-

Constable Arthur Cooper Claxton was born in 1857 and joined the force in 1886. He was a giant of a man with exceptionally large hands and feet and was reputed to be the only Constable to patrol Ber Street unaccompanied during a time when the street was normally patrolled in pairs and was flippantly known as 'Blood and Guts Street', a possible reference to the number of butchers' shops but also likely to refer to the human blood so often spilt by drunken revellers, none of whom were over fond of the police. This imposing officer retired in 1912 and died in 1940. (B.Huntingdon)

uinely unemployed, especially when they moved off and attacked shops in London Street. The International Stores and Coes' photographers suffered broken windows and the press quaintly reported that at the former shop 'venturesome spirits helped themselves to fancy cakes, fruit etc'. They also noted that 'customers hurried to the basement' and kicks were aimed at the police (presumably by the same venturesome spirits) with 'more than one member of the force showed marks of rough usage': some would say it was ever thus. The riot was quelled and the police counted their bruises.

That the police were aware and attentive to reoccurring trouble was shown by the Watch Committee's instruction in 1924 to 'adopt the same measures as last year' to deal with 'disturbances'.

The General Strike of 1926 brought Trade Unions to the fore, workers protesting in support of the miners, and themselves. This nationwide problem was greater in some cities than others. In Norwich the Chief Constable was reported to have acted as a 'mediator and peacemaker in disputes with the tramways and buses' and 'in cases of other likely disturbances in this city'.

On the Monday of the strike groups of police were drafted to likely trouble spots in the city, notably the bus depot in Recorder Road where 'a large body of men was required'. Policemen were reported to be 'in full strength along Prince of Wales Road and Recorder Road'. Mounted officers were much in evidence. A reserve force was kept at both police and fire stations.

Eighteen to 20 hours' continuous duty was the lot of some officers and those coming off duty at ten o'clock on the Wednesday morning had to report for duty again at four o'clock. During three days of simmering unrest not a single riot or arrest for disturbance was reported and a grateful citizen wrote to the press on the subject of 'our silent force' saying, 'These men have deserved well of our city'.

The effectiveness of the police in dealing with the protest of the General Strike was commended by HM Inspector of Constabulary and resulted in a collection of money by Norwich citizens to provide the police with a recreation room. The sum of £170 was realised and applied to a room in Pottergate.

Clearing the Market Place of stalls for use as a

Senior officers c.1909. Chief Constable Edwin Winch, centre, took the force into the 20th century, in which he received a King, saw the death of that King, dealt with the turmoil of floods, suffered the indignity of a public inquiry and the pain and disruption of a world war and moved the force to the dawn of a new era: the rule of John Henry Dain, beginning in 1917. The identities of the senior officers of the force at the time of this photograph are known but relating them to the picture is an exercise fraught with the possibility of mistake. There is, however, sufficient evidence to apply names to the back row, left to right: Chief Engineer Stanley Shaw who served from 1895 until 1914, Inspector John Wentford, 1888-1914 (see swimming section photograph, and chapter nine for the abrupt end to his career), Detective Inspector Charles Elliott High who joined in 1880 and died in service in 1910 (see above and chapter seven), Inspector Henry Windsor who joined in 1897 and become Chief Constable of Scarborough in 1913 and Inspector Horace Burdett (1885-1911). The officers flanking the Chief Constable cannot be named with confidence. Remaining Inspectors of the time were William Ebbage (1887-1917), Frederick Tolworthy (1889-1924), George Mills (1884-1910) and Jacob Southgate (1897-1923). (Force archives)

political arena brought the various factions to one amphitheatre, next to the police station and instant policing, and this could be seen as forward thinking; or was it just circumstantial?

Retired police officers recall that Sundays in the 1930s were not looked upon as potential leave days. A stand-by force waited in the Guildhall for Norwich's equivalent of Speakers' Corner to erupt as opposing views were reinforced with violence on the adjoining Market Place. It was the time of strong political argument (some might say it was always so) and included the Blackshirts, Oswald Mosley's fascists, marching from an office they had acquired in Redwell Street through London Street to a soapbox oratory in the Market Place. As elsewhere, the Blackshirts quickly found a crowd of unbelievers.

On 27 October 1935 Oswald Mosley himself marched into the Market Place surrounded by body-

This photograph, remarkable for its clarity, shows the force on parade at the Chapelfield Drill Hall on 25 July 1910 for inspection by HM Inspector of Constabulary; (chapter seven depicts other such parades). Constables identified in the front row, left to right, are: 95 William Brown, 89 George Jennings, 24 Percy Capon, 10 Alfred Shepherd, 21 Thomas Holland, 67 Edward Male, 61 Chandos Storey, 63 William Sheldrake, 107 Alfred Easton and 110 William Hopes (see chapter seven re duty at Nurse Cavell's funeral). This photograph came from the effects of Constable 6 Frederick Starling, third row back, with prominent moustache, visible between 24 Capon and 10 Shepherd. (Force archives)

Trouble in the Market Place. The artist, Harry Potter, was born in 1890 and died in 1972. He was, as well as an artist, a news reporter, window cleaner and sign-writer. He rode the streets of Norwich on a cycle bedecked with his pictures, looking hopefully for a sale. He was reputed to paint only what he had seen. His depiction of the Market Place above shows a protest being sorted, putdown – depending upon viewpoint, by the police during the week of the General Strike in 1926. That no arrests were made or riots took place in the city during the General Strike appears at odds with this picture. Perhaps it was a skirmish tinted by artistic licence. Potter painted himself into the picture as a reporter and is the man in the trilby being 'assisted' by the Constable, and the papers strewn across the ground are Potter's scattered notes. The original of this picture is privately owned. (S.Jordan)

Strikers and cheerful policemen. Constable Henry Blackburn with striking busmen in Prince of Wales Road in 1937 and, in 1957, another bus strike, Sergeant Johnnie Johnson and Constable Ken Grist pose with a bus inspector at the Bus Station. (R.Brighton (Tester) and K.Grist)

guards and cordoned by police. He addressed a crowd estimated at 10,000 and described as 'lively'. There was much scuffling and shouting and Mosley called upon the police to arrest the hecklers, without result. The whole thing passed off without major disorder though Mosley was not well received and was hurried away.

The political unrest of the time was to lead to the Public Order 1936. Then war clouds began looming again.

Chapter Three
Fire Engines, Ambulances and Horses!

The evolution of the emergency services, their stations and transport

THE police fire brigade did not escape public criticism over 'Chamberlins' fire'. There was a suspicion that but for the assistance of the private brigades much more would have been lost. Were the city police professional enough and adequately equipped to deal with serious fires? The question surfaced again in 1900 when they, again reinforced by private brigades, failed to contain a serious fire at a shoe factory and adjoining timber yard in Fishergate.

Former veterinary premises in Pottergate became the new fire and ambulance station in September 1898, hosting men, horses and equipment severed from the all-embracing Guildhall Police Station where horse drawn and hand-propelled fire engines, and an ambulance, had been lodged on and off for many years.

Engines and horses had also been deposited in several available and convenient, unofficial as well as official, lodging places within range of the Guildhall. A public house yard in Gentleman's Walk was regularly used and the shop of Mr Kent, bag and skin dealer, opposite the Guildhall, was converted to house a fire engine donated by Norwich Union.

In the years following its inception the Pottergate station received an increasing and updated complement of vehicles to be used under different auspices. The vehicles bursting into Pottergate could be horse drawn or motorised, police, fire or ambulance, large or small, on two, three or more wheels. Enthusiastic exits demonstrated the narrowness of the archway and of Pottergate itself, and scars on adjoining brickwork lasted long after the demise of the station. The Chief

Constable, Edwin Winch, expressed concern at the perils of egress from the fire station and his successor, John Henry Dain, was similarly perturbed, telling the Watch Committee the station's location in an area of narrow streets was dangerous. Collisions and inci-

Horse-drawn fire engines on Gentleman's Walk. A graphic impression from Harry Potter. The original of this picture is held at the Norwich Headquarters of the Norfolk Fire Service.
(Norfolk Fire Service)

dents in this area were more numerous than records reveal. The horse ambulance skidded sufficiently to warrant a special report to the Watch Committee in 1921 and another report followed in 1926 when it collided with a car in Exchange Street. There is every reason to believe that Pottergate travellers knew of the dangers and proceeded warily.

The Council acquired other property in Pottergate, beginning a period that captures several of today's personal memories. In 1914 a section house was included on the opposite side of the road at number 13, and in 1925 they took over number 17. Other accommodation in the street was secured for police personnel at different times.

Twenty-four single police firemen were in resi-

The first motorised fire engine, CL 67, was purchased in 1911, seen here after attending a fire at Upper Hellesdon Mill in Press Lane in 1913. The Chief Constable, Edwin Winch, is standing left in the picture, surveying the engine. This photograph has been shown in several books featuring old Norwich and is part of a postcard collection relating to the Upper Hellesdon Mill fire.
(Force archives)

dence at the section house, with an Inspector or Sergeant living in a house nearby. The section house men performed normal police duties and were on stand-by for fire duty at other times.

Police firemen now received an additional wage for their fire duties, no longer gratuities at the whim of the Watch Committee. In 1935, at the end of the Pottergate era, a police fireman was receiving 3s per week on call money, 2s 6d for each fire attended and 5s if water was used.

An Inspector, Sergeant and two Sub-Engineers were used as full-time firemen, though Chief Constable Dain was firm in his belief that all police-men were firemen, designated or not. To make his point he ordered one hour per week fire drill for all. Police pay at this time was 58s per week, rising to 70s after 17 years. Boot allowance was paid at 6d per week.

Life in the Pottergate Section House had some compensation for the men billeted there. A visiting cook provided a hot dinner each day, free of charge, and, in addition to the normal rota leave days, the men were granted spells when they were not on call: not exactly a gift of relaxation because if they stayed in the building they were expected to answer the bells. Every Sunday morning the two duty drivers scrubbed the engine house floor, on hands and knees.

Firemen at Pottergate c.1927. The most senior officer, seated centre, is Superintendent Alex Christie, who joined the force in 1900 from the Metropolitan Police and rose to the position of Deputy Chief Constable (see chapter nine). He retired in 1933. Sub-Engineer (Sergeant) Colin Bell, front left, served from 1900 until 1927 and Sergeant George Parker, front right, served from 1904 until 1935 (promoted Inspector 1929). Bell and Parker can be seen later in this chapter as ambulance drivers and Christie and Parker appear in the Mounted Branch. (Force archives)

Firemen at Pottergate c.1920 with a mixture of horse-drawn and motorised engines – favouring the horse-drawn. The central figure, the Chief Engineer in charge, is Inspector William Thompson who held the post from 1914 until 1927.

(Force archives)

Police firemen who could not be accommodated in the Pottergate Section House were placed in lodgings. This was no bar to a call-out. Constable Ernie Croxson gives a chronological example of 'duty calls' in the late 1930s. This sequence was not extraordinary but is representative in an historical record. Not officially on duty until 2pm, he was rudely awakened at 1am by a furious hammering upon the front door of his lodgings (many Constables were roused over the years by a style of imperious door knocking that shouted urgency and authority, and woke several other houses in the vicinity). The upturned face of the patrol Constable relays the message to be at the fire station at 2am. Constable Croxson obeys, sleepily, travelling in his police uniform, then changing into a fireman's tunic and round unpeaked hat. He is taken in a police van to Horsford (a fee-paying protected parish for fire brigade purposes) to relieve a fire-crew fighting a stack fire, eventually pulling the burning straw apart at

The Theatre Royal fire of June 1934. Within a charred framework, through a mist of smoke, a hosing policeman abstains a fireman's uniform – and wearing a white scarf? (A.Rix)

8am. Refreshment consisted of hot coffee brought to the scene in a huge earthenware jug and liberally spiced with rum by the stack owning farmer. Back to the fire station to unroll and scrub down the used hoses, finishing at 9.30am with the reminder that the next duty (police type) was scheduled for 1.45pm.

Reporting to the police station 15 minutes before a duty time was obligatory, though there is an earlier record of ten minutes being stipulated. Earlier still, shortly after the force was constituted, the Watch Committee required officers to attend for duty 15 minutes before the beginning of a shift. How and exactly when five minutes was won and lost is not clear. Neither 15 nor ten minutes apply today.

Calling out off-duty officers for fire purposes exercised Chief Constable Dain's mind on two particular occasions. In 1921 he reported that he had enough men to answer two fire calls at once but to cover this eventuality he wished to use a room at the Guildhall to sleep a number of extra stand-by men. The Watch Committee approved and the selected men were paid the extra fire money. That this arrangement did not last is evidenced by the Chief Constable's instruction in 1932 that a motor cycle was to be used to call officers directly to a fire or to the station on stand-by. In this same year he reported that in the case of 'large fires' he had men 'properly trained and drilled' from the First and Second Police Reserves and they would 'attend fires when required'.

The Chief Constable was also the chief fire officer and his official uniform hung on a peg in the fire station alongside his fireman's tunic, helmet and axe. On the opposite side of the road, at the section house, the firemen's apparel was in a state of readiness. The abrupt clatter of the alarm bell would galvanise men into a flurry of action, leaping into fire brigade trousers and rolled leather fire boots before running across the road, dodging traffic, to snatch tunics, helmets and axes off pegs. The sequence of frenetic activity continued with the designated engine driver scrambling into the driving seat and, in the motorised version, roaring off through the archway with men clinging to the sides with one hand and buttoning tunics with the other.

The routine for the horse-drawn engine was necessarily longer, though not so long because an automatic harnessing contraption slotted over the horses who, well used to the routine, would be trotting smartly into position. Some quick and well-practised fastening and the horses would be galloping through the archway with the driver hauling and slackening opposite reins to negotiate the rearing animals into the tight turn into Pottergate, firemen behind him gripping the rattling engine and bumping up and down in concert with the solid wheels. To the public meandering upon their daily business it was a stirring sight. A roaring, exhaust belching engine or hoof clattering, eye-rolling horses pulling a creaking, rattling fire engine lined with serious faced, comb-helmeted men. The urgency was obvious. If water was placed on the fire the duty firemen were entitled to an extra payment.

On 18 March 1904 the Watch Committee inspected the fire station and watched the brigade turn out in 54 seconds. It was noted that the committee 'approved'.

In November 1934 a new fire station was opened at Bethel Street and Pottergate was consigned to history. The horse-drawn engines had gone and the fleet was by now totally motorised, even fitted with pneumatic tyres. Living accommodation was provided above the new station.

Soon the duties of police, fire and ambulance were to begin the process of divorce. The National Fire Service was born in August 1941, arising from the Fire Service Act of 1938, despite the misgivings of the Chief Constable who expressed his doubts as to the efficiency of two separate organisations. Police firemen were offered the choice of services. The majority joined the police service. A united service no longer the new fire service later refused the police the use of recreational facilities in the new fire station.

After the war the fire service was to return to local authority control, not exactly a happy union because they went on strike in 1951, following which the Chief Constable ordered that police officers would not be used to eject firemen from the fire station; someone must have considered the prospect.

The move from Pottergate, and the separation of fire service duties, resulted in a new section house. In 1941 a Victorian house at 7 Unthank Rd was acquired for single police Constables and was connected to the police station by telephone. Policemen were never off duty.

But the section house living-on-the-job syndrome was fading with the loss of the fire service – Constables were not hauled out of 7 Unthank Road with anything like the same frequency as Pottergate. And another arm of the emergency services was shortly to go. Ambulances had followed the evolutionary path of fire engines with military and private organisations supplementing the police service, responding when asked; in fact the Red Cross had offered to run a regular service during World War One when the availability of Constables was at a premium. Now, in the 1940s, like the fire service, the end was in sight, from a police point of view.

The very first police ambulance was a handcart kept in the Guildhall, later improved to a covered 'hand ambulance' – still a cart. A patient hurriedly transported over stone set and cobbled streets usually remembered the journey. The evolving horse drawn ambulances were faster, if no less painful to the ill and injured. The last horse-drawn police ambulance was offered to the Red Cross in 1927.

The police motorised ambulance was a giant step forward but the service was understaffed and the driver leaving Pottergate would often pick up a patrol Constable to assist with accidents, suicides and body removals. The Chief Constable more than once complained that the ambulance service was deleterious to his police strength. In 1945 he reported 'great difficulty' in manning ambulances. At the time he was under strength as a result of the war and he was allowed to recruit seven ambulance drivers and seven attendants. His complaint was, however, on delicate ground for the Home Office had warned him in 1944 that the ambulance service was no longer considered to be a police responsibility. The Watch Committee and Chief Constable had noted the Home Office warning and made a decision not to make a decision, at that time. Wait until after the war was the minuted response. The strength of the force was then 127 against an establishment of 156.

Interestingly, the 999 emergency call facility came into being in 1946 with the dulcet toned telephone operator greeting of 'police, fire or ambulance?' They had been one service, had become two, and shortly would be three. In 1948 the local authority took over the ambulance service.

The first motorised police ambulance was a Cadillac, painted dark green and equipped with a foot operated gong to warn of its approach. A report says that the large glass side panels were replaced by smaller ones (possibly to allay the nerves of unwell prospective passengers who may have thought a hearse was approaching), but available photographs of this noble carriage do not reveal the change. This vehicle came into service in 1918, an impressively contrasting forerunner of the garishly coloured, noise jangling, light flashing, speeding vehicle of today. It was presented to the city by S.L.Witton, shoe manufacturer of Muspole Street, who later paid for a conversion from solid to pneumatic tyres thereby improving the lot of the person in the back. Note the open sides, which created a through draught that could, and did, eject policemen's helmets. At the end of the Cadillac's service, in the 1930s, it was cannibalised and parts were fitted to a replacement vehicle.

(Force archives)

An Austin, left, joins the Cadillac at Pottergate, c.1928 (to be joined by a Dennis in 1930 – see photograph chapter five) with posing crews destined to experience varied careers. Left to right: Constables George Lee, Hugh Murray, Harold Godbold and Sam Bussey. Lee joined in 1920 and became Inspector and Chief Engineer of the police fire brigade, then joining the newly formed National Fire Service. Murray served for 34 years (1923-57) retiring as Traffic Department Inspector. Godbold served from 1925 until 1931 when he was forced to resign through ill-health. Sam Bussey joined in 1926 and was promoted to Sergeant before, in 1941, he too joined the new National Fire Service. He was killed on duty in 1942 and his story is told in chapter eight. (M.Dixon)

Policemen in their ambulance driver role c.1927. Left to right, back row – Constables John Pye, Jimmy Sanders, Frank Trollope, James Godbolt; front row – Constable George Lee, Sergeant George Parker, Constable Harold Godbold, Sergeant Colin Bell, Constable Hugh Murray. Sanders (served from 1920 to 1945) was also an accomplished horseman seen at several ceremonial events. He served in World War One where he earned the Military Medal. (Force archives)

Some historical vagueness and misconception has existed over exactly when Norwich police horses were used, where they came from and when they finished. The research and record that follows has been obtained from the records of the Watch Committee and other reports of the time, combined with recollections noted then and now.

Horses served all three services – police, fire and ambulance. They had a continuing role until the very end of the force itself, though their significance waned through succeeding years as police horse patrols were discontinued and, slowly, the fire brigade and ambulance services became totally motorised. The Watch Committee of 1840 minuted that they were considering the formation of 'horse police' but deferred making a decision. The next reference appears in 1849 when it is noted that N.Beddingfield was paid £20.16

A white ambulance in the fire station yard c.1941. The Constable in the background is John Burton. The policewomen are wartime auxiliaries and have been identified as, left to right, Eve Ellis, Peggy Cockerill, Dorothy Taylor and Kathy Whall. (G.Burton)

'for hire of horses for police during royal agricultural meeting'.

In July 1857, horse patrols began, one patrol only but later in the month two, and the riding Constables were issued with cutlasses. These first horses were hired and not used for fire brigade purposes. It is a moot point exactly when they began hauling fire engines. The patrols were discontinued for reasons unknown six months later, only to reappear again towards the end of the century, hauling fire engines and patrolling. These early horses were stabled in the Guildhall, emerging from the basement via a ramp, but later, like fire engines and policemen, were kept in various places in the city.

The Mounted Branch was at its peak in the early part of the 20th century, using riders experienced through military service and competent through training that was at one time undertaken at the cavalry barracks in Barrack Street, where some of the 'police' horses actually came from. The extent of this training is not fully documented but there is a note that it was for the horse as much as the rider because the animal had to become used to a sword (cutlass) slapping against its flanks. This sword, alias cutlass, was not necessarily a ceremonial accoutrement. A witness to a

disturbance in the Market Place recorded that he was impressed by the sight of a police horse charging the mêlée with the officer drawing his cutlass with a loud scraping sound that was both alarming and disconcerting to the rioters, and the witness. Scraping the cutlass from the scabbard, or along the road surface, was a tactic that has a modern equivalent in a row of padded, visored officers methodically advancing upon rioters and beating truncheons upon shields.

Researching information on police horses revealed the statement of a long serving Norwich officer that 'there never was a Mounted Constabulary as such', meaning, a separate force. True! What did exist was a number of horses ridden by accomplished Norwich police horsemen, used for patrol purposes in both centuries, but more consistently after the Boer War (1902) up to World War One (1914), less so into the 1920s. In both centuries they were specially used for civic occasions and to combat threatened public disorder. In those peak years it was unquestionably a Mounted Branch. This does not disguise the fact that the horse was also an animal of labour in the eyes of the force, used to haul fire engines and ambulances. How much training the horses received in their tripartite role is open to doubt, especially as they were mostly borrowed or hired. Police ownership can only be confirmed from the early 1900s, and then only in part.

On 2 October 1896 the Watch Committee were informed that a fire had occurred and 'Mr Wigg was not able to supply horses to take the engine to a fire'. They were additionally told that firemen dragged the engine there. The committee resolved to ask Mr Wigg, a dealer of Cattle Market Street, 'his charges'. Some serious horse-trading followed.

The first recorded purchase of horses took place in 1903 when four were acquired, one for the use of the Chief Constable. After this date there were hirings and purchases. An agreement with Mr Wigg and a Mr Fiddy to supply horses was extended in 1914. There followed a number of single purchases and unknown number of hirings. The last confirmed recorded purchase of a horse by the police was in 1927 (but see later) when it was decided that Rose had to be replaced at a cost of £30. She was sold at auction for £11 16s 6d, an ignoble end to years of loyal police service.

At the commencement of the Pottergate Fire Station three horses were stabled at the rear of the building, two on stand-by for fire and one for patrol. These horses appear to have been hired. As patrols increased the number rose to five and included purchased animals. It is possible this number at Pottergate rose again, though it is more probable that recourse was being made to other stabling facilities or to an immediate hiring facility. A brief reference by the Watch Committee to stables in Bethel Street does not take the matter any further. The force certainly had the use of more than five horses in the early 1900s. Photographs of the time show 16 horses on parade – see later.

The sometimes spoken belief that police horses finished shortly after World War One undoubtedly comes from the decline in regular patrols but is contradicted by the 1927 purchase. It is a belief further put to rest by the record in February 1930 of the Chief Constable reporting that in the event of 'horses used by the mounted police becoming unfit' they will not be replaced and that only two horses will be kept in future. Two months later it was decided that Prince was unfit for duty and was to be 'destroyed under supervision'. But in September of that year the Chief Constable was authorised to purchase two horses offered to him. If he did purchase them it is not recorded and the final record in this chapter of purchased and retained horses is the Chief Constable's report of February 1931. He decided, and noted, that 'two horses kept at the fire station for police purposes be sold to Mr Bacon-Palmer'. The Watch Committee approved the decision and authorised him to hire the horses back at 10s 6d per horse per day, as and when required. History therefore records 1931 as the end of the police horses, in the propriety sense. Others would follow, some with distinction, but they would not truly be a part of the Norwich City Police. The Mounted Branch was to be replaced by the occasional need to find a horse and then find someone in the force who could ride it.

Horses have their special place in the force history. In the early 20th century they provided their own arm of community relations, a distinctive, imposing and salutary presence, reassuring and yet inhibiting, symbolic of the credible authority of a police force that had moved a long way from 1836. It was recorded that children frequently appeared at the Pottergate stables to see the horses, armed with titbits. Apparently, one horse was adept at begging for carrots.

Police horse Charlie was another who went on record as canvassing for treats. He was a sturdy animal, the mount of Constable Robert Beales who was 18 stone and 6ft 6ins tall. The Constable's son records that they lived in Pottergate and when Charlie was passing he knocked on the door of their house with his hoof until rewarded with a lump of sugar. Constable Beales joined the force in 1890 and retired on ill health grounds in 1911.

In January 1917 HM Inspector of Constabulary asked the Chief Constable to release as many mounted officers as he could spare for military police service in France.

In 1918 the Mounted Branch provided a more mundane and domestic service: the Chief Constable approved the use of police horses for collecting firewood for members of the force.

Police horses Charlie, Rose, Albert, Marie, Prince and Tom all found their way into the records of the force, for varying reasons. Sometimes, sadly, it was the end of loyal service and life itself, though Charlie was ordered in 1914 to be 'turned out on the marsh for a few weeks', seemingly a beneficial move for Charlie because he went on until 1923 before he was 'destroyed' and a new horse purchased. Albert did not fare so well, suffering a severe loss of status. He was sold to the unfortunately named Sewer and Irrigation Committee and later it was reported that he was ill. His fate from then on was not recorded but can be guessed. Tom was sold to Whitlingham Farm in 1918 and Rose (preceding the Rose of 1927) went the same way in 1919 the Watch Committee having been informed that she was 'blistered and tired'. In 1929 the Watch Committee told the RSPCA, presumably following inquiry, that horses were always disposed of humanely.

Ormonde, exotically and euphemistically named after a Derby winner, was a Norwich police horse. According to a recollection passed to the press by a Norwich officer, he saved his dismounted rider from a threatening gang of poachers by 'prancing and kicking around the group' until they were all driven back and

Constable Arthur Chaplin was born in 1876 and joined the Norwich City Police in 1900. Records show him acting as the mounted escort on several ceremonial occasions. He retired in November 1922 and died in February 1947. (J.Watts)

This compelling photograph of members of the Norwich City P[...] Mounted Branch was taken at St Andrew's Plain on 25 Oct[...] 1909 on the occasion of the visit of King Edward VII. These h[...] men are worthy of some detailed reference. The Sergeant in ch[...] first on the left, is Alfred Harrison, collar identification P, who jo[...] the Norwich police in 1896 after military service but was recall[...] the 7th Dragoon Guards in 1899 to fight in the Boer War whe[...] obtained the rank of Sergeant Major, note the insignia carried [...] the police uniform, a practice permitted by the Watch Comm[...] He returned to serve in the force until retirement as Inspecto[...] 1923. He then went onto the First Police Reserve. He was an ex[...] tional horseman, accomplished swimmer, physical training inst[...] tor at the Lads' Club and drill instructor for the force. Among[...] awards was the Royal Humane Society Certificate for saving a [...] from the river at Pulls Ferry in 1908. He died in 1961 at the a[...]

arrested. Such exploits would be seen in Western films 40 years later but were less familiar at the beginning of the century. Whoever strayed from the common practice of allocating homely names to police horses must have known something for the racing Ormonde was never defeated and was reputedly the greatest racehorse of his time.

The practice of using untrained, unknown horses was fraught with danger. A heavyweight policeman

then the oldest police pensioner. Following on, left to right, ·ers are: Sergeant G Alex Christie, served 1900 to 1933, pro-·ed to Superintendent, see firemen's picture earlier; Constable ·rank Dean, became a Sergeant in the Norfolk force in 1910; ·enjamin Stewardson, ex-6th Dragoons but left the force in ·0; 99 George Leatch, joined in 1902 after service in the 7th ·cers, was promoted to Inspector in 1924 and retired in 1929; ·lfred Towers who joined the Norwich City Police in 1898 and · recalled to the colours in 1899 for the Boer War where he ·ed with distinction as a member of the mounted infantry, ·iving the Queen's South Africa Medal with clasps for the ·ef of Kimberley, Paardeberg, Driefontein and Transvaal, also ·King's South Africa Medal 1902. Towers returned to the city ·ce in 1902, becoming a member of the Mounted Branch. In ·· 1911 he escorted King George V on his visit to the city and

received the George V Coronation Medal. In 1915 he rejoined the Army to fight in World War One, serving in the Military Mounted Police and achieving the rank of Squadron Sergeant Major. He was mentioned in despatches. In 1918 he was wounded and sent home where he joined the Norfolk Regiment and became a Temporary Second Lieutenant. He rejoined the city force in 1919, was promoted to Sergeant in 1921 and retired in 1923. Alfred Towers died in 1949 having well and truly left his mark on police and military history. Resuming left to right: 79 William Fuller, ex-5th Lancers, served in the force from 1886 until 1912; 22 Frederick Noller, ex-Army, served in the force from 1890 until 1917; Sergeant H John Varley, served from 1884 until ill-health in 1911. At the end of the line is Constable 41 George Parker, 1904-35, promoted to Inspector, seen earlier in fire and ambu-lance roles.

(B.Harrison)

A smiling Inspector Harrison (promoted 1914) sees his horse patted by HM Inspector Leonard (later Sir Leonard) Dunning, watched approvingly by Chief Constable Edwin Winch. The location is Chapelfield. (Force archives)

Mounted Superintendent (and Deputy Chief Constable) Robert Hodges converses with HM Inspector Leonard Dunning, watched by members of the Watch Committee and the Chief Constable – helmet just visible. All in this second picture, again at Chapelfield, were to have significant differences within a short time, or perhaps this was the time (1914). (See chapter nine.) (M.Dixon)

urging towards a disturbance or leading a noisy parade may not have been part of the horse's experience. One case has been well documented. The Deputy Chief Constable, Superintendent Herbert Balls, was riding a hired, fine white horse that was much admired by the crowds lining the route of the coronation parade of 1937. They also admired the Superintendent's display of horsemanship prompted by the horse being a hunter and not used to a band marching closely to its rear. The press advanced the opinion that 'rider and horse must have been thankful when the procession was over'.

A horse allocated to a Chief Constable has escaped photographic confirmation of carrying a Chief Constable, though Robert Hitchman, 1859-97, was reputed to have ridden the streets of Norwich. Edwin Winch, 1897-1917, was allocated a steed but it is likely that the animal pulled him in a gig (a light two-wheeled carriage) that was part of the force transport until disposed of in 1926. It should also be noted that

Another imposing equestrian line-up at Chapelfield, headed by Superintendent Robert Hodges. Note the number of horses on parade, most of which must have been hired. Constable 23 Arthur Chaplin is first on right, 45 Alfred Towers fifth from right, 103 Richard Davison sixth from right.
(M.Dixon)

Mr Winch's weight had reached 25 stones by the time he retired.

John Henry Dain, 1917-43, was the beneficiary of a motor car – and a pedal cycle, which also has escaped record of use. It can be recorded with absolute certainty that Alan Plume, 1943-63, preferred Humbers and Wolseleys and Frank Brown, 1963-67, would have recoiled from a horse.

The disappearance of the Mounted Branch was not the complete end for horses fulfilling a police role. A local brewery helped with horses to pull the civic coach at the opening of the Assize and striking ani-

In this striking photograph, c.1915, Inspector Alfred Harrison is in the centre. On his right (picture left) is Sergeant Alex Christie and on his left is Sergeant George Leatch. (A.Brown)

mals they were. (There is no evidence to support the oft-recounted story that they held up the civic parade by hesitating outside the brewery's public houses.)

Memories of proud equine years were stirred in the 1950s by the emergence of a famous, still talked about, Norwich police horse. To be exact, Starlight was not a police horse. He belonged to a policeman with a love of horses, the ability to ride them following service in the Queen's Household Cavalry and a willingness to lend himself and Starlight to special occasions in the city. Sid Cole joined the Norwich City Police in 1935 after service with the Gloucestershire Constabulary. Sid's career was distinguished by CID and uniform service and particularly by his appearance on Starlight at ceremonial occasions.

Constable Philip Hemmings rode Paddy, supplied by a local riding stable, backing up Sid Cole and Starlight. Philip was an ex-Royal Artillery soldier of World War Two experience and competent with horses. This competence was, however, tested when the riding stables began to produce new mounts instead of the tried and tested Paddy. An untrained substitute police horse could turn a solemn civic occasion into a diverting spectacle for the crowd and an embarrassment for the rider who would later have to explain rodeo antics to an unsympathetic senior officer who knew and cared nothing of horses. One example has already been quoted.

Fame is the spur. Sid Cole rides Starlight ahead of a street parade in St Giles' Street in 1956, surely the only Norwich police officer to provide an autographed photograph. Starlight, a chestnut with hunting and point-to-point experience, was 22 hands high and 27 years of age in 1956. He died in 1957, four months after Sid Cole's retirement from the force.

(Force archives)

Constable 'Paddy' O'Brien and ex-War Reserve Constable Alfred Salmon followed Sid and Philip, riding hired horses as required, but the special occasions became less horseworthy as imperious black limousines made their processional appearance behind a motor cycle vanguard. By this time knowledge and experience of horses was scarce; the police force's great love affair with the horse had gone in the name of progress. In the 1960s, the force was offered the gift of a horse, declined by a suspicious Watch Committee who resolved to hire as required and preferably to use motor cycle outriders.

Horses went into history, along with section houses and a three-pronged service.

Philip Hemmings on Paddy outside the Guildhall c.1951.

(P.Hemmings)

Sid Cole and Starlight escorting the civic coach at the Cathedral in 1955.

(A.Brown)

Not quite the magic of the horse. These 1947 outriders are Constable Thomas 'Paddy' Mulrenhan, left, and Constable John Burton, right.

(G.Burton)

CHAPTER FOUR
Backbone of the Force

On the beat: communications, police stations, property inspection and traffic control

THE early grinding years and the consolidating middle years of the force gave way to a transformation that picked up between the world wars and accelerated after the second great conflict. Changes were allied to the developing motor vehicle and new communications and training. The new century saw invention, diversification and development, the decline of the horse, the advent of police patrol cars, vans, motor cycle combinations, beat motor cycles, police dogs and frogmen, the development of the CID, the inauguration of cadets, the integration of women, new police stations and police designated telephones. New duties proliferated.

The force continued fire and ambulance services along with the registration and supervision of pedlars, hawkers, aliens, firearms, explosives, petroleum, weights and measures, places of public entertainment, lunatics, cattle, dogs, birds, drugs, lost and found property, the testing of gas meters and the training for, and application of, first aid. All have been recorded as the responsibility of the police. Later, a more sinister subject would be allocated regular training – Civil Defence. Two world wars left their mark on the city and its police force.

Other duties were domestic and menial, not to be found in any manual. Cleaning the station lavatories, windows and brass plates were examples. Some of these tasks lasted through to the 1960s when it was still possible for early travellers past Bethel Street Police Station to be caught by the station reserve Constable appearing on the steps vigorously shaking the mat that umpteen inquiring citizens had trodden the previous day.

Constables cleaning the Chief Constable's car, tending his garden and running errands for Inspectors were other examples of extraneous and quasi-official 'duties' that persisted in the 20th century and could still be found almost to the end of the force, duties that sit uneasily within modern thinking.

Some official extraneous duties were discarded in the name of progress. In 1918 the Watch Committee resolved that the police would 'cease to extinguish public electric lights' and in 1933 HM Inspector of Constabulary said the force should no longer collect rate arrears. The police acting as court ushers lasted until 1966.

The Chief Constable undertook duties that have no place in modern policing. In 1946 he reported to the Watch Committee that the film 'Snow White and the Seven Dwarfs' could be safely shown to the Norwich public. A well received decision.

But from the beginning of the force consistently to the very end, one fundamental police duty was enshrined in the policeman's lot, the cornerstone of police and public relations from which all other duties flowed, a duty that has now also passed away in the name of progress; well, nearly. In the beginning it was called 'simple patrolling', later known more emphatically by those who did it as 'pounding a beat'.

Senior officers were disposed to refer to the backbone of the force. This announcement was often made in a stirring speech to assembled officers in the manner of a general rallying his troops, but sometimes it was on a one to one basis in an office in the police station, directed at a Constable who was starting his career or had already started it and inflicted some

DAY DUTY BEATS.

First Relief and Fourth Relief.

No. 1.—The Walk.

From Corn Hall to Briggs' Street, Corner Rampant Street. Straight up and down.

No. 2.—London Street.

	1	2	3	4
Guildhall	6.0	7.15	8.15	9.25
St. Giles' Gates	6.20	7.35	8.35	9.45
Dove Street	6.40	7.55	8.55	
Bank Plain	6.55	8.5	9.5	
Guildhall	7.15	8.15	9.25	10.0

No. 3.—St. Stephen's.

	1	2	3	4
St. Stephen's Church	6.0	7.0	8.0	9.0
Victoria Station Yard	6.25	7.25	8.25	9.25
Top of Surrey Street	6.40	7.40	8.40	9.40
St. Stephen's Church	7.0	8.0	9.0	10.0

No. 5.—1 H. and 5 Min.

	1	2	3	4	5
Start at the Nelson P.H. Timberhill	10.10	11.35	1.15	3.20	4.50
„ Brazen Doors	10.30	11.45	2.5	3.30	5.0
„ Finket Street	10.40	12.10	2.25	3.50	5.20
„ Ber Street Gates	10.50	12.20	2.35	4.0	5.30
„ Rose Tavern	11.0	12.40	2.45	4.15	5.45
„ Horn's Lane	11.10	12.50	3.0	4.30	
„ Thorn Lane	11.20	1.0	3.10	4.40	
„ Nelson Corner	11.35	1.15	3.20	4.50	

No. 6.—1 H. and 45 Min.

	1	2	3	4	5
Start from White Lion Street	10.5	11.45	2.10	4.10	5.45
„ Castle Street, London St.	10.15	12.10	2.30	4.25	5.55
„ Plough Corner	10.30	12.35	2.50	4.40	
„ Davey Steps	10.40	12.45	3.0	4.50	
„ Rose Corner	10.55	1.5	3.15	5.5	
„ Scoles Green	11.10	1.20	3.25	5.15	
„ St. Stephen's Plain	11.30	1.45	3.50	5.30	
„ White Lion Street	11.45	2.10	1.40	5.45	6.0

An 1880 beat book: day beats 1 to 3 and night beats 5 and 6 are reproduced. 'Straight up and down' on 1 beat must count as some flexibility. This beat book numbered 40 night beats and 12 day beats. (B.Kybird)

blemish upon its progress. The intention was to emphasise the importance of the Constable, especially in his role as the man on the beat: he was the backbone of the force, repeated with firmness. It was never denied; nor should it be.

The man on the beat, on foot, operating singly, distinctively wearing a helmet, talking to people, even 'idling and gossiping' (the words of police disciplinary regulations), declined coincidentally with the end of the Norwich City Police. He began with the start of the force as a tentative, probing, top hatted, unloved emblem of an unwanted authority, often patrolling with a colleague for confidence and protection. Change was gradual, acceptance muted and suspicious, but then, in time, he was welcomed, looked for and appreciated. At the end the public mourned his disappearance with the intensity they opposed his first appearance.

Management of the beats and the Constables working them was initially *laissez-faire*, especially at night. The original night watch officers were slaves to a system that required them to open a clock with a key and move a peg to record the time of their visit. These clocks were so positioned on the beat as to ensure the officer kept on the move, clocking every 15 or 30 minutes. There was, however, little direct supervision at night and the clocking was not all that it should have been. Constable Crome is recorded as missing '16 pulls' and was dismissed from the service. Constable Springfield 'set his key fast' two nights running and was fined 2s 6d. Undeterred, two months later he missed '13 pulls' and disappears from the records. (His only other record is that he missed his swearing-in ceremony.)

A Watch Committee note of 1839 refers to the formation of four divisions with a sequence of overlapping shift times. Each Constable was labelled with a divisional letter – A, B, C and D, changed according to his seniority in the division, a move further complicated by supernumeraries being allocated to a division and also numbered. This system, combined with a regular turnover of personnel, had little regard for probing historians.

An 1842 note refers to 'Night Constables' remaining on duty until 8am to be paid an extra 1s per week.

Another early system of beats divided the men into three divisions, including the night watch, each division tied to a shift. One division commenced duty at 6am and patrolled in pairs until 8am, then worked separately until they went off duty at 2pm. The relieving division patrolled singly, or in pairs as required, until the night watch took over and patrolled in pairs throughout the night – though the individual misdeeds of the night watch indicate that the pairings were theoretical or related to a different time.

Two Constables working together was not a normal fact of life on the beat. Any multiplicity meant a purpose, an anticipation of event, incident or something out of the ordinary. It some areas of the city at certain times in its history it meant protection, safety in numbers. Other reasons for a plural of Constables were a recruit being chaperoned (a practice more of later years when, freshly back from training school, he was accompanied and guided over two months of night duty), or an impromptu meeting leading to the heinous disciplinary offence of idling and gossiping.

A fact of beat policing was a manual of instruction, a tome of navigation that ignored discretion and initiative. Beat books, issued to each officer, were instruments of compulsion designed to ensure a

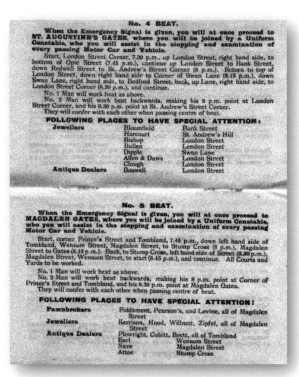

In this example, in use during World War One, beat numbers 4 and 5 are reproduced. Note that named shops were singled out for attention. 'Man will work beat backwards' should not be taken literally. (Force archives)

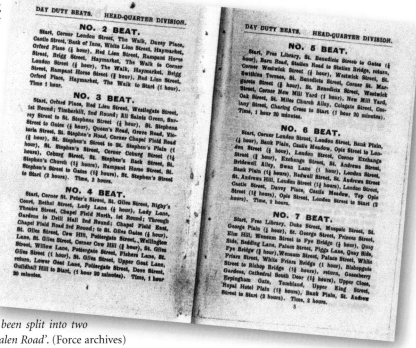

This beat book, dated 1919, shows the dictated progress on daytime schedules for beats 2 to 7, Headquarters Division. The city had been split into two divisions of 'Headquarters' and 'Magdalen Road'. (Force archives)

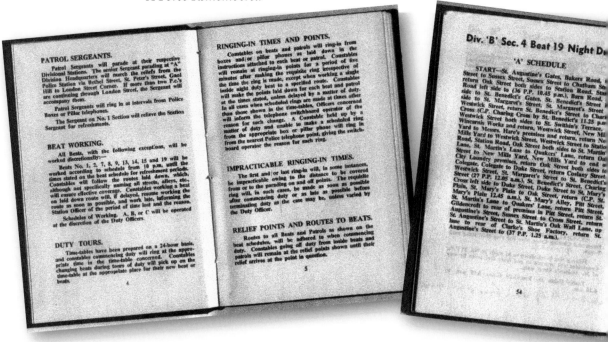

The beat book of 1938 dealt with boxes and pillarphones and took the beat Constable into and through World War Two, into the 1950s: instructional pages 4 and 5 are copied.

(Force archives)

robotic circulation through the streets during which, outside of normal business hours, the beat Constable was required to vigorously examine lock-up property. A beat book pinpointed the street position of a Constable at a given time, to the advantage of senior officers and, sometimes, the discomfit of the Constable. And the schedules allowed little or no time to admire the passing scenery, look for burglars or gossip. Many an officer was heard casting aspersions upon the character, sanity and soberness of the author of a beat book.

The original confidentiality of these books has been subverted by time and in an illustrated history it would be less than a reader's expectation not to reproduce certain examples.

Before the coming of pillarphones, after wayward rockets and exploding mortar shells, the beat Constable became the object of a new system of visual communication; primitive ingenuity unrecognised by

The man on his beat in 1928 in Orford Place – a lurking Constable taking stock of nothing much. Today the same scene is a concourse of pedestrian and vehicular traffic. (A.Brown.)

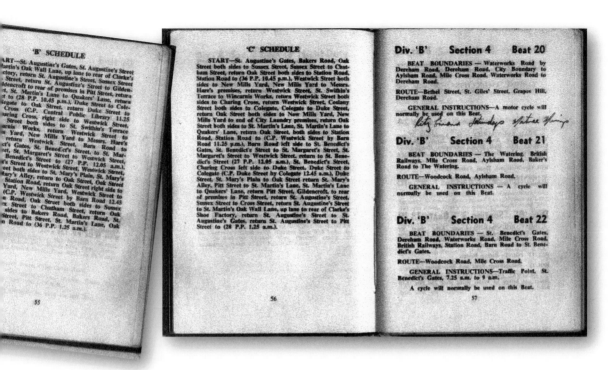

The last beat book, from 1956. The reader can choose a working schedule for 19 beat (the schedule for the day was decided by the early turn Inspector) and study the boundaries of 20, 21 and 22 beats. (20 and 21 were normally worked together on a motor cycle.) Note the written note of the Saturday matinee at the Ritz cinema (Dereham Road opposite Larkman).

(Force archives)

Man on the beat c.1928. Constable Harold Beaumont on the move in a deserted White Lion Street (just a solitary van), changed now to a bustling thoroughfare. (J.Stimpson.)

Lonely and wet, framed by darkness and light. A beat Constable hesitates for the camera at the junction of Botolph Street and Magdalen Street.   (ECN)

beat books. When a Constable was needed a block of wood was wrapped in white paper and pressed against the window of the Guildhall Police Station facing down Guildhall Hill, a prominent position overlooking the junction of five roads.

Refreshment for the beat Constable was acknowledged in later beat books, taken in all sorts of non-refreshing places and delivered by a barrow wheeled through the streets or, further afield, with the advantage of new transportation, by a police van or motor cycle combination.

In 1927 the first official refuge on the beat appeared: five police boxes of an eventual 13 were situated at Bracondale, Dereham Road, Magdalen Road, Earlham Road and in the garden of the Jenny Lind Hospital, Unthank Road. These wooden structures, in shades of dingy grey and brown, the forerunners of something more stylish, blue and better known, were fitted with a candle-stick telephone connected to the police station. More importantly, in the eyes of the beat Constable, they had heating rings for warming tea or soup.

Cycles gained their place in beat books, as did light-weight motor cycles but horses were not accorded a place and were fading as a patrol feature as beat books were developing.

In 1938 the beat system was enhanced by the introduction of pillarphones and police boxes of the type made famous by the *Dr Who* television series. They were strategically placed, although some Constables would argue otherwise, at various points in the city. Enveloping communications had arrived.

Watching the world go by, Gentleman's Walk pre-City Hall. (ECN)

The necessary new beat book detailed 25 beats and identified 19 police boxes and 35 pillarphones. The beat Constable was required to ring the police station at a stipulated pillarphone or box every hour and 20 minutes. In the intervening period he was required to answer what the book called a 'scintillating light' from any box or pillarphone. Members of the public were prone to cheerfully advise an idling street corner Constable, 'Your light is on!'

Such was the importance of the new communications the new police telephone box at Larkman Lane was opened on 12 July 1938 by the Lord Mayor, Mr Charles Watling. It is reported that he made a call and the police arrived within four minutes, impressing all concerned. A Panda car driver would be hard pressed to repeat that performance 60 years later; but then he would not be responding to the Lord Mayor, or have known in advance that the call was coming.

Advances contained in later beat books were

refreshments of 45 minutes (approved in 1949) – and taken in police stations! Old sweats continued to mumble about the 'good old days' of 20 or 30 minutes and sandwiches on the GPO steps.

Daytime fixed schedules disappeared and an element of discretion crept into the beat Constable's working life, subject to the stipulated 80-minute rings and that scintillating light. But the beat book of 1938 containing these improvements was to be the most disrupted. World War Two was near.

From 1956 a new beat book, the last, ruled the Constable's life. It basically left the beats unaltered, but reduced the number of police boxes to 15 and pillarphones to 19. This final manual of the streets was eventually to be overtaken by a new invention, one that heralded the passing of the beat Constable in the form and numbers known, coinciding with the passing of the Norwich City Police: but in the 1950s a panda was known only as a black and white furry ani-

'82 at 21'. Constable 82 Barry Catchpole rings into the police station from number 21 pillarphone at Pottergate by St Gregory's Alley. The comb type helmet came into use in 1961 and the pillarphone he is using was replaced by a new slimline model in 1963. Compare with the second photograph, which shows Sergeant Leslie Sturgess ringing in at the new type pillarphone. These street lighthouses disappeared completely in 1967 as personal radios heralded a new age of technology, but by then the force was on its way out. Note the Sergeant's shoulder where holes in the cloth denote the promotion and the removal of his Constable number, in this case 114. For nearly the whole of the force's history letters of the alphabet were allocated to Sergeants, a practice discontinued when the number of Sergeants exceeded the alphabet.

(B.Catchpole and force archives.)

mal and the thought of a beat Constable in a car was laughable.

Working a beat was a rigid exercise in both the physical and disciplinary sense. Physically came with the required stamina of body and mind and the night hazards presented by poorly lighted narrow streets,

Ringing-in, by token. The greater part of the force history was without established police communications, unless rockets, blocks of wood and a whistle counted. Tokens that operated the public telephone system were issued sparingly and briefly in 1927. The telephone company returned them to the force after use. Many officers serving in this era never saw the tokens and recall using only the public telephone system having been instructed never to go onto the beat without having tuppence in their pocket. (A.Brown)

and times, with an hour and 20 minutes in which to roam between scheduled telephone rings, out of sight of scintillating lights, there were certain shops, bakeries, commercial premises and watchman guarded buildings that provided a life restoring liquid together with agreeable company. Only a Constable who has tramped round 19 Beat (large, fast and disliked) during the first half of a night shift, in freezing temperatures, can appreciate the succour of a steaming hot mug of tea provided by the night custodian of the machinery at the New Mills Yard pumping station. And the baker in Ten Bell Lane would become upset if a heat seeking Constable did not visit him.

The cycling officer on 23 Beat, ravaged by the cutting east wind that penetrates even a police greatcoat, was even better off. He would be putting the world to rights with the night watchman in the Lido Ballroom and savouring the table of the recently finished dinner dance. Predatory Sergeants and Inspectors looked suspiciously upon such places, they had each been a beat Constable, and they occasionally made a foray designed to capture a Constable restoring his circulation and working his digestion in lieu of working his beat.

Doing something improper on the beat, like taking unauthorised refreshment or idling and gossiping (much later it was to be approved and called community relations), was potentially a disciplinary matter, usually a verbal admonishment of searing ferocity that relied on a repetition of expletives in lieu of a wider vocabulary.

A memorandum of 1947 directed 'gossiping to cease' and 'saluting to be strictly complied with'. Saluting was always seen as very important and police orders required that Magistrates and Councillors should be so recognised.

In 1954 the Chief Constable issued a memorandum of his image of the man on the beat. He disapproved of many things, notably 'leaning on doorways, bus or guard rails, leaning on car doors while speaking to drivers, hands in mack' pockets', and, 'chewing gum in recognised American fashion'.

In 1964 the Watch Committee complained that gossiping was on the increase but failed to record how they knew.

High treason for a beat Constable was being off his

A bulls-eye lantern. A poor light but a useful handwarmer in the early years of the century. (A.Brown)

winding black alleys and cobbled postage stamp yards that served a surround of over populated dwellings. The resulting criss-cross of washing lines over an unevenly surfaced, rubbish strewn, murky yard could garrote the unwary Constable, that is if he wasn't already smothered by an unseen sheet.

Bulls-eye lanterns issued to Constables cast a tired oil driven light and a later issue of battery charged Wootton lamps were a failure of illumination in an illuminating age of invention. These heavy, ponderous metal boxes, allegedly charged during the day to a light emitting capacity, were an impediment to any sudden movement and prone to drip acid if used in anything but a level position from which they revealed only a struggling watery light.

Fixed schedules kept the Constable on the move and some beats were regarded as bone breakers because of the route and times declared in the beat book. But away from that inhibiting dictate of streets beat without good reason. Murder and earthquake were probably good reasons. Stepping across the road to the next beat to look skyward for rogue lights on his beat was viewed with suspicion as an excuse.

Inspection of lock-up property was central to the beat Constable's existence. Outside of trading hours such property should be locked and without lights, other than display. Any deviations from this state of affairs required an immediate report and inquiry, before the passing public made a report or, worse still, the Sergeant or Inspector noticed the irregularity. Working a beat at night meant checking the property on the beat twice, at least, and physically. A memorandum of May 1962 said that shining a torch on a door was not acceptable. More than once a bored Constable, stifled into a routine of twist and push, turned a handle and leant on a door thinking of something else, only to unexpectedly pitch inside the premises. Insecure discovered, dignity lost – off to the pillarphone to ring-in for a keyholder.

If an irregularity was found on a second or subsequent property check there was a dilemma for the finding officer. Why had he not found it on the first check? He would be asked, very pointedly.

Irregularities found on the early shift, like a burglary, usually discovered by the shopkeeper, could, and usually did, lead to the sleep of the night Constable being rudely interrupted. He would be summoned to

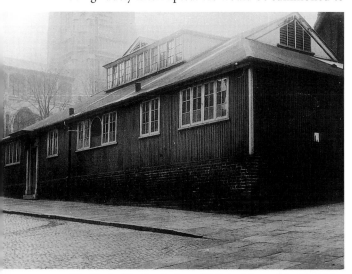

The 'tin hut' in the shadow of St Peter Mancroft in 1926 (also pictured in chapter five). (Force archives)

the police station to make an explanation as to why he had not found what someone else had found.

Police stations grew in number and varied in size throughout the 20th century. The Guildhall, the founder station, adapted and enlarged, was supplemented by a new station in 1911. From an aesthetic view it was a crash dive painful to the eye, but from a practical and logistical view it was progress. The 'tin hut', situated above the Market Place by St Peter's Street, became the Headquarters home of the Norwich City Police until 1938 and is still spoken off with the kind of affection that comes with nostalgia and a selective memory. It housed the Chief Constable and senior officers, the General Office and the parade room. It was the administrative centre of the Norwich City Police. The public continued to use the Guildhall.

From 1904 the Magdalen Road Division (also to be called Northern and B Division) was housed in a Victorian house at Magdalen Road at the corner of Marlborough Road. It served as a police station for receiving the public, parading on and off duty and refreshments. A hand propelled fire pump was parked in the parade room alongside a black, ominous looking stretcher that was fitted with a covering hood. For much of its existence this station housed a resident senior officer, firstly an Inspector and later a Superintendent; and it created more extraneous duties. There was a period when the early duty Constable had to go into the living quarters to clean out the grate and set the fire ready for the Superintendent's wife to light. The early duty Sergeant had to wind the station clock. The station was shut between midnight and 4am (sometimes longer depending on officers available) and the front door key was then kept under the mat. Crime prevention had some way to go.

In 1937 a small brick building was built in the yard of The Artichoke public house at Magdalen Gates and equipped with a representative blue light. A new police station was born, replacing the Victorian house next door. Attempts to sell the old station were unsuccessful and it was used as a stand-by station during World War Two and then converted into two police houses.

The new station, variously known as Magdalen Gates' Police Station, B Division Headquarters (from 1947) and 14 Box (listed in the beat book) was painfully small, struggling to parade three Constables and the supervisory Sergeant. Circumstances often placed more than four officers in the building at one time and there was much juggling and sideslipping of large bodies accompanied by grunts and expletives. During the day a clerk Constable received the public who were preferably unaccompanied and small in stature.

For many of the post war years the Magdalen Gates' station was ruled by a regular day clerk Constable, a studiously polite man who assumed father confessor status to the locals and Chief Constable rank to the beat Constables. Philip Salt had previously been a motor patrol officer and, having passed his promotion exams, was ambitiously considering his future when, in 1951, he was the victim of a serious road accident on a police motor cycle. Relegated to light duties he served first on River Patrol and then became the permanent B Division Clerk, retiring in 1965. Shortly afterwards the building died for police purposes, declared by the Chief Constable as unwanted because, in his view, the public telephoned or went to other police stations. It exists today, the property of a brewery, a reminder of policing that could be seen and felt as a reassuring presence within a community, a memorial to Philip Salt who died in 1990. The increasing use of police cars and radios made for an efficient, fast response but eroded the personal touch and made dinosaurs of old systems and buildings.

More police stations arrived in the 1950s. They were called Section Boxes and rivalled B Division HQ in size. The Chief Constable, Alan Plume, created these satellite stations; the idea obtained from an essay competition within the force the winner of which was Bernard Tester, later to be Superintendent.

Section Boxes were positioned at Earlham (Colman Road roundabout – the first to be opened – on 24 May 1952), Mile Cross (Woodcock Road), Tuckswood (Hall Road) and Kett's Hill (the last to be opened – on 29 August 1955). They were manned between 10am and 10pm, in theory, and used for parading on and off duty, refreshments and receiving the public. Section Box Clerk was a much-prized duty, especially in winter and during bad weather, and a beat Constable allocated this duty was thought to be much favoured. The expression 'Olympic Torch' was reserved for those who became clerks too often – never went out.

Magdalen Road Station c.1920. The Inspector has taken the time to pose for the camera. The board behind him advertises a garden fete. (Force archives)

Section Boxes did not have regular supervision, though the police house next door would contain an inquisitive Sergeant or Inspector, and were sometimes the scene of forgery and deception as weary, weather beaten Constables entered in the station book a commencing refreshment time that took account of a fast watch and later left the building on a timepiece that had slowed considerably. It was not unknown for lurking Sergeants and Inspectors to run time checks intended to prove the elasticity of an individual 45 minutes.

Magdalen Road Station c.1960. Undersized and overused: and then neglected. (A.Brown)

Mile Cross Section Box. Sergeant Alfred Wheatley meets Constable Peter Everest, and Constable Gordon Postance peers from the window. (ECN)

Tuckswood Section Box. Constable Jimmy Downes greets the public on opening day. Section Boxes are still in use today with the exception of Kett's Hill, which was closed and sold in 1999. (ECN)

The blue light entrance to Bethel Street station so well known to Norwich citizens. This station came into being on Good Friday 1938, replacing the 'tin hut'. It is part of the City Hall building opened by King George VI on 29 October 1938. Above the entrance are two embossed carvings: a policeman and a fireman – a record for all time of the dual duty of the city police. This entrance, now disabled, had the atmosphere and ambience of a police force of the time but has now given way to the corner entrance in the extension built in 1967, leading to a more spacious, brightly lighted foyer that must be better in practical terms but is more representative of a Post Office. (ECN)

There were two main planks to life as the backbone of the force. The protection of property had been essential from day one, but the other regular demand upon the beat Constable was initially a phenomenon, then a curiosity, and finally an everyday acceptance; but a nuisance for all that. The motor vehicle, mentioned as changing the beat Constable's life, began to dominate it during the working day.

Traffic supervision was initially a reactive exercise for the man on the beat. The imposition of the focal point of a distinctively garbed Constable measuring and guiding the order of things was to come with the motor car.

Point duty could be sudden and unforeseen – leaping into the road to disentangle opposing traffic that had glued itself together, or designated – specified places at specified times. In the 1950s and 1960s specified places included certain pedestrian crossings at times when the consistent flow of pedestrians threatened to permanently bisect the road traffic.

Traffic control as a skill really began in 1918 when the Watch Committee agreed that officers should be trained in the art of point duty, but not more than six officers because these new specialists were to be paid 1s per week extra. Approved traffic directing signals were later described in both force and Home Office booklets.

Many years later, when traffic duty was a routine part of a policeman's tour of duty, and extra payments had long gone, training was to be abrupt and based on the 'deep end' philosophy. It formed part of the induction course for probationer Constables, which was based at the Lads' Club. The Deputy Chief Constable's observation in 1954 that 'many young Constables were in need of instruction on point duty' ensured that great emphasis was applied to this part of the course.

Probationer Constables were taken in a group to Foundry Bridge and, after the traffic lights had been switched off, in turn placed in the middle of the road and told to 'get on with it'. Imperious signals lost their edge under the gaze of uniformed colleagues shepherded onto the pavement.

Bus drivers leaving Thorpe Station were sympathetic to these training spells, displaying a patience and cheerfulness that, after the demise of the city force, became as hard to find in the bus service as a Constable on the beat. Those who claimed that point duty Constables looked kindly and preferentially upon bus drivers were usually right. The bond probably started at Foundry Bridge.

The hazards of point duty were recognised in 1925 when white gloves and white coats were issued for this purpose, though white straw helmets and white gloves had been in summer use since 1912. The summer white straw helmet was discontinued in 1919 according to the Watch Committee record, possibly later in practice.

White helmets of a more solid composition were placed in police stations for traffic duties. These unfortunately were of a consistent size in a force of inconsistent heads and some officers wore them as an ornament, hoping the wind did not get up, while others settled uncomfortably inside to peer owlishly from below helmet rim level. They did not last beyond the

1930s. White armlets did last the course, stored in various places in the city for collection by point duty officers.

Different Constables offered different signalling styles, whatever the training, and could be recognised by stance and flourish by those in the know long before the face was visible. Constable John Fletcher had style on or off point duty. He was tall and well built, softly and politely spoken with a voice that leant more towards Oxbridge than Norfolk. His kindly and courteous approach disarmed many an outraged citizen looking for a fight, physical or otherwise. The tale of the vegetable lorry heading for the Market Place past a traffic duty John Fletcher is authentic. The extended white clad arm not only held two lines of traffic it fastened upon a large passing cauliflower, inspired by the call from the driver of 'Take a big 'un Jack'. For the remainder of that traffic duty a large cauliflower rested between polished boots.

In the 1920s-1930's period, preparatory to installing the new invention of traffic lights, the force had four regular traffic points: Foundry Bridge, GPO Plain, London Street corner (Market Place) and Charing Cross. The Foundry Bridge duty had an advantage provided by the Foundry Bridge Café, freshly cooked bacon and eggs in the police box outside Thorpe Station.

The London Street by Exchange Street point is best remembered, probably because it lasted longer, not receiving traffic lights until 1938. Ironically, in 1999 it is the only one of the original four points without traffic lights, struck by pedestrianisation in the last year of the force.

The Charing Cross duty rated the lowest appeal. It had a number of distinct disadvantages, all related to its narrowness. The centre of Charing Cross, with passing double deckers and A47 heading juggernauts, might have accommodated a thin ferret but it was no place for a sturdily-built policeman. Hence the system of yo-yo traffic control in which the timing of the hand signals and the Constable's dart to safety before they were obeyed were all-important.

A particularly distasteful aspect of the Charing Cross point occurred on Saturday mornings, especially wet Saturday mornings. As a main road into the city, and the Cattle Market, it attracted cattle drives that would have been in more in keeping with the Wyoming plains than the narrow crossroads of an ancient English city. And cattle did not understand the stop signal, and they liked all of the road, frequently the pavement as well – many a pedestrian bolted into a shop they did not want to go in.

Cattle drives lessened and cattle floats increased from the late 1930s, and traffic lights were installed at Charing Cross. But some hazards remained. The beat Constable learned never to stand too close to a laden cattle float, just wave the driver through and step away, quickly.

Traffic lights first arrived in 1929, at St Stephen's Gates, slowly spreading to oversee other junctions. By 1933 the city had five sets of traffic lights.

After the war came the most talked about point of all, the most famous and infamous (with apologies to Dickens): the Rampant Horse Street by St Stephens by Westlegate by Red Lion Street amalgam of roads was to leave its mark on the memories of many, not all of them policemen. Positioned in the centre of the bombing destruction and consequent rebuilding, it did not give way to traffic lights until 1964. It started with the signalling Constable standing at road level, exposed and threatened, then partly relieved by the prominence afforded by an orange box purloined from the fruiterers opposite. The fragility of orange boxes was recognised and relieved by something more substantial, 'knocked up' at the police station though the handyman skills of Constable 'Bodge' Newby. The offer of Mr J.Cook in 1956 to supply a free canvas cover for the new skeleton structure was accepted, qualified by the force insisting on paying the cost price of £2. So arrived the black and white striped box so well remembered by those that swirled around the surrounding roads or peered grimly through a windscreen awaiting a waved instruction.

Drivers who misinterpreted the hand signal cast from the all-powerful box could, depending upon the Constable delivering it, be the subject of a long range verbal dressing down eagerly and attentively absorbed by crowded pavements, or something worse. One Constable of undying fame was known to emphasise his remonstrations by punching the roof of any passing vehicle that had offended him. Some who performed at his junction were not averse to vacating the

box and marching menacing towards a frozen driver to deliver a homily of severe proportions, during which nothing else, on road or pavement, moved. It was said that people came especially to watch certain Constables on the St Stephen's point. There are authenticated reports of shamefaced drivers leaving the scene with ringing ears and an unwanted assessment of their driving ability, all under the gaze of fascinated bystanders. It is possible the 'aren't our policemen wonderful' saying died at St Stephens.

There were occasions when the drivers at St Stephens unwittingly got their own back. More than once a passing vehicle clipped the square box and turned it into a spinning container in which a disoriented policeman struggled for equilibrium and dignity. One much talked about case refers to an elderly

A job well done. The Foundry Bridge point duty Constable strides away, perhaps to his bacon and eggs. (ECN)

Directing with discretion. The ghost like Constable demonstrates the safety position essential to guiding traffic at Charing Cross c.1932. (Force archives)

lady who made better contact by ramming the box and pushing it, and the frantically stabilising Constable, into St Stephen's Street. She then politely asked for directions to Bonds' shop.

Unscheduled traffic points occurred with infuriating frequency at vulnerable places, usually caused by a sudden avalanche of traffic but sometimes by a traffic light failure dutifully reported to a Constable three streets away by a passing member of the public, probably the same one who persistently saw scintillating lights. Failure of the Charing Cross lights was an invitation to relive road-hopping history.

The GPO Plain traffic point still required the human touch even when liberally covered by traffic lights. The Prince of Wales Road junction with Upper King Street, opposite the GPO (now Anglia Television), provided a refuge island upon which the traffic lights control box was situated, still there today. For a period in the 1950s and early 1960s, when the evening rush hour was excessive (a bus strike in 1957 did not help), the age of push button control came to the Constable's aid. He was armed with a key that opened the box and revealed a row of control buttons. For an hour he became safe and omnipotent, happily pressing buttons according to his perception of traffic flows. There is no substance to the story that certain Constables calculated the speed and distance of an approaching car and pressed the red light button at the most inconsiderate time possible, accompanied by a stern gaze at the frantically braking driver.

Regular manned traffic points remained almost to the end of the city force but, eventually, the wheel was to go its full circle and consign point duty policemen to history, even the impromptu leaping into the road Constable. Traffic Wardens were invented in 1966 and beat Constables would not long after metamorphose into Panda cars. But by then it was not a city force.

The Foundry Bridge and Thorpe Station point framed by 1935 Silver Jubilee decorations. The point duty Constable has forsaken a white coat and is standing on a small platform that does little for his elevation. (ECN)

London Street corner and more 1935 Silver Jubilee decorations behind a well-whitened Constable. (ECN)

Almost London Street corner, more Market Place corner. The first picture dates to 1925 on what appears to be a filthy day and shows a Constable using only short white armlets. This photograph has been reproduced on greeting cards. The second photograph offers a different perspective and shows the white traffic helmet. This picture dates to 1937 and is rare because it shows the Municipal Buildings and the City Hall – peeking into view on the far right of the picture. Note the 'tin hut' and St Peter Mancroft far left. (ECN and force archives)

St Benedict's Gates. A traffic point of the post-World War Two period, operated weekdays at peak times when it was believed the city traffic was too much for the crossroads. Constable Albert 'Dixie' Dean is seen in action (one who directed with a recognisable style), the traffic flowing from St Benedict's Street into Dereham Road. (A.Brown)

Constables Peter Everest and Alfred Salmon guide schoolchildren over the pedestrian crossing at Tombland, c.1949.
(Force archives)

Traffic duty and crime prevention in 1953 from three policemen, though presumably the safe being moved from Martins' Bank in London Street is empty. (A.Brown)

Agricultural Hall Plain looking into Castle Meadow c.1925. A white-coated, white-helmeted policeman stands by a sign that says 'Caution – Drive Slowly': for obvious reasons. The building on the left is the Norfolk Constabulary Head-quarters. (A.Brown)

St Stephen's Street traffic approaching the point in 1955, showing that traffic congestion is not a symptom of modern times; it also shows, with careful exami-nation of the 'Keep Left' sign, where the point duty Constable left his coat.

(A.Brown)

An imposing presence at the junction of Prince of Wales Road and Upper King Street from Constable Edward Grint who joined the force in 1905 and retired in 1931. He died in 1933.
(R.Fowler)

A dark and wet GPO Plain and a lone policeman facing the traffic in Prince of Wales Road, c.1959.
(A.Brown)

St Stephen's point through changing times. The first picture, taken in 1955, shows a free standing point duty Constable and the stirrings of the new Curls' store.   (ECN)

Next, Constable Fred Jolly is the 'night time' (the point started at 8am and finished at 6.30pm) officer backed by a Vauxhall Velox (or Wyvern).   (ECN)

Constable Don Seager provides the contrast, photographed in 1956 by the press and described as 'something never seen locally before – a policeman on point duty in shirt sleeves'. The press immediately tackled the Chief Constable, Alan Plume, who had previously refused to sanction policemen in shirt sleeves, and he observed, 'The man on point duty at this spot is in the sun all day long, whereas other men do get some periods in the shade'. The remainder of the force continued wearing jackets during the hot weather though eventually shirt-sleeve order arrived for all and the St Stephen's point ceased to be privileged and envied.   (ECN)

Now an enclosed box, and the end in sight. (Left) Constable Laurie Harding is performing in wet weather in 1964 shortly before the point gave way to traffic lights. (The rain must have stopped or been light because the white rubberised coat hangs over the side of the box.) Then the end and a beginning in two pictures. (Top) December 1964, the last tour of duty and Constable Cliff Jessop takes a famous traffic point into history. Men can be seen connecting the new traffic lights. (Above) Next day the lights are working and there is a button to push to cross the road. A thoughtful Inspector Frank North and an interested youngster look to the future framed by Curls' Christmas lights. Note the redundant box in the background. (ECN)

CHAPTER FIVE

Detectives, Drivers and Divers

The CID, police cycles, Traffic Department, River Police and Diving Squad

THE evolution of policing was not confined to the man on the beat, as important as he was. Improving transport and increasing traffic, new techniques and new equipment, brought new specialists significant enough to be a separate department or branch of the force. The CID had long been so, the River Police off and on – subject to wars and winters, the Mounted Branch briefly within the context of the force's whole existence and, later, the Traffic Department, born of the motor car, a department rivalling the CID in strength and in-force desirability.

The Norwich CID began in 1856 under the direction of Detective Inspector George Steward, though it appears that initially he had only one detective to direct: Detective Sergeant Robert Rushmere, the holder of five merit badges for which he received 6d each per week.

Early in their existence detectives were briefly titled as Sub-Inspectors, which may have helped the élitist image maintained over later years.

Detective Constable William Beeston was one of the early Detective Constables, described, and pictured, in chapter two and in 1884 by the press as 'a wily detective'. The press noted that he was 'determined not to lose a good case'. The case in question was historically significant.

Ann Andrews complained that 'while proceeding to get a situation for the purpose of bettering herself' (a job) she was accosted and robbed of a silver locket and chain by two young men in Unthank Road. Constable Beeston 'with the assiduity which characterises the Norwich force made every search for the persons who were likely to answer Ann's description', said the press.

The assiduous detective's search was unsuccessful, but then the wily part came into play. He took Ann Andrews on a tour of dealers in the city and at the premises of Mr Freeman in Charing Cross found the locket and chain, sold earlier by Ann Andrews for the sum of 8s. Triumph for a detective through persistence and shrewdness. The rejoicing press waxed biblical and said of Ann Andrews, 'She goes on her way with a reputation equal to Ananias and Sapphira'. They called for some punishment to be devised for 'those who make false accusations' and concluded, 'We hope our police will always act as discreetly as they have done in this and similar cases'. Constable Beeston's success was far reaching. But he would not live to see the legislation called for by the press; that would take another lifetime.

Calling in Scotland Yard (established 1878) or the Metropolitan Police (1829) was a glorified tactic of provincial police forces, and the writers of detective stories, openly encouraged by the Home Secretary in 1906 but not overly practised by the Norwich force. London assistance was first noted via an intriguing Watch Committee minute of 1847 which states that £9 was paid to Daniel Forrester, a 'London police officer' for his attendance during Jenny Lind concerts at St

Andrew's Hall. Nothing more is known of Forrester's mission or expertise.

Who invited Inspector Swanson of Scotland Yard to Norwich in 1886 is unclear, probably the Chief Constable although that cannot be taken for granted in an age when local politics had much to say in what the police did and how they did it. Presumably the Scotland Yard Inspector knew something about explosions.

Inspector Swanson was met by Chief Constable Robert Hitchman and taken to Victoria Station where severe damage had been occasioned to a goods reception room and adjoining front entrance hall by an explosion heard throughout the city, attracting, according to the press, 'thousands of anxious folks' to the scene. Also visiting the scene was a formidable list of officials that included HM Inspector of Explosives, the Mayor, Town Clerk and the upper echelons of the railway company. If the CID had any part in the investigation it escaped mention. No person was hurt in the explosion because nobody was in the vicinity, but the damage was extensive.

The contribution made by Inspector Swanson to the discovery that leaking gas was the culprit is unknown, but the press reported that 'Chief Constable Hitchman is entitled to commendation for desiring that the debris should remain undisturbed, and for taking steps to prevent any intrusion upon the ruins till it had been determined whether there should be any detailed investigation by a Government officer'.

In 1886 identifying a decomposing body was an exercise in detective work and practicality, a process not blessed with the scientific methods of later years. In January of that year a female was retrieved from the river at St Martin's in an advanced state of decomposition, which did not prevent William Thouless of Old Palace Road making an identification of his wife, from whom he was separated and paying maintenance. The promptness of the identification may have related to the maintenance payments but another comment of the time suggests it owed something to his wife's burial society account.

Sarah Ann Thouless, formally identified and subject of a formal inquest, was formally buried. William Thouless drew the burial money and the matter passed from the public domain; until two months

later when a cabman at Victoria Station, who had known Sarah Thouless all his life, was startled to see the lady arrive at the station. He hailed her with, 'Good God, Mrs Thouless! You have no business here; you were buried these two months'.

Mrs Thouless, the cabman, and others, celebrated the lady's resurrection with several glasses of beer, so much so that the lady moved on and inflicted herself upon Constable Barlow in Gentleman's Walk, announcing, 'My husband has buried me once, and I have come to see him again.' She was arrested.

Mrs Thouless told the Magistrates, 'If I was drunk it was a curious thing', adding, 'I was very much excited at the time, for I heard that my husband had buried another woman and got my club money'. The Bench were unsympathetic and fined her 5s with 4s costs, with five days imprisonment in default.

The body from the river was, apparently, never correctly identified.

Norwich tradesmen in April 1896 were not impressed with detectives, more specifically the lack of them. They formed a deputation and 'waited upon the Watch Committee', complaining that when fires occurred, the police 'in and about the Market Place' were called off their beats leaving one of the most valuable property areas in the city without protection. They spoke of recent burglaries and asked for an increase in plain clothes men and the detective force, pointing out that Preston and Bolton, of similar size to Norwich, had detective forces of six and eight officers respectively, whereas there were only two at Norwich. The Mayor replied that the Committee was considering the 'advisability of increasing the detective department'.

The department was not increased. What followed the deputation was a realignment of police supervisory duties by the Watch Committee, leading to a clash between them and the Council (mentioned in chapter two) who called instead for 'the more efficient administration of the detective department'. Some of the deputising tradesmen were probably on the Council.

The number of Norwich detectives increased but slowly. In 1926 they numbered six, a Detective Inspector, Detective Sergeant and four Detective Constables.

Detectives in both centuries had a working procedure that involved human perception, local knowledge and a sound reasoning of who was doing what, and when, and how best to talk to them about it. Local policemen knew local criminals and vice versa, and a criminal could, more often than not, be related to a crime by personal knowledge of his habits and modus operandi, knowledge that was gradually eroded by an increasing population and a more complicated, faster pace of life blurring the recall of the know-everybody-and-everything-that-moved beat policeman and stunting the selection list of the wider ranging name dropping detective.

Cameras were invented just before the Norwich police and in 1924 a room in the Guildhall Police Station was designated for CID photographic use. In 1926 a camera followed, purchased from George Swain the well-known local photographer. This apparent dilatory response to an invention so essential to modern police work must be set against the pioneering action of the force in 1865 in employing a local firm, Boswells, to photograph prisoners for record purposes – six prisoners for six shillings with reductions for greater quantities. There is every reason to believe that Norwich was an innovative first in this field.

The development of forensic science and the advance of fingerprint technology opened up new scenes of crime horizons. Increasingly, the theory of relativity (police type) was applied: that no person could enter and leave a place without leaving something of themselves at that place and taking something of the place with them; and wafting black powder over a crime scene produced results. But basics applied before and after this progress – talking, observing and discussing with colleagues 'who's out'.

Working accommodation for Norwich detectives was geographically insecure over the years. They moved around in pinball fashion from the start at the Guildhall to the finish at the upper floor of Bethel Street, occupying en route buildings and rooms in Lower Goat Lane, St Peter's Street, St Giles' Street and Pottergate. From a room in Lower Goat Lane they moved, in 1915, to an office in St Peter's Street, but in 1926 the Watch Committee were informed that this office was 'dilapidated and unhealthy'; those of sufficient age recall it as grubby with whitewashed windows.

Next stop for the CID was 'Lavengro', an ex-education department office at Tuck's Court in St Giles, the building also serving as a force canteen, later cleared with a miscellaneous collection of similar buildings to build the new City Hall. From Tuck's Court they moved to a room in the redundant Pottergate section house, backing on to St John Maddermarket. The canteen moved with them. This was their last stop before the new Bethel Street station.

The CID caught up with the transport revolution. They progressed from detective work on foot and cycle to bus passes and their own CID car, a vehicle instantly known to all those with a vested interest. Years later it doubled as dog van.

Progress in the 20th century recognised the need for detective training. After World War Two newly-appointed CID officers were trained at nationally run schools, the force using London, Preston and Wakefield, but mainly Wakefield run by the West Riding force. The initial course was ten weeks and fail-

The CID of 1919 behind the bike sheds. Chief Constable John Henry Dain and HM Inspector of Constabulary review Norwich detectives at the Bignold School, Crook's Place. Left to right: detectives Walter Crome (later Head of CID), Herbert Balls (to become Deputy Chief Constable), William Fish, John Adcock, Edwin Buttle (see war duties – chapter eight) and Robert Nixon who became Chief Constable of Salisbury.

(M.Dixon)

Spot the CID, and the Chief Constables. This photograph was taken outside the Guildhall on the occasion of King George VI's opening of the City Hall in 1938. John Henry Dain (Norwich Chief Constable), right, is seen with Captain Van Neck (Norfolk Chief Constable), on his right, a rare picture of the two Chief Constables together; (it was said they did not like each other). The two trilby-hatted men are Norwich detectives with Sid Cole, of horse and Starlight fame, on the right. The uniformed Constable is Thomas Byland, later Sergeant, who joined in 1925 and died in service in 1955. He had a nickname in the force that in those days was cheerfully applied to any sallow or dark skinned person but is now deemed to be racially offensive. (A.Brown)

The CID of 1959. From left to right, back row: Ken Statham, Dick Bass, John Riches, John 'Jock' McLennan, Reg Taylor and Geoffrey Neville. Front row: Howard 'Baron' Ellis, Melbourne 'Tiny' Tythcott, Neville Ball (son of Herbert Balls – Neville dropped the s), Edward Lloyd, Ronnie Farman, Tom Jones and Jack Dunnell. (Force archives)

ure or a low mark brought a frowning response, a stiff talk on the cost involved, and a return to uniform duties.

Police specialism increased with new-found mobility. The majority of 19th-century traffic offences had involved the 'furious driving' of carts and carriages of varying descriptions, including a case of a dog cart, though parking did occasionally incur police wrath. In 1882 Constable Kirk summoned John Doubleday for leaving a horse and cart for ten minutes in Ber Street. The unfortunate Mr Doubleday was fined 5s with 8s costs.

Trams appeared in the city in 1900 and by the time they left, 1935, traffic had become a serious consideration. But at least you knew where a tram was going.

Police pedal cycles were irrefutably in use from

Police and cycles in Chapelfield Gardens in 1914, part of the force annual inspection. The first five officers, from right to left with identifying numbers and letters, are: Sergeant K John Harrison (wearing the 1911 King George V Coronation Medal and to become Chief Constable of the St Albans' force); Constable 89 George Jennings (also wearing the 1911 King George V Coronation Medal); Constable 109 Stanley Murrell (to become Inspector and die in service – see chapter seven); Constable 55 Cubitt Elvin and Constable 79 Cecil Waterson. Note that the officers are wearing cycle clips. In 1918 the Watch Committee authorised 'knickerbockers and puttees' to be issued to men working 'outside beats' on cycles. (Force archives)

1911 because the force had a contract from that date with 'Mr Kirby' to supply them. Without the internal combustion engine there would undoubtedly have been a pedal cycle department. In 1922 the Chief Constable reported that he was very satisfied with the cycle patrols.

It is interesting to note the purchase of nine cycles in 1919 with one allocated to the Chief Constable, one to the Deputy Chief Constable, three to 'central and CID' and one each to the Warrant Officer, Weights and Measures, Local Taxation and Magdalen Road Division. The fact the Watch Committee had approved the purchase of a car in 1917 for the Chief Constable's use indicates the unlikely use of his pedal cycle.

A Chief Constable on a cycle requires imagination. It was not an image of dignity, such as would be provided by a horse and a sword. A police issued cycle was gaunt and heavy and had riding characteristics of a Sherman tank. The invention of three speed gears was a step forward except that the only cycle so fitted was kept at the station for the use of Inspectors. Early machines were equipped with an oil lamp, requiring the beat Constable to have a plentiful supply of matches.

Many officers in later years opted for a cycle allowance and the use of their own cycle, which was permitted provided it was not a drop handle-barred racer in purple and yellow.

Police cycles cannot be left without reference to

Constable Ernest Kidd (served 1903 to 1930) poses with an early cycle. (Force archives)

Sergeant Frank 'Flash' Huntley who joined the force in 1937 and was promoted in 1949. He earned his nick-name through a whirlwind display of speed cycling that refused to acknowledge obstacles such as wintry conditions (Fye Bridge parted him from his machine one icy night) or foreign bodies in the road (a drunk lying in Westwick Street had tyre marks on him). That he was of genial disposition was only discovered during his brief stationary periods, usually long enough to sign the beat Constable's pocket book.

Motor cycles were in police use from the 1920s, in combination and single form. Leavis, BSA, Royal Enfield, Velocette, Triumph and Norton all found a place in the motor cycle history of the force, the more powerful machines appearing from the 1940s and allocated to a growing Traffic Department. For real enthusiasts there was briefly the use of two American motor cycles, an Indian and a Harley Davidson, supplied on a lease/lend arrangement (it wasn't just warships from Roosevelt).

Motor cycle combinations were, duty-wise, all things to all men. A combination with a boxed sidecar

Constable Albert Robinson (served from 1907 to 1932) with another early cycle, with a front light. Note the Merit badge worn on this officer's tunic, awarded for stopping a runaway horse. (J.Watts)

and a stirrup pump thrown inside frequently roared off to deal with a chimney fire, much in evidence in those days of rough, smoky coal. A motor cycle combination was used as an odd job machine by the force until it was sold in 1964.

The beat motor cycle was a temporary expedient in 1945, covering the manpower shortfall of the time. The regular beat motor cycle did not become a feature until 1955 when BSAs were purchased, quickly followed by the popular Velocette, the whispering ghost that embarrassed several with less then pin sharp hearing. Four of these lightweight motor cycles covered the suburbs of Norwich, based on the new section boxes, disappearing with the force and the arrival of the Panda car.

The Chief Constable acquired the first four-wheeled police (as opposed to fire or ambulance) motor car in the force, a Ford, approved by the Watch Committee in October 1917 and first registered in February 1918 (photograph chapter six). It lasted until 1923 when a wheel fell off in Unthank Road. A Morris Oxford replaced the Ford, in turn succeeded by a grand looking Essex Super Six and then a Morris Isis.

The first patrol cars, precursors of the Traffic Department, were three BSA three-wheelers, purchased in 1930 and 1931, two of them designated as replacements for motor cycle combinations. These

Two photographs taken at the Pottergate fire station between January and March 1931. In the first picture, and holding centre stage, is the BSA three-wheeler ('tricar'), a forerunner of the powerful and colourful traffic patrol cars seen today. Far left is a Leavis motorcycle, used by the Weights and Measures Department, and far right is a BSA machine. Note the motor cycle combination on the left has a passenger sidecar and the one on the right a box sidecar – often used as a small fire brigade. Officers from left to right are: Constables Jimmy Godbolt, Hugh Murray, Walter Goldsmith, Jimmy Sanders, Ralph Keeler and Edward Thompson. In the second picture these officers and vehicles are joined by the Chief Constable's car, CL9606, far left (identified as the Essex Super Six, shortly to be replaced), the Superintendent's car, CL9014, far right, and three ambulances at the rear – an Austin, Dennis and the pioneering Cadillac. Sub Engineer (Sergeant) Henry Coles is standing by CL9606 and Chief Engineer (Inspector) William Crane has his hand on CL9014. Behind the Superintendent's car is the Superintendent, Alex Christie. The plain-clothes man is unidentified. Constable George Harris is standing to the nearside front of the Austin and Constable Walter Cobbold is at the rear between the Dennis (newly delivered in 1930) and the Cadillac. (Force archives)

splendid un-police like vehicles lived with other police transport at Pottergate and did nothing for the police image, proving to be puny and inadequate, especially when loaded with hefty policemen. There was also the problem of tramlines to the single wheel, offering a cartoon like progress as the vehicle unwittingly pursued a tram while the driver sought another direction. Such stories, retold over the years, have met with understandable incredulity but the Watch Committee meeting of 20 October 1933 noted that the three 'tricars' were worn out and should be replaced by four wheelers 'because of problems caused by the tramlines'. Two years later the trams were gone. A tricar that turned over in Unthank Road (seemingly a bad place for police vehicles) was thought to have been influenced by tramlines.

Two Austin 10hp two seater open tourers, equipped with a rear 'dickey' seat that was threateningly insecure, replaced the BSAs, and were no more impressive in the police sense. But at least there was a wheel at each corner. These vehicles were not designed or even adapted for police use and they provided a memorable sight speeding to an emergency loaded with large policemen clutching helmets.

Before the outbreak of World War Two, three Wolseley 14hp saloons were purchased, thus beginning a long association with black Wolseleys, a colour suitable to the police and in any case the only one available (as previously stated by Henry Ford). Other forces leant strongly towards black Wolseleys and they

Four wheels on patrol. Sam Bussey poses by an Austin tourer at the corner of City Road and Bracondale. (Force archives)

Don Martin shows off motor cycles in Bethel Street, firstly c.1948 with extravagant handlebar covers, and then c.1958 with the benefits of radio and a proper motor cycle helmet; and promoted to Sergeant. The third photograph sees traffic officers with their medals and motor cycles outside the steps of Bethel Street Police Station prior to a VIP visit c.1952. Left to right: Constables Freddie Beardwood, Don Martin, Dudley Brook, Lennie Coadwell and Herbert Burton. The Chief Constable's Humber Super Snipe is partly visible in the background. (D.Martin)

Constable Alfred Copeman astride a beat Velocette.

(B.Kybird)

became nationally known as the police car. The Norfolk Constabulary was an exception, adhering to the Norfolk expression of 'du different' by using Austins and Rileys, the latter in dark green.

After the war there was an increasing relationship between the police and motorist, usually instigated by the police. There was no speed limit outside the city but inside it was 30 miles per hour. It is difficult to understand how any driver was caught speeding when a towering black Wolseley steadily followed him with two uniformed faces staring intently through the windscreen. The Wolseley had to maintain station behind the speeding vehicle for 4/10ths of a mile, checked through a calibrated speedometer.

One of the Wolseleys was burnt out in a mishap

and rebuilt as a 'shooting brake' (estate car to the younger reader). Its total carrying capacity was consequently increased to eight, though whether the suspension was so tested is not known.

A Morris van was purchased for the conveyance of prisoners (formerly they had walked or been placed in a police ambulance) and a small Ford van for general duty, adding to the post-war growing armoury of police vehicles. The best known van of all, a vehicle of redoubtable constitution and fearsome reputation, a 30cwt Austin of the type seen in a multitude of military roles, principally ambulance, arrived in the early 1950s after fire service duty. It stayed to the end, known simply as GLT 1, and has a firm place in the motor vehicle memories of the city police.

In 1948 the return of petrol rationing restricted police mileage; for a time it was only 40 miles in an eight hour shift and crews were required to leave the patrol car in the garage for two hours. They were then ejected onto the streets as supplementary beat Constables, much to their disgust, and recalled as necessary by that scintillating light. It was a time when men on the beat willed the pillarphone into life.

Petrol rationing was accompanied by the sale of dyed petrol to essential users and motorists were stopped by the police patrol car for petrol testing. This was accomplished by dipping the tank of the suspect vehicle with filter paper clipped to a length of curtain rail. Liquid reagent was then placed on the paper and if it coloured the petrol was illegal.

Despite speeding and petrol checks the early patrol car crews were employed mainly as advisory and cautioning officers, referring miscreants to common sense and old laws that went into the statute books before motor vehicles were invented – when legislation described nearly all illegal traffic movement as 'furious'. These counselling policemen were dubbed as 'courtesy cops' by public and press. Then came the heavy hand of the Road Traffic Acts, traffic and vehicle legislation that was to be become more and more intense and complicated. Police enforcement was gradually to stiffen. The courtesy continued but the tag faded with the summonses.

Problems of accommodating policemen to motor vehicles were not peculiar to early days. In the late 1950s the force strayed from its regular purchase of

An array of vehicles parked outside the 'tin hut' c.1936, but no genuine police vehicles on view (and that, on good authority, includes the van, far left). This was in fact a public car park run by the Royal Norfolk Volunteer's Association and a parking attendant will be somewhere in or very near the scene depicted. (A.Brown)

Wolseleys and acquired a Morris Isis (a stretched Morris Oxford), a disconcerting vehicle because of its tendency at reasonable cornering speed for the back to attempt to overtake the front. Placing 2cwt of ironmongery in the boot kept the rear of the car on the road, to the advantage of speeding motorists. Back to the Wolseleys.

From the first Wolseley 14 there was progression to the Wolseley 18 and 25, then the 6/80, 6/90 and the Farina styled models – 6/99 and 6/110. Heaters were included from the 6/80 onwards, making the Traffic Department even more desirable. A bell in the radiator grille gave way to a siren and later a blue light appeared on the roof. Loudspeakers and wireless communication were fitted after World War Two, the latter in 1953.

The later patrol cars provided a haven of comfortable leather and opulent walnut, intended for a private purchaser of means but much appreciated by leather gloved, peak-capped Constables swishing past envious weather beaten colleagues pounding a pavement or battling a head wind on a tank like cycle.

The Traffic Department of the Norwich City Police became a coveted élite, known to all who aspired to it as 'the mobile', a reality of the progress of the motor car and the police force. It still fell to the beat Constable to struggle with point duty and traffic jams but from the late 1930s there was increasingly an overlaid motor patrol system that dealt with the motorist who escaped the jams to speed, crash or just drive without due care and attention.

Police driving schools, established pre-war by the Metropolitan and Lancashire police forces, grew in number after the war under Home Office guidance.

Some road block! The occasion of the Royal Norfolk Agricultural Show at Keswick in 1947. A mixture of the city and county forces, predominantly the city with their Wolseleys. (Force archives)

A progression of Wolseleys, though the first photograph reveals a cuckoo. The Wolseley 25 numbered DON 90 is not locally registered and is not remembered by those who easily recall other vehicles. It is clearly being used at a function at St Andrew's Hall and the driver looking at the camera is Constable Sam Bussey who sometimes drove the Chief Constable. The vehicle is registered in Birmingham, the home of Wolseleys. It is of relevant note that in 1937 the force expressed dissatisfaction with a Wolseley 18 designated for the Chief Constable's use and the Watch Committee authorised the acquisition of a Wolseley 25. In the second photograph Constable Don Martin and Constable Bert Horrex pose with a well remembered Wolseley 18, while in the third Constable Peter Fleming peers through the windscreen of a Wolseley 6/90. The fourth photograph moves to 1967 and shows a Wolseley 6/99 in the new police underground garage at Bethel Street with Constables Ronnie Porter, right, and Brian Rouse, left, and engineer Derek Ellis centre. (E.Bussey and Force archives)

THAT van. Constables Ernie Croxson and Don Martin are flanking the Austin vehicle GLT 1 prior to a Civil Defence parade in 1949. GLT 1 was used for transporting prisoners, cycles, bodies and anything else that came the police way. It was unforgiving of inexperienced drivers. What price the number plate today?   (D.Martin)

Constable Bert Horrex demonstrates the advance of technology in April 1953: radios in police cars. This press photograph heralding progress and innovation is qualified by a Watch Committee note of July 1942: 'two police vehicles fitted with radios with control at Bethel Street Police Station'. Research indicates that the 1942 'fitting' was of heavy, primitive contraptions borrowed from the Army, notable only for their inadequate performance, cumbersome handling and brief appearance.   (ECN)

Insecure load – one. A lorry moving off from the GPO traffic lights ships part of its load of sweets: on ration in 1949. The public descended like locusts and an overwhelmed Constable Don Seager opted for good public relations. A senior officer at Bethel Street Police Station later telephoned the press office and requested the photograph not be published. Now it can be seen.   (ECN)

Norwich City officers went to the Essex force at Chelmsford for five weeks and were taught advanced driving techniques. They returned to become, if successful, confirmed members of 'the mobile'.

The Norwich police also dealt with waterborne traffic. 'River Police' is mentioned in Watch Committee minutes in the first year of the force, 1836, and discussed at various points through to 1840 when riverside traders, possibly impatient at the delay, offered to pay for boats and equipment, thus ending the Watch Committee prevarication.

It was noted that two rowing boats were to be used, to commence 'on Michaelmas day next'. Four officers were appointed. Other historical records refer to a

infamy was a starting river policeman though not originally appointed to the post. George Steward and Henry Chamberlain were appointed 'inspectors of the two boats', though it is only 'Inspector Steward' who appears in a later reference (later to become the first head of CID). The Watch Committee noted that the river police were 'to account for all fees paid which will be deducted from their pay'.

Special clothing was supplied, six outfits, paid for by the traders, thus avoiding the unhappy uniform record of the force. The pioneering police watermen were issued with a 'pea coat and jacket, trowsers (sic), waistcoat, oil coat, sou'wester, hat 'like pattern provided', boots'. The Watch Committee ordered the jackets be marked RP, consecutively numbered and stamped with an anchor symbol; they also sanctioned a piratical appearance with the issue of 'six cutlasses, two dozen truncheons and one regulation pistol'.

A boathouse at Carrow Bridge is a fact of history, probably the one Samuel Greenfield offered to build on the nearby meadow and rent at six guineas per annum. There is also an 1843 record of a boathouse hired from Walter Freeman of St Anne's Staithe (Riverside) 'instead of No. 2 boathouse from Greenfield'. The Watch Committee asked a Mr Houghton of Elm Hill if he would provide a boathouse on his premises but there is no record of such a boathouse being used.

Insecure load – two. Constable Gordon Postance, a Traffic Department motor cyclist, guides traffic past fallen wood at Kett's Hill roundabout in 1957 while the errant lorry driver reloads and contemplates a summons. (A.Brown)

starter of three officers, a disparity possibly explained by the Watch Committee naming four officers and replacing at least two (one noted as unfit) before the starting date. Constable Samuel Watts of indiscipline

To further complicate the early history of police boathouses the Watch Committee recorded in 1846 'two boathouses given up and both boats to be kept at Sandlings Ferry (Pulls Ferry) at £3 per annum'. In 1848 Mr Houghton again appears in the records, described as a 'boat builder' and asked to dispose of two boats in disrepair and provide an estimate for one boat, presumably a new one.

Early patrols of the Norwich River Police were on a daily basis on the Wensum, upstream to Hellesdon Mill and downstream into the Yare. A city charter gave Norwich jurisdiction over the river for a distance of 15½ miles, from New Mills to Hardley Cross where the Yare meets the Chet, well beyond the city boundary, but how often the full distance was rowed can only be surmised. The recorded provision of a mast and some sail material indicates that it was not all muscle power.

In 1878 a four-oar race took place between the Norwich City Police and men of the 2nd Hussars from Nelson Barracks. The intent was to resolve bad feeling following the unasked for assistance of the military at a fire in Barrack Street that the police firemen were fighting, and wished to keep to themselves. Cavalrymen were no match for river policemen. The race, between 'the fieldhouse' and 'Trowse railway bridge', a distance of one and a quarter miles, was won by the police.

The Norfolk Constabulary did not have a police boat in the 1800s, despite the proliferation of lakes and rivers within its area. They relied on the city boat and where the city's river responsibility finished the county force delegated responsibility to Constables whose beats contained the riverbanks. This produced an unequal struggle of wits between wherrymen and coverted Constables seeking to spring a one-man boarding party at a critical time. One instance, there must have been more, records a successful boarding by a Constable intent upon an all-revealing search followed by the abrupt removal of a covering hatch by a keenly thinking boat master, a move which carried the inquiring officer overboard. Wherries are not easily turned and it is reported that the master apologised as he sailed away from the surfacing officer. At least the city police could chase a wherry, even if it did strain the sinews.

Twentieth-century memories and records of Norwich police boats see the end of rowing boats, gradually, and the arrival of motor launches in the shape of fire floats and patrol boats. The details, as known, present a sequential picture with some inconsistencies.

The first police motor boat, a fire float, was built by Fellowes of Great Yarmouth in 1912, following a period of severe fires and resulting agitation at Watch Committee level. This float was in use during World War One, overhauled in 1917 and disposed of in 1920. In 1928 the force bemoaned to the Watch Committee the absence of a fire float when dealing with a fire in Mountergate.

A river patrol was less in evidence during and after World War One though there is recollection of a Constable in a rowing boat putting out from the rear of the Swan Laundry near Mile Cross bridge, either by impulse or as an occasion demanded. This boat was still in being, if not in use, resting alongside the laundry in the 1930s.

In 1930 the Chief Constable was authorised to purchase a motor boat from C.W.Mollett for 'police river purposes' for the sum of £65 but there is no confirming record of such a purchase. Recollections of officers of the time are that the police borrowed and hired boats, mainly from Pulls Ferry, though relations in that direction may have been strained because in 1932 Mr Mollett of Pulls Ferry was cautioned for overloading.

In 1936 the Watch Committee noted that a rowing boat was beyond repair. In 1938 they authorised the purchase of a new motor launch and in the minutes referred to the 'existing motor launch', twice. No record or person recalls this 'existing motor launch'. In 1938 the police sold 'a boat' for £15. The price of a rowing boat?

Percivals of Horning built a new motor launch for the police in 1939. Its potential was overtaken by war and, intended or not, it became a fire float, demonstrated to a selected audience at Riverside on 29 April 1940. The press reported, 'Chief Officers of Norfolk Fire Brigades, and others from farther afield, were entertained in Norwich by the Chief Constable. They watched an impressive display by the new fire float of the City Police'.

The newly-formed National Fire Service claimed the new fire float but the now separatist police initiated a loan agreement, to be called upon if the occasion demanded.

In 1944 the city police acquired the Yare Commissioner's launch but he claimed it back promptly at the end of the war. In this same year it was noted that a police boat in a boathouse at Carrow was damaged.

In 1946 the river patrol was restarted with a newly-acquired, converted, motorised yacht, previously owned by the police surgeon, Dr Lincoln Hurn. The Watch Committee recorded that this vessel was loaned to the police but once again they appear to be out of step with the facts. Recollections are that this boat was purchased, which hopefully was the case because the force sold it in 1951.

In 1957, a police rowing boat, noted as beyond repair, was sold for £5: the languishing Swan Laundry vessel or the damaged Carrow boat noted in 1944?

The 1950s and '60s were marked by a small open launch, number Y455, which was later fitted with a cabin and, later still, a radio and hinged mast. This boat was kept at the boathouse that formed part of the city mortuary in Barrack Street, though by the 1950s this mortuary was used less and less in deference to the facilities provided at the Norfolk and Norwich Hospital. Today, the building remains in another form.

The combined boathouse and mortuary, accessed with keys kept in Kett's Hill Section Box, was a convenience that proved extremely useful for landing river bodies, especially the foul and degenerating kind. These were often kept at the Barrack Street mortuary, even after the Norfolk and Norwich Hospital had

One mortuary looks like another. This photograph, marked 1940, is of the Deputy Chief Constable, Herbert Balls, watching the Coroner's Officer, Constable Bill Hoskins, left, and Police Surgeon Dr Lincoln Hurn examining a body and the mortuary could be late King Street or early Barrack Street. There are opposing views from men of the time with King Street having the edge.

(A.Brown)

assumed the role of city mortuary. Police officers cleaning decomposing bodies were entitled to claim a small payment. Most officers chose not to go the distance that warranted them claiming.

Mortuaries tended to be situated close to the river, that of 1886 being described as a 'rude and crude shed' at the rear of the Cinders Oven public house and 'dangerous' because of its proximity to the river. Its replacement was close by, in Cockey Lane running from King Street to the river, still in use up to the beginning of World War Two.

The river patrol in the second post-war period was an April to October duty, or as the occasion demanded, and was affiliated to the Traffic Department, following the reasoning that it was another driving job involving engines. The co-pilot of the launch, two being a regular crew, was an opportunity for a Constable normally employed on more mundane beat duties. If Section Box Clerk was seen as a sign of favour from a high place then the allocation of river patrol on the duty sheet was considered bounty from the gods.

The ability to swim was taken for granted and if officers joining the force were found to be lacking that ability they were sent to the Eagle Baths for lessons. These were given in the early morning and if the Constable had been on night duty that was too bad. Also too bad was the Eagle Baths, which was a grand name for a fenced off part of the River Wensum. And there was no dispensation for cold weather. A 1912 report indicates 'every inducement' being made for officers to receive swimming instruction.

In 1966 came the vessel that was to add poise and distinction to the police river patrol, very soon to operate under the flag (metaphorically) of a new amalgamated force. N999 (which clever person allocated the number is not known) was an aluminium hulled Pearly Monarch boat. It was fast, impressive, effortlessly sweeping the waterways with a crew of two uniformed officers, a flagship for modern policing and the pinnacle of progress from a staccato progressing rowing boat occupied by oar heaving figures.

The launching ceremony for the new boat was marked by the tireless efforts of Mrs Jesse Griffiths, Vice Chairman of the Watch Committee, to smash a bottle of champagne over the bow. After five unsuc-

The pennant of the Norwich River Police, preserved but rarely displayed on the boats. (Force archives)

The Norwich fire float in 1940. (Force archives)

Y455 labelled 'Norwich City Police'. (R. Fleming)

N999, prominently labelled, cutting a swathe. (ECN)

N999 with Constables Jack Green (left) and Peter King.
(Force archives)

cessful tries the Chairman, Alfred Nicholls, leapt forward and smashed the bottle with a hammer.

From policing above the water to the force in action below the surface. Hauling bodies, stolen property and vehicles, among other things, from the river, pond or lake bed had been an exercise in throwing a grappling iron, dragging that iron, by hand or by boat, and, if unsuccessful, trying in a different place. What you got you saw when it broke the surface.

In 1956 an attempt was made to impress the Watch Committee that the police could follow the military and form a diving squad: an underwater search and rescue unit to give it its full title. It started when Sergeant Don Martin of the Traffic Division ('the mobile'), an outstanding swimmer, practised scuba diver and ex-commando, wrote a report, dated 17 July

1956, suggesting that the Norwich City Police obtain frogman equipment. Sergeant Martin described a diving suit which 'comprises an Aqualung of compressed air, which with normal light activity in 10 to 12 feet of water will last approximately 40 minutes'. He pointed out the benefits to police work. This report landed on the Chief Constable's desk via the usual route of intervening senior ranks and appended comments, none of which opposed the proposal.

The Chief Constable, Alan Plume, reported to the Watch Committee an estimated cost of £60 for 'a submerging kit'. They requested a demonstration. This was arranged by the Great Yarmouth branch of the British Sub-Aqua Club and scheduled for Lakenham swimming baths in September, postponed to 7 October at the request of the Watch Committee to allow their attendance. The Lord Mayor was invited and replied that he would like to attend.

After the demonstration by the Sub-Aqua Club, Sergeant Martin and Constables Ernie Stuttaford and Aleck Bartram used the equipment and were impressed. The Watch Committee were not impressed because they were not there. Neither was the Lord Mayor. The Chief Constable was later to write apologetic letters to those involved in the demonstration.

The Watch Committee, hung by their own petard, did not oppose moves that quickly resulted in the acquisition of the necessary equipment. £82 was spent.

Three weeks after purchase of the equipment Sergeant Martin dived the River Wensum near the Gatehouse public house, Dereham Road, to recover the body of a young boy. He found the tragic youngster curled in a hole where grappling irons would have experienced difficulty. Some later dives would be similarly tragic, it was in the nature of the job, but some inclined towards good public relations and they included the recovery of a holidaymaker's purse, the mace of an over-enthusiastic majorette and broken glass from the bottom of Lakenham Baths.

The diving squad progressed in strength, expertise and equipment, used as required and practising weekly, usually at the behest of the CID who regularly came up with a spot in the river used to deposit stolen goods.

Communication between a diver and the bank

Constable Oliver Mantle, left, and Don Martin assist another member of the diving team at Hellesdon Bridge. (D.Martin)

watchers normally relied on an attached line and expressive tugs from those directing operations, though Don Martin ruefully recalled dives when those on the bank attracted his attention by throwing stones in the direction of the bubbles. Occasionally the squad was loaned to neighbouring police forces, including Norfolk.

In June 1967 the diving squad received a tribute from an unexpected quarter. They were called to assist the military in a sea dive off Caister. An Air Sea Rescue helicopter had crashed 75 yards off the beach with loss of life. The Norwich City Police divers engaged in that incident, Sergeant Martin and Constable's Peter King and Oliver Mantle, were individually named and congratulated in letters sent to the Chief Constable from the Royal Air Force and Royal Navy. 'Your diving team displayed the highest skill', the Chief Constable was told. It was deserved praise and a good epitaph for the city police for amalgamation had been decided and was only six months away. Ironically, in 1999, as part of the county force, the Underwater Search and Rescue Unit faced financial scrutiny with voices pointing out that the expertise could be hired from neighbouring forces. As part of the city force they had originally pointed the way.

CHAPTER SIX
They Also Served

Policewomen, matrons, reserves, specials, police surgeons, cadets and dogs

THE Chief Constable said he was not in favour of policewomen. Edwin Winch offered this observation to the Watch Committee in 1914 though how the subject came to be raised is not clear, but can be guessed during a time when female emancipation was in the national spotlight. He went on to report that Mrs Trimby and Miss Clarke were 'O K'. Mrs Trimby was employed as a police station matron but nothing is known of Miss Clarke's duties in 1914, clerking appears most likely.

On 3 May 1918 the Watch Committee resolved that Miss Edith Emma Clarke of Willow Bank, Salhouse 'be appointed a member of the detective staff, not pensionable, at a salary of £2 per week, to be terminated by one month's notice on either side'. In March 1919 it resolved that a 'simple uniform' be issued to Miss Clarke for 'special occasions'. (Mrs Trimby also got a 'simple uniform'.)

Whether the Edith Clarke of 1918 is the Miss Clarke favoured and disfavoured by the Chief Constable in 1914 is not positively known. The balance of probabilities says they are one and the same.

Another who got a 'simple uniform' in the Watch Committee's March 1919 minutes was Jessie Hines, described as a 'motor ambulance driver'. These same minutes initiated a pay review for all female staff and listed them as a matron, Weights and Measures' clerk and one dealing with 'crime of a special nature'. Trimby and Clarke are clearly identified, but reference has to be made to police civilian records to find a Weights and Measures' clerk, shown in February 1918 as 'J.Hines'. She then appears in the Watch Committee minutes of December 1918 and March 1919 as a motor ambulance driver. Other records of the time

show her as the Chief Constable's driver. His car was first registered in February 1918.

Jessie Hines was paid 30s to 40s per week in 1918 and £2 10s per week in 1919. In this latter year she drove Chief Constable Dain at Nurse Cavell's funeral.

It does, therefore, appear that Jessie Hines had a dual, even a triple role. She disappears from records after 1920, the year in which a new Weights and Measures' clerk is noted: a Hilda Hines. And Ernest Hines, of whom more later, was a commander in the Special Constabulary. As far as can be ascertained Hilda Hines did not drive or receive a uniform. She resigned in 1921.

In 1920 the Home Office asked the force to consider the subject of policewomen. The Watch Committee duly considered the subject and resolved to adjourn it indefinitely, which was actually until 7 October when they decided that 'Miss Edith Clarke be appointed a policewoman and that such appointment date from 3 May 1918'. The force's first policewoman had arrived, officially.

In 1927 the Home Office gave unasked for advice upon the desirability of the force having policewomen: they should have them – according to the Home Office. It is not clear whether the accent was deliberately on the plural, if it was the Watch Committee were not impressed. They recorded that the force already had a policewoman and it was not necessary to have any more.

In 1931 the Home Office instituted Police (Women) Regulations under powers granted by the Police Act of 1919 and approved the appointment of Edith Clarke in accordance with these regulations, which stipulated pay, hours of duty and the nature of duties. 'Patrol duty' was listed without definition. Other matters were more precise. A policewoman must be 'unmarried or a widow' and 'shall resign her appointment on marriage or remarriage'.

That the force had a policewoman does not appear to have been obvious to the public for some considerable time. In 1941 the Chief Constable received a complaint from the Cathedral clergy who were unhappy concerning circumstances in which policemen had interviewed some girls. The Chief Constable rejected the complaint, found in any case to relate to the Norfolk Constabulary, and firmly stated that the force had 'had a policewoman since 3 May 1918'. This reply invited, but apparently did not receive, the riposte that 23 years was a long time without the position being noticed or increased.

The Watch Committee of those earlier years were not misogynists, according to other records. In 1917 they licensed the first tram conductress, 17 years after the trams came into being and three years into a world war.

Edith Clarke was the subject of further record in 1931 when she was noted as 'attached to the Detective Department for duties of a special nature'. These special duties were enquiries instigated by the concern of servicemen separated from their wives, into which much can be read and would essentially be correct.

Edith Clarke.   (Norfolk Reference Library)

She checked upon the wives' welfare. It was a service peculiar to that time.

Edith Clarke stayed with the force until her death in 1933. That she was issued with a uniform is a matter of record but those who recall this first policewoman of the force never saw it. She is recalled as working in the CID office, a small woman with a foot infirmity that handicapped her movement. Her duties indisputably leaned towards women's welfare but it is doubtful whether her original appointment was instigated by this motive alone. She was the product of the politics of the early 20th century and the reluctant evolution of women into jobs originally seen as the province of men. Edith Clarke deserves her place in the history of the force.

There is an understandable view that Lucy Evans was the first Norwich policewoman. She enrolled on

Jessie Hines with the Chief Constable's car at City Station c.1919.   (A.Williamson)

Within the stilted views of the early years of the century it can be no surprise that the force did not enthusiastically embrace the concept of policewomen as opposed to female searchers, matrons, drivers and clerks and that as late as 1927 they brusquely dealt with a Home Office reference to the subject. But by the 1940s there was more flexible thinking, initially compelled by war, later influenced by changing circumstances, and it was no longer a lone policewoman but a growing department within the force.

Women, as opposed to policewomen, could be found in the force from very early days. Initially there was a 'female searcher'. The title speaks for itself and indicates that a woman had to be available in this professed man's world, indeed, the very first recorded arrests by the newly instituted force in 1836 were of two disorderly girls, aged 15 and 12 years.

The first incontrovertible record of a woman employed as a searcher is unfortunately the dismissal of the woman. In 1860 Mrs Springer was reported to be 'too old to perform her duties'. Apparently it took her half an hour to get to the Guildhall from Globe Lane.

Female searchers evolved into the grand overseeing role of matron, a post occupied by Emily Jane Trimby for nearly all of 30 years. She was appointed in January 1897, described as a woman of 'kindly disposition and pleasant appearance who won the esteem of all who came into contact with her'. First-hand accounts reveal that she projected an aura that invoked respect and support. A small room in the Guildhall was reserved for her use and was approached by hardened policemen with due deference.

Jane (as she was known) Trimby spent much time both comforting and reproving women, reportedly dealing with as many as half a dozen cases of drunkenness on a Saturday night, escorting prisoners to Holloway and attending to female prisoners in the Guildhall cells and at the court. She was subject to call-out and her retaining fee was 10s per week with an additional 3s per week clothing allowance. She supplied prisoners' meals at 6d each meal and cleaned the CID office each morning between 8am and 9.30am. In addition to her time consuming and often arduous employment she raised a family of eight children.

Jane Trimby fell ill in August 1926 and her duties

Posed on the roof at Pottergate. This little assembly has been dated to the April-July period of 1919 and the common denominator is the Weights and Measures' Department, which had its front access in Lower Goat and rear exit into the Pottergate fire and ambulance station. The standing Constables are 111 John Muttitt, left (recently returned from World War One and given a period of internal duty because of the injuries he suffered), and 93 Edward Burroughes, right (to die tragically in service – see chapter nine). The Inspector is William Thompson (Chief Engineer of the fire brigade and from 1919 also in charge of the Weights and Measures' Department.) The demurely seated woman appears to be Jessie Hines. (Force archives)

17 March 1933 as a Constable and had already been a Constable in Liverpool. Her duties remained a dilution of the men's work and her uniform was no more apparent than that of her predecessor. She married a serving Norwich officer and became Lucy Tester, serving with evident uniform during World War Two as an auxiliary policewoman. Later, living with husband above Bethel Street Police Station, she undertook matron duties in the station.

were taken over by her daughter. In September, in failing health, Mrs Trimby was sent to a convalescent home at Lowestoft for three weeks, the expense being voluntarily met by subscribing members of the force. She was admitted to the Norfolk and Norwich Hospital in December and died on Christmas morning at the age of 60. At her funeral, to which the force sent an 'immense wreath', she was described as 'the mother of the Norwich police force'. Six uniformed officers (two Sergeants and four Constables), carried her coffin from her house in Pottergate under the direction of Inspector Leatch, and duty men at Pottergate Fire Station paraded and stood to attention as the cortège passed. The Chief Constable and other senior officers attended the service at St Laurence's Church and 40 Constables processed to her graveside at Earlham Cemetery.

Another remarkable and much-respected woman followed Jane Trimby. Rosa (Rosie) Woodbine became police matron in 1927 and retired in 1947. Rosie continued the outstanding service of her predecessor, taking responsibility for all female prisoners, but was given a new duty – to collect money from public lavatories. She experienced the move to the new police station in Bethel Street and, like her predecessor, saw a world war, this one with a home front bringing terrible damage and severe loss of life in the city. It was said that she spoke of the 'hard times', the increase in prostitution and 'the dreadful state' of some of the girls who found their way into the police station.

Rosa Woodbine. (Force archives)

Emily Jane Trimby. (P.Monteath)

Rosie Woodbine and Jane Trimby were two outstanding long-serving police matrons carrying out strenuous duties in a male dominated empire. They met the worst and the best, comforted, counselled and cajoled, and had always been available. Their work was to continue in a fast changing service, carried out by other shorter serving matrons before the emerging policewomen's department swallowed the greater part of their duties.

In 1925 it was decreed that female prisoners were to be kept at St Augustine's Lodge in Lady Lane, another example of the fragmentation of police services through inadequate accommodation.

When World War Two threatened the Norwich City Police still retained one policewoman, soon to change dramatically. Kathleen Holman followed Lucy Evans in 1936 – later to marry a serving officer, William Key, and she was in turn followed by Margaret Grant – later to marry a serving officer, Leslie Goffin. Then Lucy Tester returned, with reinforcements. War brought women into men's jobs in many spheres and the police were no exception. Regular officers went off to fight for King and country and male War Reserve officers and Women Auxiliary officers stepped into the gaps.

The women drove vehicles, manned switchboards, marshalled prisoners, sometimes patrolled, and did a policeman's job while the enemy above set about destroying the city. The auxiliary women numbered 13 in 1941 but quickly increased to 21 and then 26. When the Home Office ordered their disbandment, effective from 31 March 1946, there remained only ten. Their roles at that time were identified as 'five tele-phonists, three drivers, one clerk and one reserve'. All but one of these women would be re-engaged in a civilian capacity.

There were some concessions to femininity during the 1940s. The Deputy Chief Constable forbade the practice of women officers taking over beat duties although he sanctioned an unaccompanied woman officer driving the police van to deliver coffee to beat Constables. Then, in 1944, he ordered by memorandum that Constable Barbara Allen and Constable Jessica Dewing would perform patrol duties, 8.30am to 4pm and 2.30pm to 10pm, but would not go alone in the blackout. These officers had returned from training school to join Margaret Grant as regular officers, a genuine increase in the establishment, the first since the one and only Edith Clarke of 1918. Now there were three, plus of course the auxiliaries. The decision to increase the establishment had been taken in November 1943, influenced by the 'problems of

girls and servicemen'. After the war Jessica Dewing joined the Norfolk Constabulary and was promoted to Sergeant.

May Neale joined the auxiliaries in 1944 while her husband, Detective Constable John Neale, was fighting with the Army in France. He was killed in action in 1945. She then joined the regular force and became attached to the CID, attending a national training course for female officers. From there, in 1949, she attended the men's ten week detective course at Wakefield, coming top with an 86 per cent mark. The Chief Constable, Alan Plume, was sufficiently impressed to report her achievement to the Watch committee. He then talked to the press about women police officers, saying, 'Their usefulness has been proved without any shadow of doubt, and they have decidedly come to stay.' Others before him had not been so definite.

May Neale had a successful career and later married Superintendent Edgar Dain, Deputy Chief Constable and son of John Henry Dain.

The 1950s saw an establishment of six Norwich policewomen and in 1955 there was another first, a policewoman Sergeant. Audrey Thomas transferred from Cambridge to achieve the promotion but returned after seven months. She was replaced by another transferee, from Lancashire, the popular and long-serving Eileen Craik. Her replacement in 1966 came from Yorkshire. Claire Petty became the Sergeant in charge of the policewomen's department through to the year of amalgamation.

Policewomen continued as a specialist department, receiving nine tenths the pay of their male colleagues, dealing with all matters female but also proving that police work was not all a man's world. After the city force had vanished the transformation became total, official by national decree, equal pay and duties via an act of parliament. But the proving ground had been the 1930s and 1940s. It took a war to make the point.

In 1962 policewomen were given their own transport. The force purchased a Lambretta scooter solely for their use. Most of them refused to have anything to do with it. Then came more recognition – they were praised by the Watch Committee. A Councillor drew attention to the 'efficient way' the policewomen carried out traffic control at the pedestrian crossing at

Policewomen at war. This 1943 photograph of policewomen and Chief Constable Dain was taken in the grounds of the Bethel Hospital when the force had one regular policewoman but was augmented by the auxiliaries. Margaret Grant (Goffin) is in the front row, second from left and Audrey Martin, wife of Don Martin is second from right in this row. Lucy Tester (née Evans) is fourth from right in the centre row, next to (fifth from right) Norah Bussey, wife of Sam Bussey. Barbara Allen, later to join the regular force, is first right in centre row. (Force archives)

Castle Meadow by the Bell Hotel. Chief Constable Plume replied that he was considering an increase in their number. And the Watch Committee was again moved to praise a policewoman who bettered the men in national training. Sheila George came joint top of 80 on her training course in 1964. It was progress all the way from Edwin Winch in 1914. But by the 1960s time was running out for the force as a whole.

In February 1912 the formation of a police reserve was discussed at Watch Committee level without a decision. In June the subject reappeared and it was noted that an Army Major and Captain were willing to assist in forming a reserve. Eleven police pensioners were reportedly available. What transpired, in March 1913, was the selection of 35 men and the beginning

Now we are three; the new establishment. This photograph, taken in London Street, shows the regular policewomen of the force in 1944, left to right, Jessica Dewing, Barbara Allen and Margaret Grant (Goffin). (ECN)

They Also Served

A 1966 photograph of Constable Beryl Baker, who joined the force in 1948, and Claire Petty, the Sergeant in charge of the department. (ECN)

This photograph is of the force first aid team c.1960 and two other long-serving policewomen are shown. Joy Greensides (later to marry CID officer Ronnie Farman) is on the left and Daphne Davey is on the right. The Chief Constable, Alan Plume, sits in the centre alongside the first aid instructor, Mr Linder. Holding the Pim Trophy Shield is Sergeant Stan Furlonger. Back row, left to right: Bob Harmer, John Bloomfield, Peter Everest, George Cox and Arthur Abbs. (A.Brown)

This caricature arose from the publicised praise of policewomen on traffic control. The artist was Terry George, distinctive within the force as Constable 1 and an artist of significant ability who rarely missed a chance to highlight a current event, the result appearing via the canteen or some other suitable wall in the police station. This particular picture was retained by Woman Police Constable 1 Jean Duffy and copied with Terry George's permission for this book.

of the First Police Reserve, ex-police and Army men who were trained and accustomed to discipline. They were to be employed as replacements for Army reservists or other Constables who had been withdrawn from regular duties to perform special duty. World War One was near.

In August 1914 regular officers were being 'recalled to the colours' and 29 members of the reserve were employed on police duties. Police leave was cancelled. A second police reserve was discussed. At this time of local and world tension the Watch Committee approved the purchase of 12 automatic pistols at £3 13 6d each, officers to be armed at the Chief Constable's discretion.

Norwich policemen continued to leave to fight in 'The Great War' and names filtered back of those who would not return. Others connected with or related to the force were lost, including the son of the Chief Constable, Edwin Winch, killed in November 1916. Mr Winch had earlier suffered a nervous breakdown and given notice of his retirement.

After the war the First Police Reserve continued as an available supplementary strength. In 1920 they were authorised an annual payment of £4, reflecting the city's awareness of continuing tension.

The reserve was not just a hidden force of police pensioners waiting for the call to save the city from revolution, invasion or something similar, it was a handy pool of experience for other less threatening but no less important occasions. In 1936 they took over the city for the centenary parade, of which more later. Overall they were occasionally used, occasionally placed on stand-by, receiving renewed attention as war threatened again and was then declared.

On 20 October 1939 the Chief Constable was authorised to 'constitute a war reserve of 50 members, recruited as and when vacancies arise'. Once again they replaced those who left for foreign shores, again some not to return.

War Reserve officers were enlisted or conscripted men employed full time as regular officers. Many First Police Reserve transferred to the regular War Reserve. They 'did their bit' as the saying went at the time.

In 1946 the War Reserve was unceremoniously disbanded, though many continued in the regular force, ageing and effective reminders of a time when Norwich truly had a backs to the wall situation, generally proving that age and conscription were no bar to conspicuous police service. They just looked older, as they were. Police reserves, war or otherwise, have their place in history. May they never be needed again.

Specials were, in their inception, older than the regular police. The Special Constables Act 1831 laid down, 'justices should appoint Special Constables where any tumult or riot had occurred or was likely to occur'. After the institution of the new police, specials became the relief force of ordinary citizens deputised to aid the regular force, the concept known today; but they were not legalised as a permanent peace-time force.

In September 1888 the Chief Constable applied to raise 200 specials and in October an undisclosed number were sworn in and told to 'await a Magistrate's summons'. The signs are that public disorder of the time influenced this action.

In 1911 the Chief Constable was called to a meeting with the Home Office to discuss the future of specials, apparently in some doubt. No effective decisions were made.

In 1914 specials took on a new significance. War was declared and in that first year 680 men were sworn into the Special Constabulary.

In October 1914 the Watch Committee authorised a Special Constabulary badge, with ribbon attached. At this time the Special Constabulary was ill-equipped and many were not uniformed. But they had a badge! Badged, recognised and hopefully established, they offered to police the city on Christmas Day and 72 men turned out. They offered again on Christmas Day 1915 and repeated the process in the next two succeeding years.

Early war duties for the specials were guarding bridges and gas and electricity works in anticipation of an invasion. They were also drilled, route marched (Norwich to Wroxham, Coltishall and back) and subjected to what was called 'a pleasant and healthy form of physical training'. Those on duty were issued with armlets and truncheons.

Specials were still not fully uniformed in 1916 when it was decreed that those above military age could be issued with caps. At the same time those of military age were to be asked why they were not in

HM Forces. At the inspection of the force at Chapelfield Drill Hall by HM Inspector of Constabulary 530 specials were on parade, including four company and 12 platoon commanders. In December of that same year it was reported that 760 specials had been enrolled, of which 233 had greatcoats!

The Chief Constable's report of 21 January 1916 said that the regular force had reached 'an irreducible minimum due to enlistment', yet doubt still persisted over the future of the specials.

In March 1917 the specials paraded at Earlham Recreation Ground to receive greatcoats, at least that is what the Watch Committee were told. It does appear, however, that the Special Constabulary was not fully uniformed until after October of that year when the newly-appointed Chief Constable, John Henry Dain, advised that greatcoats had been ordered. In between, in August, 340 specials paraded at the Norwich Grammar School to be inspected by HM Inspector of Constabulary. On this occasion Special Constable Butcher was commended for his arrest of two burglars. This was also the time when their duties first became laid down in printed form.

Still in 1917, members of No 2 Company, City of Norwich Special Constabulary, gathered at Blackfriar's Hall to make a presentation to their retiring Commander, Mr Ernest Hines. The occasion was dubbed a 'smoking concert' and humorous musical sketches were presented, according to a press report. On the more serious side Sub-Commander Keefe, addressing the company, said, 'No one would venture to put a date to which they could look forward as the time of disbandment'. Mr Hines, in reply, said he hoped that when the (special) force was disbanded their associations begun as policemen would continue as friends and that they would be able to meet together from time to time. But disbandment was never to be; and Mr Hines' retirement was illusory. In 1918 he was awarded, along with Special Commander Richard Winsor Bishop, the MBE, for services 'in connection with the war'. During the war Ernest Hines and other specials' commanders placed their private lawns at the disposal of their men for an inter-company bowls tournament, for which Mr Winsor Bishop presented a silver challenge cup. Mr Hines' company won.

Ernest Hines was the manager of an insurance company in the city and lived in Unthank Road very near to the home of John Henry Dain with whom he was a good friend, occasionally visiting him in his office in the 'tin hut'. Whether this close association had any bearing on the employment of Jessie and Hilda Hines by the force is a matter of conjecture. Ernest was, like Jessie, on duty at Nurse Cavell's funeral in 1919, and also at the centenary parade in 1936.

Mr S.L.Witton, donator of the force ambulance, was listed as a Special Constable and the Lord Mayor and Sheriff were honorary Commanders. Other Company Commanders were Mr A.T.Chittock and Mr F.R.C.Eaton. A report of the time says 'the fine organising ability of the present Deputy Chief Constable (Mr R.Hodges) was utilised in getting the force (specials) into competent working shape'.

In 1918 Special Constables Gallant and Harvey were commended for detecting and extinguishing a fire at 27 St Benedict's Street and Special Constable Mansfield was commended for stopping the inevitable runaway horse.

In 1921 the regular force numbered 147, the First Police Reserve 14 and the Special Constabulary 256.

Local, national and international unrest meant the authorities sought a constant reserve capability and the Special Constables' Act 1923 legitimised permanent special constabularies in peacetime. In 1939, on the verge of another war, the Chief Constable stated that 250 specials were required to supplement the 200 already recruited.

The Chief Constable paid tribute to the specials at a dinner in their honour at the Bell Hotel in 1940 saying, 'The zeal and efficiency of the Special Constabulary in Norwich is outstanding'. The Lord Mayor, Mr B.J.Hanly, himself a Sub-Commander in the Special Constabulary since 1914, said that he hoped more volunteers would be forthcoming for this important service. At this dinner Raydini, currently appearing at the Hippodrome, gave a conjuring turn and there were songs by William Frazer and Inspector Crawford with Mr G.Percival Griffiths at the piano. A contingent of police firemen also attended, but that was because a floor in the building was on fire: a small matter related to the hearth.

Your city needs you! Specials on parade during World War One, probably the 1916 inspection at Chapelfield. (A.Brown)

Specials being inspected by HM Inspector of Constabulary, Commander Willis, in August 1963. (Force archives)

The recruitment of special policemen was often dictated by circumstances – wars, civil unrest etc, but a recruiting instruction of September 1942 was very particular: bus company senior officials should be sworn-in to assist in dealing with bus queues. The Watch Committee did not recoil from this example of enforced ingenuity though it had a few months earlier complained at the practice of enrolling fire station cleaners as auxiliary firewomen.

Specials were unpaid, except for 'reasonable allowances'. After World War Two they lapsed in number and in 1950 the Chief Constable, Alan Plume, said that he had only 114 Special Constables against an authorised establishment of 380. But progress continued. In 1965 Helen Edwards joined her husband Maurice in the Special Constabulary, another first.

Others served and supported the force in a civilian-based capacity and particularly deserving of mention are the police surgeons. They began almost with the force itself. The first appointee was William Nicholls

Sergeant 'Jock' McLennan confers with Special Constables Hession (left) and Morgan in November 1963.   (Force archives)

(1838-55) followed by James Garton (1855-70), Robert Gibson (1870-82) and then an era of distinguished service from Robert Mills who incredibly held the post for 56 years, from 1882 until 1938. And then he only left at the behest of the Watch Committee after they apparently woke up to his advancing years. His surgery at Surrey Street by All Saints Green was a frequent port of call for gossiping, tea drinking beat Constables, so much so that in police circles the junction became known as 'Doctor Mills' Corner'.

Doctor Lincoln Hurn succeeded Doctor Mills and set up another, but smaller, record of long service by staying in post for 27 years, until 1965 when he was followed by Doctor James Hilton who saw the end of the force and carried on into the newly-amalgamated force.

In September 1928 uniformed members of the Lads' Club formed the 'Junior Police Force' under the direction of John Henry Dain. They became more easily known as 'carriage callers', which means exactly what it says because through to 1932 they could be seen whistling up carriages at events at St Andrew's Hall, Norwich Castle and Mousehold Airfield, to name a few that have gone on record. These young men were supplied with police type uniforms, supposedly cut down from real police uniforms though there is a counter view, supported by a Watch Committee note, that they were brand new.

Among those who also served was another young uniformed group, learning the trade as policemen of the future: the Cadet force, a nationally applied title to which the Junior Police Force can be seen as local forerunner.

Doctor Robert Mills (right) is honoured for a record of police service that cannot be eclipsed. Making the presentation at the Norwich Lads' Club in 1938 is the Chairman of the Watch Committee, Mr H.E.Witard. Seated are senior officers of the force, left to right: Detective Inspector John Watling, Inspectors Alec Doe, Charlie Baker, Edwin Buttle, Chief Constable John Henry Dain, Deputy Chief Constable Herbert Balls, Inspectors Frank Palmer and Arthur Bell, and Sergeant Charlie Porter. Nearly all the officers in the rear assembly can be identified. Some have found places in this book. Jesse Mayes is second from left and Fred Chenery third from left. Billy Kemp is sixth from left. John Colbron, killed in World War Two at Singapore, is 11th from left behind Mr Witard. John Neale, killed in World War Two in France, is ninth from the right looking over the shoulder of Raymond Blowers, eighth from right. Edward Gascoyne is third from the right. (J.Maxted)

The title of Cadet formally appears in Norwich police records in 1938 and several names follow only to disappear into the armed services with the advent of war. Again, some would not return. Cadet Peter Ivins joined the Royal Norfolk Regiment and was killed in action in 1942. Harry Eggbeer was a Cadet with the Weights and Measures' Department and volunteered for the RAF. He was killed in action in 1944.

During World War Two lads of 16 to 18 years provided a uniformed messenger service, braving bombs and blazing street littered wreckage to deliver messages on behalf of the police, fire service and ARP. Some of these messengers would in different times

have become Cadets and then policemen but instead moved on to military service. Donald Johnson, Joseph Clarke and Kenneth Gowing were ex-messengers who lost their lives in action far away from their city. Others were distinguished with awards for service on the home front and are covered in a later chapter.

At the conclusion of the war four messengers were retained as 'Cadet Clerks'.

A record in 1953 shows the force having five Cadets. In 1960 at least six Cadets were on strength for that was the number entered in the Duke of Edinburgh Award Scheme.

Cadets, messengers and carriage callers carried out

The Junior Police Force: parading at the Lads' Club c.1930 for the Chief Constable, John Henry Dain and marching into King Street. (Force archives)

important duties and were hopefully the future of the police force. Their duties were, however, sometimes only tenuously related to police matters, though old policemen would point out that someone had to make the tea and run errands. And wartime messengers did much more than carry messages. They filled sandbags, cleaned police boxes and traffic light bulbs and collected pies from Stannard's bakery in Bedford Street to deliver to the police station and boxes.

Cadet duties mostly occurred within the police station, though disinfecting the public side of pillar-phones did get them out and about. One genuine police outside duty was a frontline reconnaissance against a tacky bookshop in Charing Cross. A disarming and innocent looking Cadet was ordered into plain clothes and into the shop, to ask for something from under the counter. Upon his return to the station he was quickly relieved of his brown paper parcel and told to leave the room because he was 'too young'.

No record of the Norwich City Police and the youth of the city can be anywhere near complete without detailed reference to the Norwich Lads' Club. Such was the successful association between the city police force and this club countries from as far as Ceylon, the United States (New York) and Australia (Adelaide) expressed an interest and sought information. Police chiefs from Ceylon and Adelaide visited the city to appreciate the Lads' Club first hand.

The Norwich Lads' Club was born of the Norwich

Constable Aleck Bartram (known as Aleck with the K) and Cadet David Rowlands (to become a Detective Inspector) man a police road safety exhibition. (B.Kybird)

The General Office at Bethel Street Police station in 1957. This was the administrative centre of the station and an automatic posting for at least one Cadet: in this photograph there are two. Cadet Peter Barnes is top right (later to join the force proper and retire with the rank of Superintendent) and Cadet Brian Rouse (to become a Constable and later emigrate) is seated, top centre, in plain clothes. Also shown are two secretaries to Chief Constables: Doris Hall, seated right, and Freda Pye, seated centre. Freda succeeded Doris and served in the newly-amalgamated force. The Sergeant seated at the desk is the well-known Fred 'Stumpy' Chenery. He dealt with applications to join the force and greeted every prospective policeman with a degree of fierceness calculated to bring about an immediate career change of mind. The Chief Clerk, Inspector George Bailey, is far right. (ECN)

City Police, conceived in the latter part of 1917 when Chief Constable John Henry Dain formed and chaired a committee to provide a place and activities for the youth of the city who, as today, would say they had 'nothing to do' and 'nowhere to go'. John Henry Dain had not wasted much time for he only became Chief Constable in 1917, following Edwin Winch. He arrived from Canterbury where his newly formed Lads' Club lapsed in his absence.

The first requisite for the new club was a home. A derelict building at St George's Street, belonging to Norwich Corporation, became available at a nominal rent and policemen, working in off-duty hours, began the task of restoration. Many were the skills discovered within the force. Bricklayers, plasterers, carpenters and painters materialised, assisted by the enthusiastically labouring less skilled. Together they transformed the premises. Influential citizens and prominent employ-

A Cadet helps a member of the public, supposedly. This photograph was posed on the police station steps for publicity purposes. Cadet Barnes had been momentarily removed from the General Office, told to put his cap on and stand on the station steps and point. The 'member of the public' knew full well where she was and where she was going, as can be seen by referring back to the office photograph and the lady seated at the typewriter, front left, later to become the author's wife.
(ECN)

ers took notice and provided money and equipment and a comfortable club appeared from dereliction without notable financial cost to the city. A recreation room, gymnasium and theatre stage formed the core of the building, providing accommodation for approximately 200 boys.

On 8 April 1918 the Lord Mayor, Richard Jewson, formally opened the building. Initial membership was reported to be between 200 and 300 but by the end of that year it was well over 1,000.

Membership of the club, free to any lad between the ages of 14 and 18 (extended to 21 during World War Two), soared. It became necessary to find larger premises but it was not until 1924 that a suitable

building became available by which time the club's popularity was widespread and funds were more readily found. £4,000 was obtained through public subscription and the new building in King Street, catering for a membership of 6,000, was officially opened by the Duke of Gloucester in 1925. He spoke of the unique partnership between the youth of the city and the city police force.

The club was managed at minimal cost through the support of the public and business, and the personal unpaid services of many police officers. (On-duty policemen were not infrequently employed at the Lads' Club and it is reported that John Henry Dain consequently incurred the displeasure of HM Inspector of Constabulary.)

By 1943 11,000 lads had enrolled and attendance at an average membership night was quoted as 600 to 700. The diversity of activities ranged from sport and theatre to the formation of a division of the St John Ambulance Brigade and a band that was in great demand at charitable events. Juvenile crime plunged to a new low; the Duke of Gloucester said the club had 'practically eliminated juvenile crime in Norwich'. Though World War Two curtailed events it also provided a new comradeship as Lads' Club boys proudly took their heritage all over the world.

Chief Constable Dain acted as recruiting officer for the club on Sunday mornings when he conducted his juvenile cautioning sessions in the 'tin hut'. Many a youngster was sternly rebuked for an offence and then directed towards the Lads' Club. One recipient of such an interview recalls that the Chief Constable spent an inordinate amount of time reflectively examining a cane while casually discussing with a Sergeant the merits of corporal punishment, professing to ignore the avidly listening and trembling youngster: psychology that today would remove the Chief Constable from his post.

Disaster struck on 6 February 1943 when the club was destroyed by fire. Poignantly it was the year of retirement of John Henry Dain, the founder and Life President, and, tragically, a National Fire Service fireman, Albert Read, lost his life fighting the fire. In a scene reminiscent of Henry Hook in Queen Street 51 years earlier he was trapped by falling rubble.

Following a rebuilding appeal and many generous

John Henry Dain, Chief Constable of the Norwich City Police from 1917 to 1943. His portrait, commissioned by members of the force in 1938, hangs in the Chief Constable's old office at Bethel Street, now used as a conference room. (Force archives)

donations from individuals and organisations, the club rose phoenix like from the ashes and was reopened by Lord Mackintosh of Halifax on 13 September 1951. For many years it continued as a haven and sporting and cultural centre for the youth of Norwich; but then it declined, the glory days were over and it became only a faded memory. Sadly, like the Norwich City Police, it is no more.

Kim joined the force in 1959. He was aged two years and three months, fine coated with appealing eyes, and was very keen. He was an alsatian, Norwich's

Lads' Club gymnasts, c.1919. The Chief Constable, John Henry Dain, sits in front of the name board and trophies with instructor, Inspector Alfred Harrison, on his immediate left. Note that boxing came under the title of gymnastics.

(B.Harrison)

This scroll was presented to John Henry Dain after his appointment in 1917. It requires no further explanation.

(Force archives)

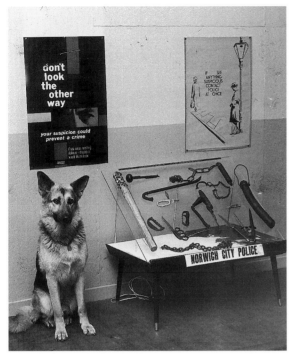

Kim is seen here at the 1963 Trades Fair. A popular dog within the force and to the law abiding public, he has his place in history as Norwich's first. He retired in 1966 and continued living with Stanley Nunn in the company of the newly-trained Nicky. Kim died in 1968, the year the force died.

(Force archives)

first police dog. After training at the Metropolitan Police Dog Training School with his handler, Constable Stanley Nunn, he returned to the force and blazed a trail that was to be followed by so many others; almost instantly in fact. Tiny, aged two years and six months, joined the force two months later and with his handler, Constable John 'Taffy' Bounds, formed another two-pronged attack that left many lawbreakers with revised views on man's best friend. The Metropolitan Police had donated Tiny to the Norwich force after Taffy's first dog failed the training course.

Constable Stanley Nunn and Kim on duty at the Cathedral.
(B.Kybird)

Constable Peter Barrett and Dolf succeeded Taffy and Tiny, forming a new partnership of one man and his dog in 1964, another distinctive pairing remembered by police and criminals alike. They went on with Stanley Nunn and Kim (then Kim's successor, Nicky) into the new amalgamated force. Kim, Tiny, Nicky and Dolf were the Norwich police dogs.

CHAPTER SEVEN
Days to Remember
Parades, processions, inspections and sport

MANY incidents, occurrences and what are indisputably notable events have already been recounted or have received some reference in previous pages, through distinction or simply as a marker or reference point in the force's history. What follows in this and succeeding chapters has missed or glanced off the story so far and yet is representative, significant, outstanding or just plain deserving of a place in the telling of the history of the Norwich City Police.

The loneliness of the policeman on the beat, his isolation and paradoxical calming obviousness to a bustling passing community, can be contrasted with the role reversal that occurs when that community stays around to form a crowd. Crowds vary in size and disposition but usually have a purpose and if uncontrolled will seek to realise that purpose in the most expedient way possible. Riots and public disturbances, more a feature of the earlier years of the force, have already received some detailed reference but other gatherings of the community are worthy of note, some of them actually inspired by the police. Whether people have assembled to view, protest or are simply gregariously curious, the police are invariably there, sometimes through pre-planning sometimes by reaction.

Parades and processions have long figured in police planning and earned places in the memories of individuals watching, marching or processing. Some of these occasions have been awe inspiring and pure entertainment. The Royal Canadian Mounted Police, resplendent in red tunics and grey Stetsons, rode through the city from Thorpe Station to the Costessey showground astride prancing, livery jingling horses, led by ex-War Reserve Constable Alfred Salmon bouncing on a hired and tiring police (for the day) horse. Elephants had their day, winding their way through city streets, trunks clasping tails, plodding steadily past wide-eyed spectators to the circus tent pitched at Eaton Park, policemen watching nervously, contemplating what form of action was required if one or more pachyderms took exception to the route, or anybody or anything on it. The police briefing had taken an icy turn when a Constable blandly asked the instructing Inspector if the procession would go via a trunk road.

Other processions were satisfying for different reasons and required a level of police planning and security that gave senior officers acute anxiety, and in some cases rank bad temper. Royal visits, Prime Ministers and film or pop stars fell into this category.

Royal events that required a celebration but were missing the royals themselves were easier from a security viewpoint and no less enjoyable. Coronations and jubilees fell into this category and the 19th and 20th centuries were not short of both. They led to a decorated city and street processions with much flag waving and expressions of pleasure from loyal subjects only too glad of a day in which something different and exciting was occurring. When a royal person actually appeared the excitement multiplied among citizens and police, though there was a difference in the anticipation.

The visit to the city of King Edward VII in 1909 combined several ceremonies and individual visits. The city's senior citizen received the King at St Andrew's Hall and was conferred with the new title of Lord Mayor. A cine film of this momentous visit has survived and is held by the East Anglian Film Archive, also copied into a video on public sale.

Six months after being received in Norwich King Edward VII was dead.

In 1918 Queen Alexandra performed the unveiling

ceremony for the memorial to Nurse Edith Cavell, executed by the Germans and at that time still lying in a Belgian grave.

Nurse Cavell returned in 1919, with solemnity and dignity, arriving in Norwich from Belgium via Westminster Abbey and train to Thorpe Station. A large crowd assembled to pay their respects to the lady of Swardeston as she was drawn through the streets, from Thorpe Station along Prince of Wales Road to the Cathedral and Life's Green. It was a day of restrained pomp in which slowly stepping horses and crawling cars formed a silently moving cortege past serious faced, some weeping, crowds, all preceded by a lone cycling Constable directed to check the route in advance of the procession. The choice of officer for this task was appropriate – deliberate or inadvertent. Constable William Hopes (photograph, chapter two) served in World War One, a member of the Norfolk Yeomanry at Gallipoli.

The police operational order for Nurse Cavell's funeral survives in police archives.

The city was not to be short of visiting royalty in the 20th century and the new Prince of Wales (later King Edward VIII and subsequently Duke of Windsor) came to the city on no less than 11 occasions. The future King, albeit of short reign, opened the new Carrow Bridge in 1923 and went on to the Royal Norfolk Agricultural Show at Eaton Park (then open ground but called a park) and once again the police operational order survives in police archives. In 1928 he officially opened Eaton Park.

The visit of the reigning monarch in 1938 was of special significance to the police. King George VI and Queen Elizabeth opened the new City Hall on 29 October, an auspicious day of fanfare and procession attracting large crowds to points of the royal itinerary. It was also a day of amalgamating police forces; officers from both city and county forces were on duty in the city. (Fourteen years later King George VI brought them together again, at Sandringham, lining the drive of the royal residence to pay last respects.)

The Special Constabulary and the Police Reserve

King Edward VII is seen leaving the Chapelfield Drill Hall where he had lunched in October 1909. The Constable looking directly at the camera, far right, has been identified by the collar number 30 as Sidney Cushing who joined the force in 1902, was later promoted to Sergeant and subsequently suffered ill health. He was admitted to Hellesdon Hospital in 1916 and died in 1917.

Death of the King, denoted by the black armbands. The Chief Constable, Edwin Winch, with officers in The Close on 20 May 1910 on the occasion of a special service held in the cathedral. The elderly gentleman in the background adds some distinction to the photograph, not that it needed any. (B.Harrison)

were represented at the opening of the City Hall, the former attracting a measure of criticism from regular officers who spoke of the sudden recruiting of local businessmen, the swift issue of uniforms – Sam Browne belts and all, and their prominent line-up before the King and Queen.

Bethel Street Police Station was already in use and had been so since Good Friday of that year, leaving the 'tin hut' to an antique collector, literally; but there had been some settling-in problems. Reports refer to 'slippery floors' and 'broken limbs'. Whose limbs and

which floors were not noted. And the walls of the Chief Constable's office were too dark, according to somebody, presumably the Chief Constable. Five Constables spent a day scrubbing the offending walls with petrol to lighten the office (another extraneous duty not envisaged by recruiting and training). Readers who hesitate over this revelation from the past will wonder not only at the smell but the risk of the Chief Constable blowing up himself and his office before the King had opened the main building.

King George VI returned in 1942, briefly, without

The long arm of the law. An autograph hunter ambushes the Prince of Wales at the showground in 1923 and is thwarted by Inspector Harrison's snaking arm and the studied indifference of the Prince. (B.Harrison)

Princess Margaret visits the City Hall in July 1952 after opening a new orthopaedic ward at the Norfolk and Norwich Hospital, watched closely by Constable John Riches. (ECN)

Prime Ministers and a Norwich Police Sergeant. Sergeant Dudley Brook watches over Harold Macmillan and Alec Douglas Home, in the latter case watched by a smiling Inspector Neville Ball, and traffic motor cyclists. Note the change of helmet style in the intervening years (changed 1961).   (A.Brown)

One looking after many. Constable Sidney Page with an intent and patient crowd at the opening of Waterloo Park in 1933.
(A.Brown)

fanfares and the blaze of publicity of his earlier visit. He was touring and reviewing troops. The country was at war.

Processions and parades featured in both world wars, the most important being, of course, the victory parades at the end. Scenes of uninhibited joy upon the receipt of momentous news would later be repeated in a more dignified manner at parades of the victorious services, though the American allies would be slightly more flamboyant. (See photographs, chapter eight.)

The police themselves marched when the occasion demanded, as it did every day for 100 years at shift changeover times. This was the routine spilling from the station of half a dozen or more men juggling themselves into formation and striding smartly along the pavement flanked by a Sergeant, men then peeling away to take over beats. This beat changeover march, begun in 1852 at the instigation of the Watch Committee, had moved its starting point through successive stations to the Bethel Street Station. It lapsed in the middle 1950s, much to the disappointment of watching old soldiers and locals who found something reassuring in watching the 'changing of the guard'.

Other parades of police officers were special, spe-

Constable Herbert Docwra stares straight ahead, aware that he has a king and queen on his right – and his Chief Constable: October 1938 and the opening of the City Hall.

(A.Brown)

cific, and formal, some annually unwelcome others suddenly and tragically unwanted, all impressive. The visit of HM Inspector of Constabulary was a parade and pretence of perfection in which hard creased and hard brushed uniforms were arrayed in poker faced ranks of individual rigidity, each hoping for anonymity as the highest rank in the police service passed by.

Funeral processions marked a loss to police and public. The death of a serving colleague demanded proper respect from a disciplined service imbued with the bonding comradeship that comes with adversity. The solemn formality of a police farewell was dignified, disciplined and the essence of comradeship. A farewell to arms, in a sense. Long files of uniformed policemen marched slowly through city streets on such occasions.

On 1 March 1936 the Norwich City Police marched uniquely, as a force, in celebration, 140 of them from Bethel Street to the Cathedral via London Street,

Collars and ties. Officers march from Bethel Street Police Station in June 1950 showing for the first time collars and ties, initially for daytime summer wear, then for winter as well; but closed neck tunics remained for night duty almost to the end of the force. Constables Brian Markham (picture left) and John Crisp (right) lead with Fred Jolly (left) and Frank Sabberton (right) in the second row. On the left in the third row is Ernest Betts ahead of Willie McLintock, George Russell, Barney Mallett and Stanley Nunn. (ECN)

The funeral of Detective Inspector Charles Elliott High, Head of Norwich CID, who died on 20 March 1910 at the age of 48 years (joined the force in 1880). The hearse heads the force procession in Earlham Road and Inspectors march alongside the coffin at the cemetery. After Inspector High's death there were many tributes, including a Magistrate who commented on the rough times of the detective's early service saying that as a police officer he was 'an exceedingly tough handful for the criminal fraternity to turn upon'. Another tribute drew attention to what was called the longest police chase in the history of the force (pre-motor vehicle), occasioned when Constable High pursued a warehouse burglar through Botolph Street into St Augustine's and on to St Martin's before effecting his capture in New Mills Yard. One of his early arrests was of Arthur Riches shortly after this local fish-hawker had stabbed and strangled his wife to death on Gentleman's Walk. Detective Inspector High's funeral was attended by local dignitaries and a large number of officers from the Norwich, Norfolk and Great Yarmouth forces. (Force archives)

Tombland and the Erpingham Gate. Regular policing of the city was given to the First Police Reserve for this special occasion, the centenary of the Norwich City Police. Never before had the city police marched as one, and never would it do so again. Never again would the people have the opportunity to witness a spectacle of rhythmically thudding feet and rigid faces set in a briskly moving long caterpillar of rippling dark blue and silver. And it snowed, the sudden driving, sleety kind so peculiar to early March. Ranks of

Marching to the beats in the 1950s. Constable Ted Fisher leads Constables Charlie Marten, Cliff Vincent, Stan Furlonger, Bob Joyner, (next is not positively identified), 'Paddy' O'Brien, Jimmy Downes and others. The supervising Sergeant is Basil Gibbs. Charlie Marten was in trouble after this picture was published, sternly asked why his gloves were not in his right hand. He replied that this was his saluting hand. (ECN)

This photograph was issued as a postcard without an accompanying explanation and one only has come to notice, found in the effects of a Norwich officer. Enquiries indicate the place is Earlham Cemetery and the occasion possibly the funeral of matron Jane Trimby on 31 December 1926 (see Chapter Six). Identifying the officers has resulted in only limited success, and some conflict of names. The picture is best left to its general impact. (G.Burton)

The funeral of Inspector Stanley Murrell, killed in a motor vehicle accident in June 1939. He joined the force in 1909. The force marched to St Faith's Crematorium and leading the procession left to right, are: Inspector Frank Palmer, Detective Inspector John Watling and Sergeant John Pye. In the second picture fellow Inspectors accompany the hearse. Edwin Buttle leads on the left (Alec Doe at rear) and Arthur Bell leads on the right (George Lee at rear). (Force archives)

polished boots smacked into running, slushy water. Any ill-informed, unprepared person engaged in an act of lawlessness can only have wondered at the odds against him as a solid phalanx of police tramped into view. In reality hundreds watched from the pavements.

The Lord Mayor attended the service at the Cathedral and the Vicar of St Peter Mancroft, a role that during the lifetime of the city force embraced that of police padre, conducted the service. The Reverend Hugh McMullan said, 'Within the comparatively short space of 100 years here, in this city, renowned for its antiquity, we have a company of officers and men to whom is entrusted the responsibility for maintaining the principles, laws and statues of civic governance, and who have created within themselves, for themselves, a tradition for discipline, integrity of character

and devotion to duty that cannot be excelled by any other service in the state'. The Chief Constable told the congregation that for the first time since his appointment a year had passed without a single member of the force being subject to disciplinary proceedings. Real progress over 100 years!

The police parade that did not attract the public, because they were not invited, occurred every year when HM Inspector of Constabulary inspected the force. Earlier inspections, in the 19th century, occurred quarterly, mostly at St Andrew's Hall, and were conducted by the Watch Committee. Preferred venues for the HMI were the playground at the Bignold School at Crook's Place, the Chapelfield Drill Hall and Chapelfield Gardens and, in later years, the Bethel Street Fire Station yard.

In 1933 HM Inspector Major General Llewellyn

The force outside St Andrew's Hall in 1920. The Chief Constable, John Henry Dain, sits in the centre with the Deputy Chief Constable – Superintendent Robert Hodges and Inspector Alfred Harrison on his right and, to his left, Inspectors Edward Doe, Alex Christie, William Thompson (Fire Brigade) and Walter Crome (CID).　　　　　　　　　　(Force archives)

The centenary parade arriving at the Cathedral led by Inspector Edwin Buttle, then halted with Inspector Stanley Murrell at the front and, behind him, Sergeants Arthur Jarmey, centre, Reggie Nicholls to the picture left, Sidney Barrett behind Nicholls, and Jesse Mayes' picture right. Next, the force is formed in open ranks and inspected: old soldiers know that a parade always has an inspection. The inspecting dignitary is the Lord Mayor, Mr W.A.Riley, accompanied by the Chief Constable, John Henry Dain. The CID were not exempt from such an important occasion, and it was the time of the bowler hat: left to right of the waiting detectives is Detective Inspector John Watling and Detective Constable Cecil Waterson. This photograph also reveals the presence of father and son – John Henry Dain does not look towards Inspector Edgar Dain. (A.Brown, A.Rix and M.Salt)

Atcherley inspected the force in the playground at Crook's Place, following which the assembled officers marched to the Lads' Club for 'further inspection'. The reasoning behind this march through city streets (three years ahead of the big one) and what was meant by 'further inspection' has not been explained. HM Inspector was not going to see more at the Lads' Club then he could at Crook's Place. It is possible the weather was inclement; HM Inspector, Chief Constable and dignitaries unitedly refused to get wet.

The Bethel Street Fire Station yard became the regular place for HM Inspector to prowl the assembled ranks and ask a rigid straight faced Constable whether he had 'had a good year?', the standing question of Commander Willis who carried out 11 such inspections. Woe betide the Constable who had not had a good year. The Chief Constable would be listening at HM Inspector's elbow.

Following the formal inspection in the fire station yard it was practice for the Constables to assemble in the police station parade room and answer questions and make statements about outstanding examples of police work they had been involved in. That they had each been specially selected and primed, and leapt up on cue, was probably within HM Inspector's knowledge.

The ideal of good police and community relations was served in many ways, not the least of which was the police participation in sport, within the force and against other forces, and competing against and displaying to the public at large. But the most important change for force members was the forming of the

Inspection of the force by HM Inspector of Constabulary at Chapelfield c.1912. Officers are formally producing appointments (truncheons and handcuffs) for HM Inspector, Leonard Dunning accompanied by Chief Constable, Edwin Winch. Officers identified by collar numbers and letters are, from right to left: Sergeant R William Ward (retired November 1913 following which Charlie Meachen took the latter R); Constable 21 Thomas Holland; 124 Archibald Snelling (killed in action in World War One, 1917); 19 Thomas Palmer; 114 George Elvin; 64 Henry Sparkes; 121 Percy Gray; 78 Joseph Bean; 56 Thomas Brown and, picture left of HMI, Sergeant E Ephraim Emmerson (see chapter nine). (M.Dixon)

This parade, also in Chapelfield Gardens, c.1913, shows St John's Roman Catholic Cathedral in the top right of the picture. Sergeant S on the left is Donald Piercy. The war left its mark on three Constables standing together in the front row. Fourth Constable from the left is a youthful 123 William Jackson who survived and returned to the force to serve until retirement in 1937. Next, fifth, is 66 Sidney Smith who fought in France, received the Croix de Guerre, returned to Norwich and failed to report his demobilisation, then replied to an inquiry from the force by resigning, took a public house at Wymondham, joined the Royal Ulster Constabulary as a drill instructor, returned to live in Norwich and claimed continuous police service (repudiated), and then dropped out of sight. Next in line to the right, on Smith's left, is Constable 47 Herbert Whitehand – killed in action in 1917. (M.Dixon)

Another inspection by HM Inspector, c.1914, and it appears to be Leonard Dunning leading Chief Constable Winch along the ranks. Note that the Constables' uniform has changed and the tunics have buttoned pockets. Summer helmets are being worn. The Inspector on the left cannot be named with certainty. The first six Constables in the front rank are: left to right, 3 George Canham, 71 Alpha Rix, 123 William Jackson, 64 Harry Sparkes, 81 Sidney Page and 67 Edward Male. First in the rear rank is 24 Percy Capon. (M.Dixon)

HMI's inspection in the fire station yard, 4 November 1958. Commander Willis asks Sergeant Jimmy Downes if he has 'had a good year?' Waiting their turn are Sergeants Johnnie Johnson, Dudley Brook and John Wright, and in the next row: Constable Alan Brown. The Chief Constable Alan Plume precedes the Lord Mayor, Norman Tillett and the Sheriff, while the Deputy Chief Constable, Arthur Burns, brings up the rear. (Force archives)

HM Inspector is accompanied by Chief Constable Dain during the 1919 inspection of the force at the inappropriately named Crook's Place. This was, unusually, a December inspection, a time of year revealed by the photograph. Inspector Edward Doe stands in front of the first rank and Sergeant R Charlie Meachen is first in line. In the second row two survivors of military service in World War One stand together: third from left is 55 Cubitt Elvin and fourth is 123 William Jackson. (M.Dixon)

Winners of the Arnold Cup 1924-25 – Norwich City Police. Back row, left to right: Superintendent Alex Christie in uniform, Hugh Murray, Arthur Jarmey (uniform), George Tubby, Alec Doe, Frank Franklin, Herbert Docwra and Inspector Bert Gardiner (uniform). Front row: Archie Turner, Percy Moorby, Charlie Baker, Chief Constable John Henry Dain, Sydney Jary, Jimmy Wanbon and Ted Burroughes. (A.Brown)

Norwich City Police Social Club and Athletic Association, an organisation that brought a number of flourishing force activities under one umbrella. Records show that the Chief Constable, John Henry Dain, inaugurated the association in 1929, and he certainly gave it his active support; but other notes and recollections indicate that the true originator was Sergeant Alec Doe who was running an embryo association in 1927.

Shortly after the official formation of this association it was reported that in open competition the cricket, football, swimming, billiards and shooting teams had all carried off trophies.

Comprehensively illustrating the city police in their sporting guise would mean pages of formal photographs of arms folded, camera conscious officers variously grinning, scowling, blankly staring, grimacing, arrayed on chairs, front row kneeling, and would not do justice to the action that led to the photograph. It is hoped that the overall picture will be conveyed by the few pictures selected and the text summary.

The national games of football and cricket had their city police devotees and many a duty sheet was

Champions of the Norwich Thursday League, Division One, 1953 – Norwich City Police. Back row, left to right: standing, Neville Garnham (linesman),Willie McLintock, Don Hooper, Ted Mileham, Terry Comer, Kenny Crowe, Albert Turner, Cliff Vincent, 'Jock' McLennan, Dan Griffiths and Freddie King (trainer). Front row seated: Lennie Bacon, Ivan Kidgell, Harry 'Chesty' Wright, Chief Constable Alan Plume, Superintendent Bernard Tester, Jimmy Tricker and Geoffrey Neville. (W.McLintock)

altered to accommodate a player, to the disadvantage of a non-player. In the post-World War Two period Inspector Harry Wright, known as 'Chesty' – an obvious nickname once his barrel-chested figure was seen, managed the football and cricket teams and earnestly interrogated every new recruit to assess his capabilities in these sports. Any who had played at a higher level were assured of a promising police career by Chesty: not necessarily realised.

The first record of a police cricket team appears in 1884, and an official football team in 1913 when the Chief Constable gave permission for officers with under 15 years service to form a team.

Football was played in the Norwich Thursday League, also competing for the Arnold Cup and playing the annual fixture of Police versus Specials at Carrow Road.

It has been said that teams in the Thursday League looked forward to playing the police because it was the only time they could get away with an assault upon police. On the other hand, there were those who claimed that the police were the roughest team in the league; something to do with a release of inhibitions. The truth was probably somewhere in between but in any event it was an involvement with the community.

While the younger officers played football and cricket their ageing colleagues tended towards bowls, a

Nearly winners. The final of the national bowls triples tournament in which the Norwich City Police lost to the City of London Police – but they got some silverware. Back row, left to right: Jack Cates, Ken Grist, Dudley Brook, John Wright and Lennie Coadwell. Front row: Fred Gravenall, Herbert 'Budgie' Lines, Fred 'Stumpy' Chenery, Harry Baughan and Ray Blowers. (A.Brown)

prominent sport for Norwich officers, especially Inspectors. The cry of 'Good wood, sir' was occasionally heard from a lesser rank seeking a better place on the duty sheet.

Tug of war would seem to be a natural sport for heavily-built policemen and some success was achieved. It was not, however, consistently popular within the force and it had the disadvantage that no senior officers showed an interest. Early training sessions were tempered by a low turnout that was further reduced by reparation to a nearby public house. It is therefore of great credit that the team went as far as it did.

Snooker was popular from the moment a table appeared at Bethel Street Police Station and some officers became accomplished upon the green baize during the 45-minute refreshment period. They tempted indigestion by bolting sandwiches to gain a place at a table, and stress by rushing to down the colours before their 45 minutes expired. Local clubs were invited to participate in matches, bringing people into the police station as genuine guests, a term not strictly applicable to many who were invited, or propelled, into the building.

Darts, table tennis and tennis became more prominent police sports with the strengthening of the policewomen's department. Some of the women, notably Beryl Baker and Joy Greensides, excelled in these games and went on to win national titles within the Police Athletic Association.

Athletics events were organised by Norwich City Police over many years, and officers accordingly ran, jumped and threw things on annual special days, held in the early years of the century at Honingham Park, then at the Grammar School playing fields, later moving to Lakenham.

Following the centenary celebration of the force Chief Constable Dain inaugurated the Centenary Cup, to be allocated in turn to each section of the sports and social club of the force and to be competed for annually.

A horticultural section was formed within the social club and was strongly supported, staging an annual show that usually coincided with the sports day. Competition was fierce and the seriousness of the rivalry was demonstrated in 1923 when a Constable appeared before the Watch Committee to explain how his entry of two cabbages corresponded with two cabbages missing from an allotment that did not belong to him. He pleaded guilty to discreditable conduct, explaining that his keenness for gardening 'carried him too far'. He was ordered to forfeit 6s per week of his 90s weekly pay for a period of 12 months. In the later years of the force the Thomas Byland Cup, in memory of the keen gardening Sergeant who died in service, was annually awarded to the competitor gaining the most points at the show.

Some sports created after affects, potentially noticed by the public. An upright citizen stopping in Tombland to inquire of the beat policeman some pertinent information – like the location of the Cathedral, would find his inbuilt healthy respect for the police seriously damaged by the startling revelation that the Constable giving the necessary guidance was wearing make-up: eye shadow and traces of lipstick without a doubt. It was all due to swimming.

There is no lack of sporting photographs of the swimming section; sporting in its widest sense. Again, not all can be reproduced but the less serious side of the police can easily be detected in those that follow. The post-World War Two period saw the police and the community at their bonding best, courtesy of police swimming galas. Relaxation and laughter were the tonics.

The Norwich City Police swimming section existed in the previous century (see 1896 photograph, chapter one) and was attracting considerable interest through its annual 'aquatic sports', as the press called them. Canoe racing and competitive swimming, some in uniform, figured strongly. World War One interrupted these events and the section was not reformed until 1928 when it was reported to have 108 members. At this time the section began giving tuition to Lads' Club members and the Lads' Club Band gave a 'fund raising concert'.

The pre-World War One public displays were held

A fashion parade, of sorts. Police officers pose on the roof of the Lido in July 1938 wearing swimming costumes dating from 1890 to 1925, supplied by a swimwear company with strict instructions not to get them wet. From left to right: Freddie King, John Fletcher, Tom Archer, Frank Barnes, Percy Moorby, Fred Chenery, Phil Salt, Frank North. (M.Salt)

You didn't have to enter the water to get wet on a dreadful summer's day c.1958. A false start in the uniform race at Lakenham.
(ECN)

at the Swan Baths (heated by the adjoining Swan Laundry). In the 1930s, the Lido was consistently used. There is one unconfirmed recollection of the Eagle Baths being used for a display and the Samson and Hercules was used on at least one occasion just before World War Two. The public were invited to galas, or something called a 'water frolic'. The 1935 frolic, at the Lido, included an invitation to other police forces and it is reported that the watching crowd numbered 1,000. A short cine film of this event was discovered in 1993.

The annual police swimming gala increased in popularity as it became more extrovert, particularly in the second post-war period when most of the available photographs were taken. These were the galas held at Lakenham and St Augustine's, the official swimming baths of Norwich, the former an open air pool – usu-

ally struck by rain and freezing cold weather on the day of the gala in high summer, and the latter a new state of the art much publicised enclosed and heated pool that has since bodily declined and been demolished.

The serious side of swimming (if a line of uniformed policemen diving into the water is serious), had featured strongly in early police galas (or sports and frolics), with humour appearing in the greasy pole and short skits, but the trend became increasingly theatrical and the people of Norwich warmed to the sight of policemen parading in women's clothes (borrowed from the WVS), and other inappropriate costumes, usually parodying some respectable institution or event. The fact that all concerned eventually fell in the water helped considerably. Make-up liberally applied in a thespian cause could be embarrassing if not thor-

On a clear day you could see the police playing a piano and drums in the middle of the pool. A boarding party approaches from the left and a not so heavily disguised Johnnie Johnson hurls encouragement, directions, or perhaps warnings, from the poolside. The piano sank. The subsequent move to the indoor pool at St Augustine's ruled out pianos and the like. (J.Johnson)

oughly removed, hence the man on the beat next day alarming the inquiring citizen.

The last gala was held in 1966, anticipating the end of the Norwich City Police.

'Crossing the line' was a popular sketch, so much so it was repeated at a later gala. Those lined up at another wet Lakenham are, left to right: Mike Leggett, Brian Rouse, Kenny Dennis, Don Seager, Johnnie Johnson, John Fletcher, Brian Roberts, Les Abley and Ted Goodenough. (A.Brown)

Nothing is more guaranteed to help community relations and leave fond memories than entertainment. Music! The Norwich City Police band was known to be in existence in 1892 though scant reference is found thereafter. That they occasionally played at force functions and more regularly in the iron pavilion at Chapelfield Gardens for the entertainment of the public was reported by ex-Sergeant Moses Giles (retired 1919) in a press interview in 1941. The press used this interview to provide a revealing insight into the band, commenting, 'the procession of burly instrumentalists picking their way up the narrow spiral stairway of the old pavilion was not without its humour' and 'on a sultry summer night they would present a perspiring picture by the time they formed up before their music stands'. The bandmaster was a Mr Widdows, well-known in musical circles in the city, and, according to the press, 'what he lacked in stature beside the comparatively towering presence of his bandsmen, he more than made up by his commanding style as a conductor'.

Four detectives as never seen before, except at a police swimming gala. They are named with their eventual rank. Left to right: John Riches (Detective Chief Inspector), Geoffrey Neville (Superintendent), Ken Statham (Detective Inspector) and Ken Grist (Detective Inspector). (K.Grist)

Confirmed police members of the band in 1892 were Sergeant Bix, Constables Ridley, Marshall, Barlow, Beeston (a man of many talents-see previous references), A.Woods (the drummer, later succeeded by Patrick Connors who retired as Inspector in 1919), Easton, Gostling, N.Miller, F.Miller and Watson.

The police band performed at police sports' days and at the force annual outing, traditionally provided by successive Sheriffs of the city. These outings had gone by or with World War One, as apparently had the band, though a police concert was

reported in December 1913, with proceeds going to police charities, and this would have seen the band in action. But by 1928 it was the Lads' Club Band performing on behalf of the police and one can only wonder at the effect of World War One on police musicians. Dissolution thereabouts seems likely.

The 'Blue Club Concert Party', formed in 1938, was different, wider ranging and more diverse with its music and entertainment;

The programme and foreword from the Blue Club performance in aid of the dependents of those killed in HMS Hood. (M.Salt)

Policemen cavorting with policewomen at St Augustine's in the name of entertainment. Left to right: Carol Downs, Peter Fleming, Maurice Morson, unidentified legs and Daphne Cullington. (ECN)

'On the Beat'. The sketch performed at the Theatre Royal, left to right: Philip Salt (police officer), Alan Brett (civilian), Tommy Webb (civilian), Norman Kefford (police officer). Note the Blue Club emblem on the backcloth.   (M.Salt)

a mixture of police and civilians, it entertained as a voluntary unpaid group and was much in demand during the war. By June 1941 the group had given 99 shows to audiences ranging from 30 to 1,000, performing at venues that included the Hippodrome and Theatre Royal. The company included three females singing and dancing and Constable John Stockdale – 'Yorkshireman – 6ft of fun', and Sergeant Ted Scott – 'organiser and compére'. The copied programme and photograph refer to the 1941 fund raising performance at the Theatre Royal in aid of the families of an early tragedy of World War Two, the sinking of HMS Hood with great loss of life. It is notable that sketches 'On the Beat' and 'Spare a Copper' were performed by permission of George Formby. Indeed days to remember. The Blue Club gave its last performance in 1944.

CHAPTER EIGHT

War is... Hell!

Norwich City Police and the Crimea, Boer and two World Wars

THE Norwich City Police was affected by several wars. (Distinguished service in the Boer War is covered in Chapter Three.) Mostly they were fought on far-off fronts, yet they reached out to indirectly impress upon the city force, with one, World War Two, having a devastating impact.

In the Crimea War the Norwich force was represented by the secondment, in 1853, of Constable John Nary to the Turkish Army police. Colonel T.B.Wright, writing on the subject of the United Kingdom police seconded to Crimea, said, 'Any good policeman will make a good soldier although by no means every good soldier will make a good police officer'. Nary duly returned to the city force and is next heard off in 1857 as a member of the 'horse patrol'.

World War One more than touched the daily lives of the people of Norwich. There was the inconvenience and danger of the blackout, the fear of bombing, and hard times got harder; and there was tragedy as families learned that the loved one who had left would not return.

The war intruded and transformed the policing of the city, though not in the manner that was to be so horrifying felt some 25 years later. Anxious eyes of police and citizens scanned darkened city streets for bearings and the night skies for Zeppelins, one related to the other. Credit for thwarting the German airships was given to the blackout and the city police.

Blackout was introduced in stages via Lighting Orders, the first printed onto 6,000 handbills and distributed by Special Constables. As measures became more stringent trams were compelled to travel with drawn blinds (later rescinded and replaced by an order to extinguish all tram lights except for an interior candle), public lighting was abolished, shop lights were dimmed (later they had to be extinguished forcing shops and factories to close early) and motor, cycle and horse transport had to make their way without effective illumination. Pavement edges were whitewashed and some pedestrians sported luminous discs to avoid collisions. It was reported that 'sober and respected citizens were unable to find their homes' and more than once 'boldly walked into somebody else's house'.

So strict were the later Lighting Orders it became an offence to strike a match in the street and several persons were fined for the offence. Early in the war lighting offences were dealt with by issuing a caution but from March 1915 until the end of that year 1,028 offences were the subject of a summons.

The city suffered 60 'air raid actions' in World War One but was not bombed once, though the Germans reported otherwise. The first threat occurred on 19 January 1915 when Zeppelins were reported over Bacton and heading for Norwich. The city's electricity supply was deliberately cut off and the enemy never appeared.

In the evening gloom of 1 October 1916, Zeppelins were seen approaching the coast and later, in more solid darkness, the distinctive droning engines were audible and moving lights were visible in the sky over Costessey. Four Zeppelins were reported to be operating over Norfolk that night but Norwich had earlier been plunged into total darkness. The police had instructed the closure of railway services at City and Thorpe Stations and all lights on trains had to be extinguished.

In the early hours of 2 October 'a Zeppelin engine sounded distinctly over Magdalen Road Police Station', reported in the Norwich War Record, and shortly after the noise had faded bombs were dropped at Easton Park, about five miles away, and it was noted that 'the noise of the explosions reverberated through

Norwich Tank Week. Firstly, the Deputy Chief Constable, Superintendent Robert Hodges, leads the tank towards the Guildhall. Secondly, the Chief Constable, John Henry Dain, stands on the tank with other speechmakers. (A.Williamson)

the city'. A Zeppelin was then heard to pass over the city.

The October raid was analysed by a contributor to the War Record as follows: 'Unquestionably this represented the narrowest escape Norwich had from being bombed, and the greatest credit was due to the police authorities for the alertness and resource which they displayed in meeting the emergency'.

The Zeppelins had not given up on Norwich. They tried again on the night of 31 January and 1 February 1916 when 'full protective measures were put into force'. The raid lasted 12 hours and again the railway stations were shut down. Zeppelins were heard over the city and bombs were dropped over a wide area in the county: some explosions were reported to have shaken houses in the city. But, again, the city emerged unscathed. The account of this raid said, 'Again the police authorities rose to the occasion'.

In 1916 the tank was introduced to World War One, and in 1918 to the city of Norwich.

'Norwich Tank Week' began on 1 April with a tank on display outside the Guildhall, tortuously delivered from Thorpe Station the previous day, part of a nationwide drive to raise money for the war effort at a time when the war was not going well for the allies. The Lord Mayor, Minister of Labour, Chief Constable and other distinguished persons assembled to address the populace and exhort the purchase of war bonds.

The Chief Constable, John Henry Dain, stood on the tank and stole the show by presenting the Lord Mayor, Richard Jewson, with a cheque for £40,250, representing 'the private investments of the special police, their wives and families'. The Lord Mayor said it was 'further evidence of their patriotic fervour'.

On the last day of Norwich Tank Week the police provided an upstaging encore. The Chief Constable presented another cheque from the Special Constabulary, for £9,750, sufficient to raise the week's total to one million pounds, quadrupling the original target. After that the Norwich police had only bad luck with tanks.

December 1919 saw the return of a tank to Norwich, presented to the city in recognition of its war effort – obviously of no further use to the Army. The proposed display, and reception committee, was on the lines of the previous visit, the Lord Mayor,

Minister of Labour, Chief Constable and others assembling at the Guildhall, this time with a band. Unfortunately the tank broke down in Prince of Wales Road and by the time it had been repaired and crept along London Street to the Guildhall everybody that mattered had gone home, including the band. The tank clanked its way to the Chapelfield Drill Hall under police escort without an official welcome.

Several years after World War Two the Army inflicted another tank upon the city, part of a recruiting drive. The metal monster was delivered by low-loader lorry, escorted by a Wolseley police car, to a display site next to the Woolpack public house in Golden Ball Street where it was started up, unloaded and steered into position, a process that saw it run over the front of the police car.

In the 1930s came growing apprehension, international threats and posturing and, finally, in 1939 – World War Two. City police officers drained away, leaving a core force bolstered by War Reserves,

Men of war. Harry Daniels VC visits Norwich in 1915 for a civic reception and Constable Thomas Smith stands to attention. Harry Daniels was born at Wymondham in 1884 and raised as an orphan in Norwich. As a Company Sergeant Major in the Rifle Brigade in 1915 he was awarded the Victoria Cross for attacking the enemy under severe machine-gun and rifle fire. He later received the Military Cross and rose to the rank of Lieutenant Colonel. Constable Thomas Smith was born in 1880. He served in the 7th Dragoon Guards and South African Police and joined the First Police Reserve in 1913, serving for the duration of the war. (A.Williamson)

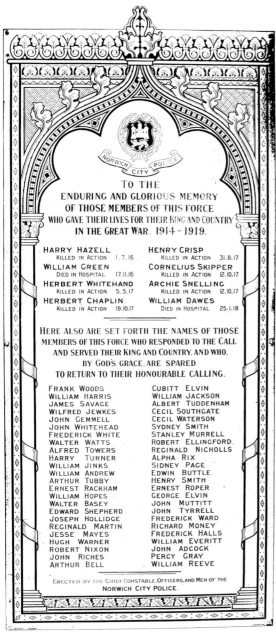

The Norwich police roll of honour for World War One, a plaque displayed in Bethel Street Police Station.

(Force archives)

The Norwich war memorial located at the Guildhall in 1927. The Chairman of the Watch Committee, Mr H.E.Witard, and Constable 55 Cubitt Elvin, who served in the armed forces in World War One, stand at ease. (A.Williamson)

Auxiliaries, Specials, Messengers, ARP wardens and other products of an organised defence to a fight that was anticipated on home ground. The bomber was expected.

The people of Norwich had not been blind to the increasing threat of war long before it became inevitable. One man and his comment epitomises the perception of the man in the street, if not the politicians of the time. The elderly citizen stood watching workmen removing redundant tramlines from the road, and, knowing they were being sold to Archie King the scrap metal merchant, and being advised that this firm was exporting the metal to Germany, he sagely observed, 'They'll be coming back'.

Police training for war on the home front began after the greatly publicised Munich agreement, showing little faith in Neville Chamberlain's waved white paper. This training centred on the recognition of gases and fitting respirators, police officers instructing newly appointed ARP Wardens.

In June 1939 a mock air raid was staged behind the

Remembering World War One and marching along tram lines. The exact date of this parade in Tombland is not known but it could not have been very long after the war finished. The supervising constable is 100 Edward Grint. (R.Fowler)

City Hall in front of a large crowd. Superintendent Herbert Balls explained the warden's services and described fire-fighting procedures and how to deal with incendiary bombs. Other speakers talked of decontamination, rescue and casualty services.

The city staged a blackout exercise. Householders were told through the press that 'complete blackout is one of the principal weapons of passive defence'. More detailed notice was given, saying, 'It will be essential in these blackouts that all exterior lights, such as petrol pump globes, cigarette machines, and advertisement signs, should be extinguished, and that shop lighting normally left on after closing time should also be extinguished. Motor headlights should not be used, and while traffic lights will be kept in operation, the signals will be masked. All street lights will be extinguished.'

To emphasise the sense of impending doom the city's sirens were tested.

The Chief Constable, Deputy Chief Constable and other officials stood at the top of the City Hall tower at midnight (an exercise their predecessors had undertaken in 1914 from the ramparts of Norwich Castle) and watched the city disappear into a blackness that was never totally complete. They reported a number of lights from the Thorpe direction and saw some car sidelights, which they said were 'easily distinguishable'. From Mousehold observers (again a repeat of an exercise in 1914) reported 'one or two bedroom windows on the housing estates were lighted' and 'one house where a light shone out from a front door which had been left open'. In the next few years such indiscretions would lead to fines at the Magistrates' Court but the first blackout was assessed as 'quite good', though one voiced opinion that it was so good that aircraft would not be able to find the city was to prove sadly wrong. Luftwaffe navigators were to be more successful than their Zeppelin predecessors.

The police put their own house in order. Pillarphones received shades over that scintillating light, police boxes were screened by badly laid concrete blocks and Bethel Street Police Station was sandbagged with such enthusiasm that, according to a report to the Watch Committee, it had to be altered to 'allow in light'.

Not from outer space. How to repel a gas attack with police tuition. (A.Rix)

After the outbreak of war the Watch Committee agreed that sandbags should be carried on buses, a decision that went unnoticed but might have explained double deckers jettisoning passengers to struggle up Kett's Hill. Later, the war effort required buses and fire engines to be painted a drab shade of battleship grey.

With speculation removed and war declared an armed guard was placed on the front door of the City Hall: a Constable was issued with a revolver and five rounds of ammunition. Other entrances were not covered, it being presumed that insurgents or invaders would use the front door.

The force was issued with rifles and this led to drilling practice where great attention was paid to the shoulder, slope and present arms. Operating the rifle received less attention. Drilling, without rifles, had

taken place over the years as part of general force training, reinforced in 1938 with the order to parade each Friday at the Crook's Place playground after school hours. (1919 had seen a similar order).

Probationer Constables were drilled as part of their induction training, at one time striding around the fire station yard saluting the petrol pump. Drilling and saluting were important even without a war.

The press performed a valuable service in updating and educating the public. In addition to advice on building and securing private shelters, and the whereabouts of public shelters, a list was published of 'horse shelters'. Drivers were advised to take their horse to the nearest horse shelter upon hearing a siren warning.

In June 1940 a public notice was issued from the City Hall listing the places where the names could be seen of 'any casualties resulting from air attacks in the

City of Norwich'. At that time there had not been any – but it would not be long. Press reports of bombing raids would be less than helpful because they were usually obliged to refer to 'an East Anglian town', a vagueness that German reconnaissance planes had no difficulty with.

The steady dilution of the regular police into the armed services, notably in the early years of 1940 and 1941, saw the increasing employment of war reserves, auxiliaries and specials. Police officer was initially a reserved occupation but many with previous military service were recalled and many volunteered. In 1942 officers under a certain age were conscripted and the Home Secretary insisted they served in combatant units.

Two probationer Constables called to the armed forces in 1939 requested the Chief Constable's permission to marry before they left. Permission was refused. One married anyway and was dismissed when he returned, only to be reinstated after HM Inspector of Constabulary had referred the case to the Home Office.

The Chief Constable decreed that in the absence of regular police officers serving in the armed forces all police promotions would be temporary only.

The Chief Constable was given three months to replace any military reserve man who had been notified of his recall to the colours, but in February 1941 the increasing frequency of air raids caused him to take advantage of Government permission to claim back these reservists. Some officers went into military service in 1939 or 1940, returned in 1941, were active in the city during the horrific and seemingly apocalyptic Baedeker raids of April 1942, then, as the city settled into a series of raids of lesser force and frequency, left again to fight elsewhere. Other city policemen followed into military service through 1942, 1943 and 1944.

Constable Philip Hemmings could not be recalled. He was already a prisoner of the Germans in 1940.

Constable Herbert (Bert) Horrex fought on several fronts. Recalled to the Welsh Guards in 1939 he was called back by the Norwich City Police in February 1941 and served during the holocaust sprung upon the city in April 1942. He was recalled to his regiment in August 1942 and served in the African campaign

During the war men in plain clothes shuffled into Bethel Street Police Station and mysteriously disappeared into the basement or in this case a little room on the third floor. Operation Starfish (the display of decoy airfields) and other secret operations, reactive and contingency, had their administrative place in the station. This photograph is a rarity. Fred Low, the manager of Coes' the photographers, is seen (background) listening to German transmissions. Known only as 'Bert' he would arrive at the station with furled umbrella and uncommunicative manner, vanishing inside for the night.

(Royal Photographic Society)

and then in Italy where he was badly wounded, spending 11 months in hospital. He returned to the city police at the end of the war, another example of duty to both city and country.

The war did more to enhance police and community relations than any previous event or social chapter. Cases were noted of elderly residents waiting for the beat Constable to pass before retiring for the night, and wardens, firewatchers and air raid shelters became social calls on the beat. Red Cross canteens were well visited by beat Constables.

There was of course a downside, frightening and sometimes tragic, but the whole picture was seen at

Others did their bit in other ways. Marion Vincent was employed during the war as an ARP Reporting Centre Clerk working under police supervision. She is pictured in West Pottergate with her police issued uniform. The arm flash is 'Reporting Centre' and the cap badge is 'ARP'.

(R.Brighton, Tester)

The Police Auxiliary Messenger Service, known as PAMS, had its own rank structure, revealed here by Sergeant Peter French.
(P.French)

the time with the pragmatism and humour peculiar to the British perception of common danger. The Constable who witnessed a daylight raid and a bomb bouncing towards him only laughed about it later because that bomb failed to explode. And the Constable who passed a building in Pitt Street and glanced over his shoulder to see it falling across the road recovered from his shock to retell the story with relish; as did the Constable in Dereham Road who, passing a bomb damaged and blazing wholesale grocers, found himself in the centre of a fast running pack of rats.

The humour and bonding between police and public of the time, comradeship in adversity, could also be found between police and local criminals; on occasions! One local ne'er'-do-well, the previously mentioned head-in railings 'Fagin', was doing his bit for King and country. He became a member of the Home Guard, as a result of which he was allocated a sentry post at the railway bridge leading to the power station at Thorpe, a job he took seriously, especially when Inspector Arthur 'Snotchie' Bell, well-known to Fagin, walked up to the bridge one night in uniform.

'Halt who goes there' boomed Fagin, ahead of his ritual demanding of the password, which Inspector Bell had forgotten. Exasperated entreaties of, 'You know me, Fagin' were vigorously denied by Fagin. A grumbling Inspector was forced to retreat. To some the war had advantages.

At the start of the war the Chief Constable reported that the First Police Reserve was up to 20. He was then authorised to recruit up to 50 War Reserve Constables but later this was increased. He also had 400 specials.

Special Constables were issued with pillarphone keys and were allocated four divisions (other records mention three), Park Lane Methodist Chapel, St Catherine's Hall, the Lads' Club and The Jolly Brewers (missing off some records). Six officers were required to sleep at each place (and were ensconced in the Lads' Club when it caught fire in 1943: unrelated to the Luftwaffe). A Special Constabulary mobile section was allocated a room at the Presbyterian Chapel in Theatre Street, later burnt out in a bombing raid, following which they moved to 'The Elms' at Unthank Road.

Policing the city during World War Two required some amendment to normal procedures. Working a beat looking for insecure property had an element of absurdity when somebody above was making it insecure, with a vengeance.

When the warning siren sounded the beat Constable was required to go to the nearest pillarphone. He remained there on stand-by or was directed to an incident or, after the all-clear, resumed his beat and the examination of lock-up property. Off duty officers were also expected to go to the nearest telephone and announce their presence. While this practice had commendable exigency value it was frustrating on the many occasions when the sirens wailed because the enemy was thought to be approaching, and sometimes actually was but only passing on to targets further north. Reports were often received of enemy aircraft over the city without bombs falling and it was later concluded that the railway line north from City Station was a route finder for a downward peering German navigator.

A number of Constables were trained to take charge of 'bombing incidents'. To effect the necessary authority they carried Sergeant's stripes in their gas masks and became Acting Sergeants during the time of the incident. Promotion courtesy of the Luftwaffe! These men could be realised from those working the beat at the time or the stand-by off-duty men, or called from a number of men ordered to sleep overnight in the basement of the City Hall. Bunks were arranged for these basement men but the venti-lation was inadequate and such was the old socks atmosphere the men were sometimes glad to be called out.

The first bombing raid occurred shortly after 5pm on 9 July 1940. There was no siren, no warning or anticipation. Roaring aircraft engines shattered the subdued bustle of early evening and startled faces swung skywards as two low flying aircraft with black crosses on their wings raced across the sky. There was never to be a raid with so many witnesses, and such a close-up view. They spoke of bombs tumbling from the aircraft then gliding downwards, and some were sure they heard the stutter of machine guns – later to be confirmed. History was being made – the first ever air attack upon Norwich.

The Dornier bombers swept low over Sprowston and Salhouse Road. They bombed Barnard's Works, and roared across Mousehold, dropping bombs on the engine sheds at Thorpe Station, Boulton and Paul's factory and Carrow Hill. Then, just as suddenly as they had appeared, they were gone, leaving raging fires, billowing smoke and strewn bodies. In the dazed aftermath people tried to absorb the sudden transformation from quiet to noise, from cold intact buildings to rubble and raging fires, and the sight of people who were living, walking, talking, and in an instant were no more.

The death toll from this sudden daylight raid was 27. They included a 60-year-old woman at Salhouse Road, four men at Barnards, seven men at the railway station, ten men at Boulton and Pauls and five women leaving the Carrow Works caught in a detonation in Carrow Hill near the old city wall. The youngest of the victims were Carrow girls aged 18 and 19 years.

Forty-six persons were injured in the raid and police, fire and ambulance resources were stretched between the bombing points, the Norfolk and Norwich Hospital and the mortuary at Barrack Street, which was full and could not receive a number of bodies arriving in a corporation lorry. A police escort was provided to guide this lorry with its tragic load to the contingency mortuary at Waterloo Park where, an escorting officer sadly recalls, they slowly wended their way past white clad tennis players darting back and forth and calling scores in an incongruous but typically English scene.

The first air raid on the city, by low flying Dorniers on 9 July 1940; depicted by Terry George.

The next raid, on 19 July, also arrived without warning, at 6am on a bright sunny morning, a lone bomber crossing the city almost in the opposite direction to the previous raiding Dorniers. Bombs fell in St George's Street (a fish and chip shop was the greatest loss), Botolph Street, Magdalen Street, Bull Close Road and at the Mousehold Aerodrome where the Aero Club was burnt out. No lives were lost but the stage was set, people knew more raids would follow.

The hat trick of no-warning raids occurred on 30 July when Surrey Street Bus Station and the surrounding area was hit and 14 persons, men women and children, lost their lives.

On 1 August a siren warning was sounded, just seconds before the bombs arrived. Thorpe Station and Boulton and Pauls were hit again. The death toll of nine was later amended to 13 and included one posted as 'missing-presumed killed'. A 15-year-old boy was originally posted as missing but later identified as dead. Two 17-year-old girls and a railway policeman, Constable Leonard Bell, sheltering under a wagon, were among the victims.

Hit and run raids, usually by lone raiders or small groups of aircraft machine gunning and bombing, continued, often with little or no warning, through the Battle of Britain and beyond. It was a daylight exercise to stand in the street and peer anxiously into an engine droning sky and ask the standard question of the day, 'Is it one of ours?' But the glorious summer of 1940, weather-wise, was fading and while the hit and run raider would not completely disappear the police

and defence organisations were going to face a change to a new pattern of bombing terror: the night blitz.

Bombs dropped on Norwich at 5.45pm on 2 December 1940, coinciding with the air raid warning, killed six people including Special Constable Arthur Pennymore who was walking near his home at 70 Bracondale. A bomb impacted near to number 58 and he was caught in the blast. Another bomb exploded in the road immediately in front of an approaching lorry, the driver of which, alerted by the increasing high pitched whistling, was flattened to the floor of his cabin. The lorry plunged into the smoking crater, which gradually flooded through a burst water main. The driver scrambled back to the road, unhurt, later to complain during interview that the explosion had made him late home for his supper.

The same area suffered again on 11 December when bombs fell across Carrow Hill and one demolished the cottage of the Warnes family and blew 83-year-old William Warnes, still in his bed, into the front garden. Mr E.West, a member of the Carrow observer team rushed to the scene, crawled into the wreckage of the cottage and pulled Mr Warnes's daughter and granddaughter from the rubble. Unfortunately the 18-year-old granddaughter was dead. Mr West was awarded the Kings Commendation for Brave Conduct.

The public in 1940 had not entirely related themselves to the air raid shelters. A letter to the press, signed 'One of the Wardens', complained that when people were asked to take shelter they ignored the request or replied with sarcastic remarks. Another letter spoke of 'a casual attitude, a studied indifference in the face of the sirens'. And those who did use the shelters were not entirely happy, complaining of poor lighting, dampness, and narrow entry and, in a letter signed 'Disgusted', rowdyism by youths.

1941 began with a mixture of night raids and harrying daytime forays from the Luftwaffe. The night raid of 17-18 February upon the Vauxhall Street and Rupert Street area was described in the police report as 'the greatest devastation seen in Norwich, with rows of houses around what was left of the Vauxhall Tavern twisted and torn into piles of rubble'. The report ends on a note of surprise: 'It seems only 8 killed, with 20 injured'. 140 people were rendered homeless in this raid.

A shattered Rupert Street, a stressed policeman and a contemplative small boy. (Norfolk Reference Library)

As the raids continued wardens, police and fire-watchers became more adept, more experienced in dealing with incidents, but could still be caught out. The late evening raid of 29 April 1941 again spread

A picture to be studied carefully to find a police cycle and hel-met resting forlornly against wreckage at the junction of Rupert Street and Union Street. (A.Brown)

explosions across the Carrow Hill and Bracondale area, but before the emergency services were on the scene cars drove into craters in Bracondale and the adjoining City Road. The Chief Warden's report of this raid attributed the unmarked and unguarded craters to a 'shortage of personnel'.

The night raid of 5-6 May 1941 resulted in three deaths after bombs fell in Bury Street. The Chief Warden's report of this raid referred to the congestion caused by rescuers crowding into the area prior to the arrival of 'a responsible police officer'.

The following night the police report identified 22 HE bombs falling across the Larkman area. A house and family were torn apart in Cadge Close and rescuers found that three children, aged 15, 13 and ten years, had died with their parents. Three other children in the house survived.

That first ever raid, in July 1940, was a swift flurry

of blows delivered without warning in minutes by suddenly visible, then vanished, low flying Dornier aircraft. The infamous raids of 27-28 April and 29-30 April 1942 were the opposite, delivered after ample warning, lasting hours rather than minutes, and were pummelling night raids by unseen cruising Heinkel, Dornier and Junkers aircraft. Known as the Baedeker raids because of the eponymous guidebook, and identified as reprisal attacks after the RAF bombing of the old German city of Lubeck, they had begun with raids upon Bath and Exeter. Then it was Norwich. York and Canterbury would follow. The intent was unashamedly admitted by the German High Command, to destroy the heritage and all that was treasured in the fine city of Norwich. At the time, to those on the ground in Norwich, guide books and the politics of the raids were academic – it was sheer hell.

Josef Goebbels, Hitler's Minister of Propaganda, wrote in his diary of his satisfaction over what he described as 'the heavy destruction of Norwich'. Norwich survived, many of its citizens and fine buildings did not.

The sirens wailed their warning at 11.20pm on Monday, 27 April, a cold moonlit night with a stiff north east wind blowing. The sleeping city noted another raid, or was it aircraft passing over? People reacted in different ways. Many turned over and went back to sleep. Others waited for the initial sounds of a raid. Some actually went into their garden shelters. They had been warned but they were not to know that the most terrible air raid the city would ever experience was about to begin. The subsequent police report to the Regional Commissioner said that 'heavy casualties were partly explained by the fact the public were taken by surprise'.

At about 11.40pm a single aircraft crossed the city and dropped incendiaries in the area of the City Station. If this was a marker it was successful for fires immediately raged in the station's wooden buildings. One report says five minutes elapsed before the 'main bombing force' arrived, others merely indicate a steady stream of aircraft cruising and bombing the city. The raid lasted until just before one o'clock in the morning by which time devastation and death were widespread, the Dereham Road area suffering greatly. The Corporation Depot at Westwick Street was razed to the

Two photographs with a tragic connection. The scene at City Station showing the remains of a train, and in Helena Road the house destroyed by a direct hit. The train driver missed the first disaster but not the second. (R.Brighton, Tester)

ground with several deaths and the loss of considerable stores, including nine vehicles.

Sam Bussey, a Senior Company Officer in the newly-formed National Fire Service and a Norwich City Police Sergeant until the division of the services, died in blazing ruins in Oak Street attempting to save trapped horses. Sam Bussey was a married man aged 39 years with two young children living in a flat above the fire station.

This first Baedeker raid killed several members of the emergency and defence organisations: nine fire-watchers, three ARP men and two Home Guard. Also to die was Private Frederick Warren of the RAOC who had been directing people into the public shelter at Chapelfield Gardens when a bomb struck. Three others died in this explosion, including two teenage girls.

At the City Station a train at the platform burned to a twisted unrecognisable frame. It was the 10.07 from Melton Constable and the driver, Albert Wallace, had gone home to Helena Road before the raid started. But fate was against him. His house received a direct hit and he died with his wife and grown up son and daughter.

Several families died together as an estimated 41

A victim of war. The funeral of Sam Bussey, This photograph, taken in Hay Hill, epitomises the closeness of two services that had only recently been one; police lined on one side of the fire engine, firemen the other. The funeral service was held in St Stephen's Church, regarded as the fire brigade's church as St Peter Mancroft was the police force's church. (E.Bussey)

tons of high explosive bombs rained down on the city: a mother and two children in Belvoir Street – the father away serving in the RAF; a mother and three children in Rosebery Road; a mother and two children in Northcote Road; a mother, father and two children in St Mary's Road, and a mother and her three children in Valpy Avenue.

Number 16 Rye Avenue was the scene of frantic police activity, just one of many such scenes across Norwich that night. The house was bombed and wrecked and Constables Don Martin, Jimmy Godbolt, Charles McCalley and John McKenna quickly arrived to begin searching the debris for bodies or survivors. Bombs were still dropping as they probed the wreckage, encouraged by the sound of faintly calling voices. Constable McKenna, a very big man, showed 'exceptional strength in removing debris' as he raised one end of a rubble-laden bed. Constables Godbolt and McCalley raised the other end of the bed and Constable Martin crawled underneath to rescue a mother and four children. Unfortunately the youngest, a four-month-old baby was dead. The Chief Constable in reporting this rescue to the Watch Committee for commendation said, 'The rescue actually took place on the top floor side bedroom, three walls of which and part of the floor were demolished. Ladders had to be used and the falling of further bombs disturbed the roof causing further debris to fall during the time these officers were engaged'.

Don Martin was another officer who went off to military service after the Baedeker raids. On 6 June 1944 he landed on the beach at Normandy as a Sergeant in the Commandos. He was mentioned in despatches, seriously wounded and returned to England where, after the war, he rejoined the Norwich City Police, going on to become a Sergeant in the Traffic Department and the pioneer of the diving squad.

Constable John Stockdale, of Blue Club fame, was on stand-by at a police box in Dereham Road during the first Baedeker raid and was ordered to assist at the Woodlands Hospital, which had received severe damage from HE bombs. He then experienced what the commending report described as 'great mental strain' by the sight of his own house being demolished by a bomb. Despite his anguish, he carried out house

checking duties in the road and extinguished several incendiary bombs. He extricated a woman from 313 Dereham Road and 'carried her to safety whilst enemy planes were machine-gunning the streets'. He found his wife uninjured.

Constable Harold Waddicor's house in Elizabeth Fry Road was severely damaged by HE bombs and his wife and children had to be removed from the Anderson shelter. Accompanied by a nurse the Constable went to another house, which had been severely damaged, and together they rescued a man and woman who were injured and trapped. As they brought them out the house collapsed.

Other police officers suffered the loss of their homes in raids, including the Deputy Chief Constable who was bombed out of his house in Aylsham Road.

Constable Ernie Croxson was bombed out of his house in Waterworks Road and later had to appear before the Chief Constable to explain why he had not handed in his clothing coupons. There were a lot of other things he could not find.

The aftermath of the first of the Baedeker raids was a city glowing with fire, littered with debris and torn by tragedy. The death toll was 162 with 600 injured. It was the highest death toll of any one raid upon the city. It could have been worse, and nearly was. A bizarre incident arose from the discovery of a crater and hole in the side of the Carlton cinema – the apparent evidence of bomb detonation and the near destruction of the cinema. A fragment of the bomb was found in the crater. Repairs were made and performances continued. The public returned to their celluloid escapism, for a few days, until the bomb fragment was displayed to an Army officer visiting Bethel Street Police Station. An apoplectic Army officer quickly advised that the displayed metal was not a fragment but a retarding ring designed to slow penetration. 'That bomb is unexploded', he told horrified listeners who knew it must be nestling underneath hundreds of intent cinemagoers. The cinema was closed, quickly, the bomb located, made safe, and hauled to the surface.

Unexploded bombs were a continual problem for police and military. A 1,000lb bomb could wreak considerable damage to a building without exploding. Many were the occasions when earnest detective work was needed to examine an entry hole in a building, puzzle a trajectory, look at surrounding damage, and then conclude if the villain of the piece was spent or just sleeping. On one occasion the examiners roped off the damaged area and went away to debate their findings only for the prime question to be answered by a massive explosion.

The following night, 28 April, with the city braced in suspense, the Luftwaffe went to York in pursuit of their Baedeker aims. It was to be a one night respite only.

At 11.11pm on Wednesday, 29 April 1942 the siren sounded its deadly warning and at 11.23pm Norwich knew the enemy was coming again as flares dropped from aircraft droning overhead. This time shelters filled quickly. There was little hesitation. The raid that followed blasted the city centre, destroyed Caley's factory and again ravaged the Dereham Road area. The death toll this time was 69. They included two Air Raid Wardens, a Home Guard, and a mother and her three children in an air raid shelter in Helena Road. People were also killed in shelters in Ethel Road and Raynham Street. The stage manager of the Hippodrome and his wife were killed in a caravan alongside the building, as were two performing artists who had a sea lion act. (The sea lion survived but later died of a heart attack.)

As before, the police and emergency services struggled to trace and rescue people amidst falling bombs and raging fires. Constables Bert Horrex and Walter Goldsmith heard a woman's voice under rubble at 75 Earlham Road and, with the assistance of soldiers and civilians, found and rescued the woman after digging for one hour.

The morning of 30 April revealed smoking ruins in the city centre and swathes of destruction radiating out into the suburbs. Firemen and rescue parties struggled to clear debris and groups of anxious people stared disbelieving at what was no longer recognisable. Could the city survive consistent attacks of this ferocity? Those who believed it couldn't began trekking into the countryside. One estimate says that the greater part of the population of North Heigham moved out.

The Luftwaffe did return the very next night but it was to drop incendiaries only and it may have been just a passing thought on their part for their main

A night at the cinema. The Carlton is hit, but had the bomb exploded? The answer is in the second picture.

(R.Brighton, Tester)

attack was upon Tyneside. The people of Norwich were not to know that the worst was over. Neither were they to know of a contingency plan for the military to take over the city upon receipt of a code word from the Chief Constable, and how close events brought the use of that code word. (There was also a contingency plan for the evacuation of Norwich in circumstances of invasion in World War One.)

Following the Baedeker raids the Chief Constable reported to the Watch Committee on the performance of city police officers referring to 'many instances of devotion to duty, as well as incidents of exceptional courage and bravery'. Commendations were awarded to 23 regular police officers, one First Police Reserve and one War Reserve, two Women Auxiliaries, one

A lone Constable against a background of ruins in Orford Place after the second Baedeker raid. Note St Stephen's Church just visible on the right.
(Norfolk Reference Library)

Unexploded, defused and safely retrieved; they are entitled to look happy. On the left is Inspector Edwin Buttle, the Bomb Reconnaissance Officer, who served in the armed forces in World War One. His assistant, Constable Neville Ball, is on the right. Captain Wheeler is the Army officer in the centre. This photograph was taken at the Cattlemarket where the bombs were weighed on the public weighbridge. One of the bombs in this picture had gone through a house in West End Street and lodged under the stairs.
(A.Brown)

St Benedict's Gates – though you would never know. One can only guess at what the Sergeant is saying to the woman. Note the crown above the Sergeant's stripes, a briefly used method of identifying Station Sergeants (much used by the Metropolitan Police). Circumstances have clearly brought the Sergeant out of the station. (A.Brown)

Police Messenger and 11 Special Constabulary officers.

Inspector Edwin Buttle, employed as Bomb Reconnaissance Officer – looking for what other people wanted to get away from, was commended, awarded a Merit Badge (possibly the last to be issued) and later received the British Empire Medal.

David Grix, aged 15 years, an ARP Messenger, was awarded the British Empire Medal for 'bravery and devotion to duty' during the 'heavy air raids of April 1942'.

The Chief Constable singled out many actions but could not possibly have covered every instance of courage and selflessness. He described many incidents, some of which have already been detailed. Others he reported were: Sergeant William Kemp climbing into the false roof of a grocery shop at the corner of Bowthorpe Road and Earlham Green Lane to extinguish an incendiary bomb; Sergeant Marmaduke Potter and Constables Arthur Turner and Walter Goldsmith digging and rescuing two trapped and injured women from a shelter in Nelson Street; Inspector Herbert Docwra, Sergeant Thomas Byland and Constable George Moll burrowing under debris and extricating a woman and three children from a house in Elm Grove Lane; Constable John Prytherch climbing buildings in Waterloo Road to extinguish incendiary bombs – then rescuing people from a shelter that had been hit in Patteson Road, and Constable John Williams entering a line of houses in Dereham Road to extinguish incendiary bombs.

The two heavy night raids of late April 1942 severely strained the resources of the city. The police formally reported that lighting, gas, electricity, water, telephones, transport and other services had suffered by varying amounts, and the city's laundry service had been reduced by two-thirds.

Further raids occurred in May and early June, the Woodlands Hospital was hit again on the night of 1-2 May, but the last heavy raid that might be listed under the heading of Baedeker (and has been by some historians), occurred on the night of 26-27 June. This was the night when Bonds' department store was lost and only feverish activity by firewatchers saved the Cathedral as incendiaries clattered across the roof near the base of the spire. The city owes a debt to those civilians who defied the height and blackness to scramble across the cathedral roof and douse the flames.

On this night War Reserve Constable Arthur Wilby was killed when he fell through the roof of St Mark's Church in City Road where he was fighting a fire, though another report says he died from a bomb blast. It is possible the two descriptions are a linked circumstance. A bomb killed an Air Raid Warden at Heigham Grove and another killed a mother, father and two children in the shelter in their garden at Vincent Road. The total killed in this raid was 18.

Adversity did not bring out the best in everybody; in some it accentuated the worst. Looting offences that occurred were usually on a minor scale but were none the less abhorrent for that. Larceny from war damaged property had been elevated to a new status by wartime regulations, becoming an offence punishable by death. Only a few came to notice. Walter Nichols was one who did and his mistake was to pass within viewing range of the police station.

Constable Tom Jones looked out of a window at Bethel Street Police Station at the very moment a solitary figure and furniture laden barrow staggered along Theatre Street past the junction with Lady Lane. It was 1942 and the city was badly damaged with many open ended houses. People had been bombed out, leaving skeletonised structures that had once been a home. The barrow pusher had to be a refugee or a looter.

Constable Jones tracked Walter Nichols and the barrow to Timberhill and found the furniture came from bombed houses in Rupert Street. Nichols was arrested. He promptly entered into a spirit of non-co-operation by refusing to push the barrow to the police station. It was no matter. Assistance arrived and Nichols got seven years penal servitude while Constable Jones received a certificate of commendation from the Watch Committee.

The raids continued, at intervals, some by day, some by night. A raid at 10.37am on 5 September 1942 killed six people with direct hits on Frazer's Joinery Works in St Martin's Palace Plain and Batson and Webster's shoe factory in Fishergate. Special Constable Vic Austin was badly injured in the Fishergate blast.

The Bus Station was hit again on 3 November and on the night of 18-19 March 1943 Harmer's clothing factory in St Andrew's Street was hit and destroyed. On this occasion a Police Messenger, Peter Smith, climbed onto the roof of the building to assist fireguards fighting incendiaries. For his action he received the King's Commendation for Brave Conduct, duly reported in the *London Gazette*. One person was killed in this raid, a 50-year-old woman in Pottergate, apparently the last death arising from direct bombing raids against Norwich. The last recorded raid by enemy bombers was on the night of 6-7 November 1943 when bombs were dropped in the Unthank Road area and a man in Gloucester Street was injured.

Sirens continued to wail into 1944 and the police, emergency services and public continued to look skywards, but only occasionally did they give up a warm bed for a dank air raid shelter. It was over. And in 1945 it was official.

St Andrew's Street; a fire rages and a policeman waits for the end of Harmer's factory. (A.Brown)

The official record of Norwich at war shows 340 killed and 1,092 injured with 30,354 houses damaged, of which 2,082 were totally destroyed and 2,651 were seriously damaged. Not many buildings escaped at the very least loose tiles or broken windows. The majority of the victims came from the Baedeker raids and the great majority of these were buried in a mass grave at Earlham Cemetery.

At the end of the war the Special Constabulary were given a special certificate in recognition of their valuable service. (They had received a similar certificate at the end of World War One.) Of the 300 specials serving at the end of hostilities 117 volunteered to keep serving.

The peace was a time for reorganisation and reflection. Norwich police officers did not return to the force in one parcel. They reappeared in groups at the convenience of the releasing military, some making it back in time for the welcome home dinner at the Lido, others returning to hear all about it. (Officers returning to the force from World War One had been entertained at a dinner at the Lads' Club.)

The Chief Constable's refusal to allow 10am-6pm duty men to finish early to get to the dinner for 7pm caused considerable ill-feeling among the ex-servicemen and they made their feelings known at the dinner. John Henry Dain, the former Chief Constable spoke on behalf of the guests and was received with rapturous applause. The Chief Constable, Alan Plume, was received in stony silence.

Inspector Alec Doe spoke at the dinner of 'the proud war record' of the Norwich City Police, point-

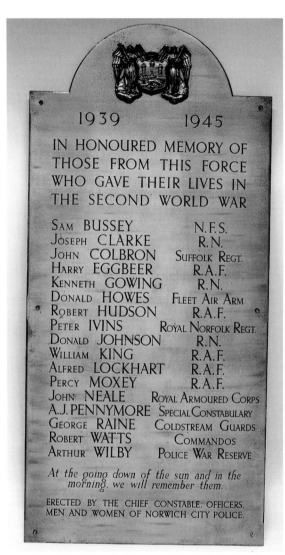

The Lord Mayor, Mr S.A.Bailey, said, 'The time when the public were hostile to the police has gone. As chief citizen of this city I must say how proud we are of the City Police Force and their record.'

Some did not come back immediately. Sergeants Tom Bellamy and Derek Canham joined AMGOT (Allied Military Government) and become Town Mayors in Occupied Germany. When these duties were finished Tom Bellamy retired from the force (joined 1923) and Derek Canham (joined 1937) continued, eventually retiring with the rank of Superintendent.

City policemen were not finished with war, or foreign service. But in the future they went away to serve as policemen, to fight terrorism or, in the case of Superintendent John Noble seconded to the Greek

The Norwich police roll of honour for World War Two is displayed in Bethel Street Police Station alongside the memorial to the first great war, both striking plaques that were more readily seen by the visiting public when the station was using its original entrance. They are now viewed only by denizens of the station and special visitors. (Force archives)

An officer who did not come back. Constable William King (right) stands outside the Cathedral with Constable John Burton, the war footing indicated by the carrying of gas masks. Constable King joined the force in 1938 and joined the RAF as air crew in 1941. He was killed in action in 1944. (G.Burton)

ing out that 51 out of a strength of 156 had joined the armed forces. He said, 'These men had marched with the most famous armies of the world, sailed on and under the sea, and flown night after night over German targets. Some have been decorated for gallantry and some have endured the horrors of prison camps. Now they have come back – right in the middle of a crime wave.'

police in 1945, to deal with the aftermath of war. In 1948 John Noble became Chief Constable of Burnley.

In 1957 Constable Allatson was seconded to Cyprus. Constables Thackeray, Hooper and Ross ('Nicky') were likewise seconded in 1958. In 1960 Sergeant Downes was seconded to Nyasaland.

Wherever, as the American General said, 'War is hell'.

Remembrance Day 1958. The Constable stands to attention as the Royal Norfolk Regiment marches past. The Regimental Sergeant Major following the leading officer is the renowned 'Winkie' Fitt, well-known to, and well-impressed upon the many police officers that entered the force via National Service in the county regiment. (A.Brown)

Victory! 'Dad's Army' (the Home Guard) march from Queen Street to London Street while the Americans celebrate with more of a swagger, and with bigger instruments, striding in the Cathedral Close from the Bishops House (where a number were stationed) to the Ethelbert Gate. City police officers line the routes. (ECN and Norfolk Reference Library)

The return of the Americans. They parade in June 1963 to open the memorial room at the city library (to be destroyed by fire in 1994). St Peter Mancroft is the background with Sergeant Dudley Brook to the right. (ECN)

CHAPTER NINE
Catastrophes and Commendations

Floods, scandal and public inquiry, siege and death, rescue, pursuit, murder, confrontation and explosion

THOSE extolling the benefits of being a policeman, or woman, would invariably draw attention to the variety attached to the work. 'You never know what is going happen' or 'every day is different' were favourite expressions; surprising news to those who regularly plodded around a beat shaking door handles and waving at traffic. Yet there was an element of truth in both statements.

Sergeant 'Stumpy' Chenery, in his role as de facto recruiting officer, would tower over an enthusiastic applicant and lead with, 'Can you fight?' A question demanded with such fierceness that the blanching applicant would wonder at the havoc that faced him on the streets. What did face him in a reasonably sized measure was tedium in a round of disciplined movement that took some of the gloss off being a visible icon of law and order. But then, something extraordinary would happen.

In this chapter of crime and incident, disaster and disturbance effecting the city police, the aim is to mark some of the extraordinary occasions and events, some individual, some all embracing, many estimable, a few disgraceful, some sad and tragic: all important.

After the great fire disaster of 1898 came the flood disaster of 1912. An unusually wet August culminated in incessant rain and a gale force wind and from the 26th to the 28th a serious and deteriorating situation developed. Swollen rivers flooded Hellesdon meadows and water cascaded into North Heigham – through Heigham Street, Dereham Road, Westwick Street and Oak Street across to Magdalen and Fye Bridge Streets

and through Bishopgate and Prince of Wales Road. The Carrow and Lakenham suburbs were similarly affected. Unthank Road, Portersfield Road and Park Lane were submerged. Four month's rain fell in just over one day. Street gullies, blocked by straw and other debris, failed to carry away the tumbling water.

Road and rail links to Norwich were cut off for two days, the tram service was suspended, gas and electricity supplies were interrupted and bridges were washed away. Buildings crumbled to the raging torrent.

Families, trapped by the rising water, which did not peak until the night of the 27th, appeared at upper windows and the streets became awash with varying forms of rescuing, communicating transport. Horse and carts struggled to transfer the trapped and isolated to drier ground, and rescue parties, official and unofficial, toured the flooded streets in an array of commandeered rowing boats. The night rescue in a rowing boat of a family from Canterbury Place ended in tragedy when a five-month-old baby, Edward Poll, was lost in the swirling water. His body was found two days later snagged on a nail in a yard off Heigham Street.

George Brodie, a 46-year-old porter who lived in a yard off Oak Street, worked through the night wading through the water to carry people to waiting Corporation carts and safety. He refused to rest saying there were still people to be saved. His body was found the following morning. He had succumbed to the water through exhaustion.

A third casualty of the floods was Mrs Kemp of

Constable Albert Farrow effecting the rescue of a trapped family; note the white summer helmet. There is a suggestion that this photograph was posed for press purposes but it is none the less important and representative for that. The original of this photograph is framed and displayed at the Bethel Street Fire Station. (ECN)

Goat Yard, Oak Street who reportedly died from fright and shock.

William Marrison, a boat owner, was reported to have rescued 100 persons. He was publicly praised and pictured in the local newspaper.

Many others worked long hours in the teeth of the floods and they included the city police, on almost continuous duty organising and guiding waterborne rescue traffic, retrieving or comforting people marooned in their houses, and organising relief for the

Constable 103 Richard Davison, a member of the Mounted Branch (see chapter three) in a river police role in Lothian Street. A postman peers over his shoulder. (A.Williamson)

Rolled-up trousers and no helmet; a policeman takes charge. (A.Williamson)

A bridge no more. Clearing up in the presence of a caped policeman after the collapse of Lakenham Bridge. (A.Williamson)

distressed. It was another time of common bonding. The son of one city policeman recalls delivering refreshments to his father at a prearranged point, his father going back to continuous flood duty, not to be seen at home for any sustainable time over a period of several days.

The fire brigade side of the force was fully employed pumping out premises, further in demand on the second evening of the disaster when a fire took hold at Thorpe Station. The blaze was confined to the gas regenerating department and extinguished after a resource and time consuming effort by police firemen under the direction of the Chief Constable.

Two thousand people were made homeless and damage was widespread. A flood relief fund was organised and raised over £24,000.

George Brodie was publicly declared a hero and a large crowd attended his funeral.

The Watch Committee commended the city police and awarded the officers two days extra pay. The press spoke of the force in glowing terms saying, 'No more humane civic force exists in England than the Norwich police'. The relationship between police and public reached an all-time high.

The praise heaped upon the force after the floods deflected HM Inspector of Constabulary from making too much of his dissatisfaction over a lack of police resources, noted at his July inspection (it is an ill wind…) and so the force wallowed in public acclaim instead of recoiling from critical review: but not for long. The most scarring scandal in the history of the force was very near.

At first there appeared to be nothing amiss. Henry Foster was a tramp, discovered on a fine night in September 1912 in a garden at 28 Newmarket Road. The discoverer, Constable Louis Debenham, possessed of only nine months service, arrested him and took him to the Guildhall Police Station, meeting Constable Sidney Smith on the way.

Constable Donald Piercy was on duty at the station and he received the prisoner with a marked lack of enthusiasm. He advised Inspector George Seaman, 'Debenham has brought an old chap in for being on enclosed premises in Newmarket Road. He is boozed and I have a good mind to kick him (prisoner) out'. This was to prove most excellent advice.

The prisoner was searched and Constable Walter Watts reportedly found a small knife preparatory to

Damage at St George's Bridge. The Boston Blacking Company falls into the river. In the corner of the photograph Superintendent Robert Hodges and Constable 6 Frederick Starling confer. (A.Williamson)

placing him in a cell, something that Constable Watts never recalled. Superintendent Hodges was later to say that he found the knife on the prisoner.

The queue of flood victims at St Andrew's Hall, described by the press as 'painful and poignant'. Each house was entitled to two candles and one box of matches and each person could receive half a pint of milk, half a loaf, six biscuits, half a pound of pressed beef and three bars of chocolate. (Force archives)

Debenham reported that the arrest had been effected after a struggle and that the prisoner had on the way to the station said, 'If you had not caught me I'd have made a dollar or two'.

Inspector Seaman ordered Sergeant Ephraim Emmerson to accompany Debenham back to 28 Newmarket Road. The Inspector followed. The three officers examined the premises with bulls-eye lanterns and saw that some flowerpots had been moved near a window but the window itself bore no unusual marks. They returned to the station.

Debenham returned again to 28 Newmarket Road, this time in the company of Detective Sergeant John Thomas, by whose order or inspiration was never resolved. Thomas thought Superintendent Hodges had instructed the visit, a belief denied by the Superintendent.

Thomas's findings were in accordance with the other officers, and Debenham duly reported to Superintendent Hodges. The Superintendent immediately ordered that two cycles be obtained and that Debenham accompany him to the scene.

The Superintendent, in possession of the knife, found corresponding marks on the window sill. He also found paint flakes on the knife consistent with the sill. The charge of being found on enclosed premises, already preferred, was changed to attempted housebreaking.

Foster had no chance. His not guilty plea floundered on the forensic evidence. He was sentenced to three months hard labour.

Foster served his sentence and disappeared, seemingly without protest. Constable Debenham was commended by the Chief Constable and Watch Committee and went on to greater things through a transfer to the CID. But there was unease within the force, particularly with Sergeant Emmerson, Detective Sergeant Thomas and Inspector Seaman. More so with Sergeant Emmerson who had earlier that night met Foster in Newmarket Road and knew him to be very drunk.

Nearly 18 months later Debenham confided to Detective Constable Crome that Superintendent Hodges had made the marks on the window frame with the knife.

Crome reported to Detective Inspector Wentford who instigated a meeting between Crome and Debenham in the CID office, with Inspectors Tolworthy and Southgate listening in an adjacent room. Crome encouraged Debenham to repeat his story. He did so and the Inspectors appeared. Inspector Southgate took a written statement from the disconcerted Debenham and Tolworthy informed the Chief Constable, though it is not clear as to the time lapses between all this telling and re-telling, a point of some importance to those involved.

The Watch Committee, the disciplinary authority for the force, began an inquiry as a result of which they concluded that the original three officers had missed the marks and Superintendent Hodges was innocent of any malpractice. They also concluded that other officers had failed to make prompt reports of their concerns and they took a serious view of the actions of the accusing officers. Constable Debenham was dismissed from the force. Inspectors Tolworthy and Southgate were reduced to Sergeants and

Detective Inspector Wentford retired on pension: jumped before pushed.

If the Watch Committee thought the matter was done with they were very much mistaken as police and public unrest promoted unhappiness in the City Council. The Council thought that the Secretary of State should be asked to look into the case, and into the conduct of the Watch Committee. The Home Office accordingly ordered an inquiry to be conducted by Leonard Dunning, HM Inspector of Constabulary.

In July 1914 the public inquiry began at the Guildhall. What followed filled newspapers for several days.

Two new civilian witnesses appeared. They gave evidence that they were present when Debenham arrested Foster; in fact he had called for their assistance. They said, to the accompaniment of laughter at the inquiry, that the officer had been reluctant to enter the garden by himself. The witnesses said that the Constable had leapt upon the sleeping man and thrown him through a gap in the hedge, briskly following to handcuff him though he was not resisting and was obviously drunk. The Constable had then insisted the civilians accompany him and his prisoner to the station but dismissed them when he spotted another Constable approaching.

Sergeant Emmerson quite firmly told the inquiry that he knew Foster was drunk and, in his view, incapable of burglary, but had not spoken out because such an action would have been 'the first step to getting the sack'. He said that making allegations against a Superintendent was the death knell of a police career and pointed to the dismissal of Debenham and punishment of the Inspectors as an example.

Debenham gave evidence to the inquiry that Superintendent Hodges found the marks on the window and used the knife against them but was now undecided whether the Superintendent had made the marks in the first place. He said that his original report of the case was dictated by Superintendent Hodges.

Superintendent Hodges, Deputy Chief Constable of the force, was severely cross examined. He agreed that he had transferred from the City of London Police, where he had been a Sergeant, to obtain the Superintendent's job at Norwich but was unaware that the person who had recommended him was related to a member of the Watch Committee. He agreed that he

Headline of a scandal.   (Norfolk Reference Library)

had gone on to the maximum incremental salary before the normal term of service in the rank but did not think that was illegal. He also agreed that he knew Debenham before he became a Constable and had used him as an entrapment in a liquor licensing case, which had failed. There was some unresolved discussion over when, exactly, Debenham had himself been arrested for a betting office offence and how much the Superintendent knew of that case.

Hodges was sure that the other officers had missed the marks on the window frame. He said Inspector Seaman had 'deficient eyesight', Sergeant Emmerson he would expect to only give a 'casual glance', Debenham was 'agitated' and Thomas had been 'slack'.

The inquiry rumbled on with a succession of witnesses, including the Chief Constable, through more disreputable and conflicting evidence. Only the perceptive Donald Piercy had got it right.

HM Inspector reported his findings in October 1914. He supported the action taken against Constable Debenham and Inspectors Tolworthy, Southgate and Wentford, but criticised Superintendent Hodges and the Watch Committee for the way they had dealt with the case.

The Watch Committee accepted his findings with the exception of the criticism levelled at them, which they rejected. They decided not to take any action

against Superintendent Hodges. A proposal by one of their number, Mr Hotblack, that reparation be made to the 'poor, helpless' Henry Foster (wherever he then was) was also rejected.

In October 1914 the disciplinary authority for the force was transferred to the Chief Constable and the Home Office produced rules of guidance for disciplinary cases. The Hodges' case had at least achieved new standards.

The case was not finished. In 1915 the Watch Committee, believed to be acting under Home Office pressure, gave Superintendent Hodges a written reprimand.

Superintendent Hodges retired in 1925, much disliked and still clouded by suspicion. It is historically of note that after his departure Superintendent Christie (1925-33) and Superintendent Scott (1933-37) filled the role of deputy to the Chief Constable without either being formally accorded the rank of Deputy Chief Constable. The Watch Committee minuted that they would not declare the rank. Both Christie and Scott were respected officers and efficiently carried out Deputy Chief Constable duties, and were so known. The 'Hodges' affair', as it became labelled, soured Watch Committee relations with the force and persuaded them not to formalise a ranking deputy to the Chief Constable.

Time heals. Superintendent Herbert Balls was in 1937 formally declared the Deputy Chief Constable.

Constable Edward Burroughes has his place in the force history through the tragedy of what today is called stress, a word not so easily found in June 1933. He had joined the force in 1907 and was a popular officer not noted for sickness or erratic behaviour, until the June day two days before his retirement date when he paraded for duty at 2pm. After a short conversation with Inspector Parker and other officers he suddenly walked from the station. Constable Walter Goldsmith, sent to catch him up, saw him riding on the top of a tram in St Giles' Street.

Constable Goldsmith was sent to Burroughes' house in Winter Road to ascertain the cause of his abrupt and unauthorised departure from the station. There he was greeted from a window by Mrs Burroughes and advised that her husband had a gun and was stating an intention to shoot any policeman who came into the house. Burroughes affirmed this intention from the top of the stairs.

During the afternoon and early evening a succession of policemen went to Winter Road and engaged Burroughes in conversation. They included close colleagues, Inspectors Bell and Parker, and Superintendent Christie. He gave them all the same message, 'I shall shoot the first policeman that shows his face at the bottom of the stairs'. Through shouted dialogue he said he would be there until 10pm, 'no longer'. He refused to see Dr Lincoln Hurn, saying, 'I have only a little longer to live'.

The Chief Constable, John Henry Dain, went to the house and Burroughes told him, 'I don't mind speaking to you, sir, provided you remain at the bottom of the stairs'. The Chief Constable obliged and prompted a conversation, which failed to move Burroughes from the top of the stairs, or from the shotgun he was nursing. The Chief Constable withdrew and a ring of officers waited.

At 7pm, for no apparent reason, Burroughes fired the gun to the bottom of the stairs. Dialogue continued without any change until 9.15pm when the gun fired again. This time there was the thud of a falling body and Constable Edward Burroughes, with over 26 years distinguished service, two days from a Watch Committee approved pension, sprawled dead at the bottom of the stairs. He had discharged the gun into his mouth. The question of 'why?' was never fully answered though his comments from the top of the stairs revealed his belief that he was being persecuted within the force, something the Coroner found no evidence to support.

Commendable police work was not always commended – 'just doing my job' the praiseworthy one would modestly say, at the same time hoping that he would be visited by recognition from a higher place. And commendation could arrive from many different directions: the Chief Constable, Magistrates and Judges were the most usual lauding points – details noted on the officer's record with an accompanying paean of praise on force orders.

Certificates were sometimes issued, formally scrolled and calligraphically worded on quality paper, emanating from societies and organisations recognising bravery and from the Watch Committee describing outstanding police work, which often incorporated bravery. These certificates were in early years handed to the commended officer with curt formality but later, certainly from the 1940s, they arrived with pomp and ceremony after the officer had been ordered before the Watch Committee. They were a tangible record to be set in family archives as well as police records – evidence for all time of what was achieved, and by whom.

Merit badges were occasionally awarded for some outstanding deed or deeds and were worn on the tunic as a visible commendation. More importantly they came with a small enhancement to the officer's wage. Time, and a thrifty Watch Committee, saw them become exceedingly rare and Inspector Buttle's badge awarded after the 1942 Baedeker raids appears to be the last.

River rescues and runaway horses were often commended at Watch Committee level. Constable John Stockdale received Watch Committee recognition and glowing press coverage for stopping a runaway horse and carriage in the Market Place in 1937, wrestling with and being dragged by the animal as it scattered shoppers in its frantic progress.

The horse and carriage continued well into the 20th century (many costermongers, coal merchants and the like were trading from horse-drawn carts through and after World War Two), but they were fading in number and purpose as the motor vehicle gradually, and then more rapidly, took over. The two did not mix well, as Constable Ted Mileham discovered in June 1953 when a horse pulling a four-wheeled trolley bolted in Thorpe Road and was pursued through heavy traffic by a hooting motor car intent upon drawing attention to the danger, which increased as the horse was scared to a greater effort. Constable Mileham ran alongside the frightened animal, grasped the reins and, after a struggle worthy of a range cowboy, pulled the animal to a halt at the Harvey Lane junction. The Watch Committee awarded Ted Mileham a certificate of commendation and the local newspaper published his photograph.

Constable Philip Salt achieved the double, both river and horse: Foundry Bridge in 1937 when he abandoned his traffic duty to leap into the river and save the life of a nine-year old boy, for which he was

NORWICH CITY POLICE

Certificate

THIS IS TO CERTIFY THAT
at a Meeting of the WATCH COMMITTEE
held on the eighteenth day of July, 194_
Police Constable No. 11 PHILIP SALT was highly commended
on the action he took when called to a house where a
woman gave birth to a child in the absence of a doctor or
a Midwife.

H.E.W.Ford
Chairman of the Watch Committee

J.H.Dain
Chief Constable

Constable Philip Salt, thrice commended at Watch Committee level, and a certificate of commendation. (M.Salt)

water to save a woman from drowning and duly received the Royal Humane Society certificate.

Sergeant John Wright entered the river from Foundry Bridge to save a man in 1955 and in addition to receiving the Royal Humane Society certificate he got 25s from the Watch Committee for his damaged watch.

1937 was seemingly a vintage year for police heroism and included two feats in which policemen leapt upon moving cars, actions that became nigh impossible in later years as car manufacturers dispensed with running boards. Constable Raymond Blowers occupied the running board of a stolen car, the driver of which had refused to stop, and brought the car to a standstill and the driver into custody and was duly commended. Then came a more violent incident.

During the evening of 3 July Sergeant Sidney Barrett was in a police car driven by Constable 'Paddy' Mulrenhan accompanied by Constable 'Chesty' Wright, in Dereham Road, stationary, lurking and looking. A Morris car was seen in Sweet Briar Lane (now Road) and was recognised as belonging to Mr Montague, a city dentist. Mr Montague was not driving the car. The value of local knowledge! The police car set off in pursuit.

The Morris driver did not want to stop for the police and went off at a fast speed into surrounding

awarded a Royal Humane Society certificate, and Charing Cross in 1946 when he stopped a bolting horse pulling a railway cart. In between, in 1941, he collected a Watch Committee certificate of commendation for promptly and efficiently assisting in the delivery of a child in a house in Sussex Street, action carried out in the absence of a doctor or midwife and during a bombing raid.

Another Foundry Bridge river rescue occurred in 1937. Constable William Baldry plunged into the

Sergeant Sidney Barrett and medals. The KPMG medal is to the right of his World War One medals, inscribed 'To Guard My People' and 'For Gallantry'. (J.Green)

The scene of the crash in Larkman Lane, looking towards the Dereham Road. This is the official police photograph taken shortly after the incident. (J.Green)

roads, eventually crossing the Dereham Road into Larkman Lane where the police car overhauled and forced the fugitive vehicle to stop long enough for Sergeant Barrett to leap onto the running board. He reached through the driver's window but was then compelled to do no more than hang on as the car accelerated away. The police car followed.

The Morris driver swerved to each side of the road in an attempt to dislodge the tenaciously clinging policeman, zig-zagging progress that crashed the car into a lamp standard and hurled the Sergeant into the road, at the same time bringing the car to a halt. The driver, Albert Cubitt, ran away but was caught and sat upon by an enraged 'Chesty' Wright. Cubitt later admitted 22 offences of taking motor vehicles without consent and was sentenced to three years penal servitude.

Sergeant Barrett suffered multiple injuries that included a broken leg. He was commended, received a Merit Badge and was awarded the King's Police Medal for Gallantry, a rare award and the only one received in the entire history of the force. Sidney Barrett retired in 1954 and died in 1957.

In 1939 Constable Robert Pearson tangled with a motor car on fire at Rose Lane by King Street. He tackled the blaze with a police car extinguisher and was still employing the extinguisher when the burning car rolled forward. He stopped and held the car, which then exploded as the flames reached the petrol tank. Constable Pearson was burnt on the hands and face. He was duly commended and received a Merit Badge.

Constables Andy Anderson and Peter Everest braved fire on the river for their certificates of commendation, awarded by the Society for the Protection from Fire. And they were off duty. In July 1952 they were enjoying a peaceful day boating on the river when they passed a stalled motor launch containing several persons, including a family with children. Several hundred yards past, nearing Surlingham Ferry, they heard an explosion and saw the stalled launch was on fire. Returning quickly, they braved the spreading fire and took on board all the panicking boat occupants before the vessel became engulfed in flames.

Those saved from the burning launch were never to know that Peter Everest was an ex-naval man who knew what it was like to see his vessel go down, cast into the water for more than 24 hours after a U Boat attack in World War Two. Neither did they know that their gratitude was not matched by the Chief Constable, Alan Plume, who expressed extreme displeasure because the officers modestly did not leave a report. He answered their plea that they were off duty with the retort that a policeman was never off duty.

Fire was the challenge to Constable Terry Moore, earning a certificate of commendation from the Watch Committee in 1963. Walking the beat in Colegate he was made aware of a house in flames, the fire quickly taking hold as a result of an accelerant used by one of the occupants. He entered the building and led and carried a family to safety and while in the building applied a tourniquet to a man with cut wrists. Nearly 100 years earlier, and not too far away, Constable Edward Chambers had rescued a drunken man from a smoke filled room at the Garibaldi Tavern in St Mary's and been awarded £2 by the Watch Committee.

Initiative and bravery appeared in many forms, the danger always real. In 1955 the Watch Committee commended Constable Terry Comer for rescuing a kitten from a tree.

The action of Constable Charlie Marten on 21 November 1956 received the award of the Carnegie Hero Fund certificate framed in oak, presented to him by the Lord Mayor, Mr Arthur South, who publicly praised his 'courageous act'. The courageous act was a race to save the life of a child seen to be sitting on a railway embankment, reported to Constable Marten while he was at the Cavell School. The child, only three

Charles Marten and the Carnegie Hero Award.　　(ECN)

THE · CARNEGIE **HERO** FUND · TRUST

FOUNDED　SEPT. 1908.

PRESENTED
BY THE TRUSTEES TO
Pol. Const. CHARLES H. MARTEN,
NORWICH,
IN RECOGNITION OF
HEROIC ENDEAVOUR
TO SAVE HUMAN LIFE
ON 21ST NOVEMBER 1956.

Dunfermline.　*Vrd AE unningham*　Chairman.
31st January 1957.　　　Secretary.

years of age, could be seen opposite the school playground but separated by a high wire-mesh fence. As the report was made to the Constable he saw the plume of smoke from an approaching train.

Calling for the boy to remain absolutely still Constable Marten furiously rode his cycle to the Mansfield Lane bridge, a point about 100 yards from the boy. As the train came into view he scaled the bridge parapet and at the same time the boy toppled down the embankment onto the railway line. The Constable's sprint along the track towards the boy was, as the Chief Constable later pointed out, extremely dangerous, for any trip or stumble would have seen the train upon them both. Constable Marten snatched the boy away with 25 yards to spare.

At the presentation ceremony the Chief Constable reported, 'In forwarding this award the secretary of the Trust intimated that the Carnegie Hero Fund trustees also decided to have the name of PC Marten inscribed on the illuminated Roll of Heroes of the Trust'.

Courageous action in the face of discovered crime earned Constables Alfred Turner and Douglas Ross commendations, and head injuries. Working a night time plain clothes patrol in Magdalen Street in 1958 they saw an intruder in a lock-up café. Constable Turner climbed through a window to apprehend what he could see only as a crouching figure and was then attacked from the side by a second intruder. In the fight that followed, joined by Constable Ross, Constable Turner was struck over the head with an iron bar, receiving a severe injury. It was abundantly clear that neither of the men surprised inside the café had any intention of 'coming quietly'. Constable Turner slowed the iron bar man by striking him with a chair and the fight moved outside the premises where the men were eventually overpowered, but not before Constable Ross had received a wound to his chin.

Percy Nicholls, the wielder of the iron bar, and Walter McDonnell, his accomplice, were later to say they only wanted to get away, something patently obvious to the officers. Nicholls was sent to prison for five years and McDonnell, the lesser man, was placed on probation.

Richard Dunphie was a criminal of a different order, a 'raffles' type jewel thief who included among his victims the Duke of Marlborough and the Duchess of Windsor. Jewels he confessed to stealing from the Duchess were valued at £20,000 in 1946, and later assessed as priceless. They were never found and stories were told that they were disposed of among Norwich dealers. What is certain is that Dunphie was jailed at Suffolk Assizes in October 1960 after admitting thefts totalling £90,000.

He did not stay in custody very long. Two days after sentence he escaped from Norwich Prison. The press report said, 'He is thought to have got away over the sports ground at Britannia Barracks'. This, ironically, was the place where police dog training took place and one senior police officer had recently gone on record as saying, 'There is a psychological advantage in choosing this training ground – the prisoners can see the dogs at work'. Dunphie had not been there long enough to see the dogs though they now turned out to look for him, Kim with Constable Stanley Nunn and Tiny with Constable John 'Taffy' Bounds.

The media, already sated by the daring exploits of Dunphie in aristocratic and royal circles, leapt upon the promptness and simpleness of his escape, raking over his only to recent court appearance and the charismatic calendar of crimes that put him there, also affording lurid detail to his 'scarlet pimpernel' disappearance. This was not going to be just another prison escape. The police gave press interviews, made public statements, carried out inquiring interviews and road checks, circulated information to other forces, and hoped that this already much publicised criminal did not assume undeserved fame. His published photograph, titled 'the wanted man' showed a bow-tied, good looking man with sleeked hair and a quizzical 'James Bond' look.

Dunphie did achieve an amalgamation of the city and county police forces. County officers were drafted into the search straight from a football match at Thorpe Recreation Ground where they had just finished beating the city police team 10-1 (the city police would point out it was their reserve team). Later, search teams responding to reported sightings in the county were composed of both city and county officers.

On 25 October 1960, five days after Dunphie's escape, with press and public interest still buzzing, a

Forestry Commission warrener walking in Thetford Forest saw a man sleeping in bracken near to the Mundford to Brandon road. He cycled to Mundford and told the wife of the village Constable and the Inspector at Methwold was informed. Inspector Churchyard and Constable Hooper drove to the spot and Richard Dunphie was woken and arrested. He was described as pale, tired, cold and hungry. It was reported that the Head of Norfolk CID, Detective Superintendent Tom Smith, went to the scene, shook Dunphie by the hand and said, 'Hello Richard'. An Eastern Daily Press reporter, also smartly in attendance, reported that Dunphie smiled at him. A car stolen from Swanton Morley was found nearby.

So ended the myth of the master criminal, the debonair, raffish, man-about-town who preyed upon the society of the rich and famous, and himself became, briefly, famous rather than infamous. Somehow he had lost the aura garnered from his illegal exploits in high society. He had made an impulsive, unplanned prison break and committed car theft and burglary to sustain his wayward progress across Norfolk before collapsing drained and starving into the cold, damp darkness of a Norfolk wood, and then into the clutches of county policemen making an easy arrest. But he did unwittingly forge a working relationship between officers from the city and county forces, to formally join together again in less than eight years time. And the city police did avenge the football match.

The publicity and potential embarrassment of the disappearance of a professional thief was within a few

Constable Stanley Nunn and Kim searching Mousehold for Richard Dunphie watched by the beat Constable, Velocette motor cyclist, Constable Derek 'Tug' Wilson. (ECN)

Police forces unite. Pictures reproduced from newspaper cuttings. City and county officers in the search for Dunphie are briefed at Reepham. Constable Ron Lingwood is in the centre, in wellington boots, and Constable Peter Tooke has hands on hips. Detectives Cyril Scott, also in wellington boots, and Douglas Ross and Alan Brown are to the right of the picture. GLT 1 is parked in the background. In the second picture city officers are queuing for refreshments. Detectives left to right are, Alan Brown, Douglas Ross, Cyril Scott and Roy Hipperson (centre). Uniformed Peter Tooke and Cliff Jessop are on the right. (ECN)

money barring £40. He had, he admitted, just helped himself.

Someone helped themselves to the antique china collection in the Strangers' Hall Museum in August 1963, breaking into the ancient building after climbing a wall at the rear. The importance of this crime was reflected in the personal attendance at the scene of the Chief Constable, Alan Plume, and the Head of Norwich CID, Detective Inspector Ted Smith. Three men were arrested, charged and convicted, but the china collection was not recovered: not until 1965

Detective Constable Ken Statham shows the recovered Stranger's Hall china to Curator Rachel Young for formal identification while Constables Ray Norton and Basil Kybird rejoice in the background. Another picture from a newspaper cutting. (ECN)

months matched by another case. This time the thief was strictly amateur and the embarrassment belonged to Norwich City Council, more specifically the City Treasurer's Office. £15,000 was missed from the official safe – easily missed because it should have contained £17,000. Also missing was a junior clerk, aged only 18 years.

The press headlines that followed the loss of this large sum of ratepayer's money made for uncomfortable reading in the City Hall, partly alleviated by the discovery of the missing clerk in Dorset with all the

when, to the delight of the Chief Constable and others in high circles, Detective Constables Ken Statham and Gordon London recovered the collection following 'long and patient enquiries' and 'weeks of observation far into the night'. The officers were commended for outstanding detective work and 'enquiries far into the night' became a meaningful and much used phrase in CID reports.

Crime was sometimes detected almost immediately in a fury of discovery, response, pursuit and capture – a sequence of unfolding drama that charged adrenalin and raised all the instincts of tally-ho and up and at them. This sudden and abrupt contrast with routine blurred time, boundaries and, sometimes, reasoning on both sides.

Big city criminals occasionally visited what they saw as the provincial land of easy money, the home of slow moving, tractor driving yokels; and came to grief on the rock of such supposition. Such a gang dropped through the skylight of Laurence and Scott's factory in Kerrison Road in October 1962. After cutting open three safes they were busy removing the £11,400 payroll when they were spotted climbing a gate by a Carrow Works' security man.

The three villains panicked, dropped wage packets over the road and drove off in the opposite direction to their second car, stashed in Argyle Street. They found the nearest A class road to take them out of the city and then went the wrong way, for them, travelling towards Great Yarmouth with three police forces ganging up against them, later four as the Suffolk Constabulary joined Norfolk, Great Yarmouth and Norwich. Another amalgamation.

The thwarted villains were further thwarted by the discovery that the road beyond Great Yarmouth led to the North Sea. They consequently raced to Lowestoft where the swing bridge was closed specially for them, and the police. Their car crashed into the barrier and they ran away leaving the remaining bags of wage packets. So ended the visit of the out of town gang, in full flight and empty-handed. One, a Londoner, found hiding under a Lowestoft caravan, dubbed the lookout man (obviously not a very good one), got four years in prison, another, arrested at his Leicester home, later to grumble, 'We were dead unlucky', got ten years preventive detention. The third was luckier. Much later a man was detained but not convicted.

A 1963 chase in Norwich involved local criminals who knew their way around but still failed to make it. A smash and grab raid was reported in the early hours of the morning at a jewellers in Magdalen Street. The suspect car was seen in Sweet Briar Road and pursued by a Wolseley police car, 'the mobile'. Radioed information alerted a CID van containing Detective Constable Gordon London, Constable Stan Limmer and Constable Taffy Bounds with Tiny the police dog. The CID van entered one end of Shorncliffe Avenue as

the pursued vehicle entered the other. Placing the CID van across the road seemed a good idea at the time.

The fleeing car rammed the CID van, throwing Gordon London into the road, clutching a suddenly insecure and still chattering vehicle radio, and Taffy Bounds out of the back. Stan Limmer and Tiny remained in the dented, metal ringing van, relatively uninjured though Tiny was clearly impressed by the upturn in noise and the sudden departure of his handler. In the absence of any instructions from his handler Tiny declined to pursue the fleeing perpetrators.

Gordon London and Taffy Bounds recovered from their injuries, Tiny went on to less noisy successes elsewhere, and two local criminals wasted their energy running away because they were on first name terms with most of the force and had already been identified.

The number one crime in the calendar of crimes occurring in the city police history was, of course, murder, invariably successfully investigated, though a case in 1851 was unsolved through initial investigation and had been consigned to history, until 1869 when things began to happen. Several ex-policemen found themselves delving into memory recesses; not entirely successfully.

It began when a dog rooting in undergrowth at Bracondale found a human hand, which was handed in at the police station by the dog owner. Other body parts were then found in the areas of Trowse, Bishopgate, St Augustine's and Hellesdon. The grisly collection included the hand and a foot, a leg, thigh and pelvic bones, various pieces of flesh, entrails and part of a breast. The Mayor issued the following public notice under the heading of 'Supposed Murder'.

'Several parts of a human body belonging to a person supposed to have been recently murdered, and to be that of a young female between the ages of 16 and 26 years, having been, within the last days, found in the environs of the city of Norwich, information is requested to be given to the Chief Constable, at the Police-office, Guildhall, Norwich, of all females who may have been recently missing, together with any particulars which may lead to the detection of the person or persons who committed such supposed murder. The portions of body already found comprise the right hand and foot and several bones with numerous pieces of flesh. Further search is making for the head and remaining parts of the body. Signed. H.Woodcock, Mayor.'

The police began receiving all manner of body parts handed in by a well meaning public, mostly that of domestic animals. The final human collection included both hands and feet and part of the backbone, but not the head. The body, such as it was, remained unidentified and was eventually buried in a vault in the Guildhall. The case faded from public attention and the police were left with speculation, for nearly 18 years.

On 1 January 1869 William Sheward walked into Walworth Police Station, London, and told an Inspector that he wished to charge himself with the wilful murder of his wife, Martha Sheward, in Norwich on 15 June 1851. He said he had cut up her body but the details were too horrible to talk about. He later, with the help of legal representation, decided not to talk about it at all and at his trial at Norwich Assize he pleaded 'Not Guilty' to murder.

The police retrieved the body parts from beneath the Guildhall for re-examination, or most of them for some were now inexplicably missing, as were various items of bloodstained clothing originally said to have been found nearby but now no longer recalled.

Witnesses of the yesteryear were hunted down and memories were put to test, particularly to the circumstances of William Sheward who had by now remarried, significantly perhaps to a woman he had known while his wife was alive.

William Sheward's advocate submitted to the court that Martha Sheward was not proven dead, was in fact 54 years of age (the Mayor's notice had, on medical advice, presupposed not older than 26), the body parts had not been identified (could have been the result of a medical student's dissection, advocate said,), the vital part – the head, had not been found, and not a spot of blood had ever been seen at his house in Tabernacle Street (near Bishopgate), on his clothes or possessions, or at his place of work, Christies the pawnbrokers in Orford Hill.

After a retirement of one hour and twenty minutes the jury found Sheward, 'Guilty'. In response to the inevitable sentence Sheward bowed to the Judge.

William Sheward became a milestone murderer because he was the first to be privately executed in Norwich, meeting the hangman at Norwich City Gaol out of sight of a morbid public. He took with him the secret of the whereabouts of his wife's head – it's still out there somewhere.

Dennis Moore was another murderer who gave himself up, telephoning Bethel Street Police Station in 1950 to report that he had just murdered his girlfriend. He was less than convincing in his call and the Station Sergeant was not impressed, guffawing to a colleague that he had a lunatic on the line. Nevertheless, a Constable was dispatched to meet Moore near Catton Grove Road. From there it became very real. Moore's 21-year-old fiancée, Eileen Cullen from Buxton Road, lay in a cattle shed in a field in Oak Lane, strangled and suffering from cuts to the neck, which a court would be told had been caused after death; after Moore had gone home to Woodcock Road to obtain a bread knife.

Moore also brought about a brief amalgamation between city and county forces, caused by an intense discussion as to whether Oak Lane was in the city or the county. It was found to be in the county.

In April 1951 Dennis Moore became another milestone murderer when he became the last person to be hung at Norwich Prison.

The arrest of double murderer Henry March at Wymondham in 1877 is worthy of mention, because the arresting officer, Sergeant John Scott, a member of the Norwich force, was not only outside his normal jurisdiction he was off duty. His action was rewarded with a merit badge and a gratuity of £3 from the Watch Committee.

The facts were simple. March battered his blacksmith workmate, Henry Bidewell to death and when his employer, Thomas Mayes, a local man well-respected and of some substance, intervened, dealt with him in a similar fashion. As news spread of the double tragedy, and the identity of the suspect, Sergeant Scott, on a purely social visit to the town, was guided by excited informants to March's house. He there detained March without difficulty.

In 1894 Sergeant Scott made another notable arrest outside the city, with difficulty. The *Eastern Evening News* recorded, 'The Norwich police are to be congratulated upon the manner in which the speedy capture of the prisoner was brought about'. The case was one of a lunatic without a hat.

Constable Henry Goldsmith stopped John Wilson in St Benedict's Street at quarter past two in the morning for the simple reason that Wilson was not wearing a hat, seemingly a matter of some suspicion in 1894. The Constable demanded to know where Wilson's hat was and was informed it had been lost, which was true. It had been left at Mountergate where, earlier, at half past one, Wilson had attacked a man and woman with a knife, inflicting severe head injuries upon the man. Constable Goldsmith did not have the benefit of modern communications and was unaware of the Mountergate assault. After some jousting dialogue he allowed Wilson to continue.

Constable Goldsmith, later to be Detective Sergeant and become one of the longest serving 19th-century officers (34 years), related his encounter when he returned to the police station and the hat found at Mountergate was promptly connected. A posse was formed, how many is unclear, but they included Detective Sergeant Slaughter and the redoubtable Sergeant Scott who, according to the press, 'procured a trap' and set out of the city on the Dereham Road. At nine o'clock that morning they found Wilson drinking in a public house at Hockering. He was arrested and taken to Norwich. The press reported that on the way he 'attempted to turn Sergeant Scott out of the trap'.

The press acclaimed the arrest, and their story was gilded by Wilson's antics in court. He called the Town Clerk (prosecuting) an 'old humbug', demanded that everyone speak up because he was 'greatly interested in the case', and told the injured witness giving evidence, 'If I come across you again I will take good care. I will not make half a job of it,' a statement that did not help his 'Not Guilty' plea. At the end of the hearing he swore at the Chairman in the 'most copious language'. Appreciation of the police became even greater when 'burly Constables' removed him from the dock.

The Magistrates committed Wilson to Norwich Assize where he was found unfit to plead and ordered to be detained during His Majesty's pleasure, the Judge remarking that he should not have been loose in the first place.

After the case of a lunatic without a hat came the case of the lunatic without a coat. George Daisley, not wearing a coat and carrying a basket, found himself the object of Constable 27 Jacob Southgate's attention in St Giles' Street just after midnight on 10 August 1899. Southgate wondered over the absence of the coat and asked to look into the basket. Daisley obliged and presented an agreeable manner, before running away.

The Constable took up the chase, which took an alarming turn when, near the junction with Willow Lane, Daisley turned and fired a revolver. The bullet went wide, later claimed by Daisley to have been fired in the air – a statement that must have been incontrovertibly true in any circumstance.

Detectives Edward Doe and Robert Chapman appeared and joined the chase, which culminated in Chapelfield Road when Daisley ran round the Drill Hall and was seized by Constable Patrick Connors. The revolver was found to be fully loaded.

Daisley could offer no coherent explanation for his actions; the basket was innocuous and the only clue was his two previous spells in a lunatic asylum: a third was in the offing.

Policemen checking late night citizens was not unusual in an age when night was different to day in more than just the degree of light, times when the blanket silence of empty streets was infringed only rarely by a homeward hastening pedestrian or swishing motor vehicle, or even a policeman's truncheon winging in pursuit of a scurrying rat. After the city force had gone, in name and procedures, a new age of nocturnal community behaviour took over. The one to one pavement confrontations of police and citizen in hollow surroundings gave way to prowling police vans overseeing groups of noisy, jousting revellers against an all-night background of pavement ringing footsteps, calling voices and revving traffic.

The night of 15-16 October 1963 saw a police check with a knock-on effect. Inspector Edward 'Butch' Gascoyne walked through Exchange Street and saw a young man at the corner of Lobster Lane apparently going no where in particular, just hanging around. He spoke to the man, this being the natural inquisitive instinct of a policeman faced with a listless citizen, and was informed the man was 'waiting for a mate', which was true.

Inspector Gascoyne went on his way. The city was settled, quiet, except for the furtive activity of three local men commissioned by an Exchange Street café owner to fire his premises for insurance purposes. He had not chosen wisely.

The three men and the café owner had earlier entered the café and deposited cans of petrol, the café owner then leaving, the lookout man taking up position and the remaining two conspirators sprinkling fuel on different floors. That they had sufficient petrol to burn down most of Exchange Street indicated thoroughness or unthinking recklessness, probably the latter because the café owner had only paid them £25 out of which they had to buy their own petrol.

The lookout man became an instrument of panic after his encounter with Inspector Gascoyne and fled, leaving his accomplices inside the café. On his way home he had a change of heart and stole a cycle to return to the scene, or at least nearby. He stopped in St Giles' Street to telephone the café owner to advise him that it had all gone wrong. (It hadn't, but it was about to.) Unfortunately for the panicking ex-lookout man

he dialled the wrong number and relayed his all gone wrong message to a bemused householder who had no idea what he was talking about. (Later he did, and gave evidence in court.)

Having primed the café owner, or believing he had, the failed lookout man returned to the café and met the other two who had poured petrol liberally around the premises. Outside the building, in the early hours of the morning, the prospective fire raisers found that they did not have a match and there was a significant delay while they found a cigarette lighter and some paper.

The admitted intention was to light the paper and thrust it through the pavement grille, letterbox or other suitable orifice of the now reeking café, and 'Spud', as he was colloquially known, shortly to be even better known, and the redundant lookout man strived for ignition. The other man, the oldest at 21-years of age, strolled away, luckily for him.

The lighter jostled into life and from then on indi-

News of the Exchange Street explosion. (ECN)

A curious public in Exchange Street closed to traffic. (A.Brown)

vidual recollections became hazy. The explosion took Spud across the street into the Corn Hall door and moved the ex-lookout man into the road under cascading debris. The front of the café spread outwards and succeeding floors dropped down to the cellar. Adjoining buildings collapsed.

By a quirk of circumstance the beat Constable was nearby, window shopping in London Street. The bang brought him hurrying into Exchange Street to find buildings in smoking ruins (later to be demolished and rebuilt), debris blocking the road (Norwich traffic lost the use of Exchange Street for several days) and, sprawled dazed and speechless in the wreckage, two scorched and tattered bodies.

A chastened lookout man was not badly hurt and was quickly discharged from hospital into the eager hands of the CID. Spud was in a more serious condition and lay in the West Norwich Hospital for several weeks in a rueful, blackened state that was not improved by the unsympathetic comments of guarding policemen. He also lost, along with his fellow fire raisers (the unscathed third was arrested at his home), three years of liberty.

The café owner contested the admissions of the three arsonists but a jury took 15 minutes to find him guilty. He was sentenced to six years imprisonment.

Death from a daytime confrontation. Wild animals were not an everyday occurrence, although this one was not wild in the fuller sense until it met the police in 1959. The coypu is a South American animal akin to a giant rat, and was introduced to Norfolk and much in evidence during the 1950s and 1960s. It was accused of causing damage to riverbanks and this led to a campaign of ruthless extermination. Occasionally they strayed along the river and caused consternation in the city. Children trapped this example in an alley off St George's Street, where it turned at bay. Members of the public informed the beat policemen in the picture, Constables John Pask, on the left, and Mike Henry, of the impasse and they dispatched the animal with truncheons. The news reporter holds the beast for the photographer's benefit. (ECN)

CHAPTER TEN
Last Days

Amalgamation, county and railway police forces, Crime Squads, police station extension, notable persons

EVENTUALLY it was to come: amalgamation, take-over according to some. Whatever it was called, or would turn out to be, the Norwich City Police was on terminal notice. It would look back with pride, forward with apprehension.

Rumours, rumblings, protests and speeches over possible amalgamation with the county force had fermented since the Government had set up a Royal Commission in 1962 to look into policing in the United Kingdom. Those with foresight saw the inevitable. Successive governments had sat uneasily with the concept of small police forces and a Royal Commission appeared to be the means to the end, and so it was. The Royal Commission recommended a massive reduction of individual police forces, to be achieved by a programme of amalgamations, preferably on a voluntary basis. A threatened alternative was a national police force.

The Norwich Watch Committee went to London in 1965 and stated their case for the Norwich City Police to remain as the police force for the city, and consequently for the committee to remain in existence, but it was an exercise in futility. They stoutly defended the status quo of one city and one police force but the national dictate prevailed. The Home Secretary, Roy Jenkins, told the Norwich Watch Committee to negotiate with their neighbours and told the world through the House of Commons on 18 May 1966. Norwich City, Great Yarmouth Borough and Norfolk Constabulary would become one force.

Mr F.P.C. (Peter) Garland, Chief Constable of Norfolk, was in the house for the announcement and said, 'It was very well received by both sides'. He was to become Chief Constable designate of the new force.

Frank Brown, Chief Constable of Norwich (he had succeeded Alan Plume in 1963), was not so sure. He

expressed disappointment and said he had hoped that Norwich would remain a separate force. He must have known that such a chance was remote. He declined the opportunity to become Deputy Chief Constable of the new force and retired with the end of the city police.

Alfred Nicholls, Chairman of the Watch Committee quite bluntly said, 'I take a very dim view of amalgamations'. He called it a 'shotgun union' and 'not in the best interests of the city'.

The idea of union between city and county was not new. In 1852 Superintendent Dunne had thought amalgamation a good idea. He was a lone voice and 100 years later most Norwich officers still viewed the prospect with anathema.

Not all city officers were averse to policing in the county. In 1843 Norwich Constables Hambling and Charlesworth offered their services to the county force. The city force learned of their action and dis-

missed them. Henry Hambling went on to become Superintendent at Wymondham.

In 1848 the Watch Committee noted that chief officers of the county and city were to arrange for a union for the 'next two months' for 'preventing and detecting robbers during winter season'.

Scares and threats of a permanent amalgamation existed long before it finally happened. In September 1942 a House of Commons Committee proposed to amalgamate forces 'where it is considered desirable', creating a storm of protest with strong criticism from MPs and municipal representatives. Chief Constables, some of whom were present at the committee meeting, were said to be 'perturbed'.

The wartime Home Secretary was given the power to 'make amalgamations of police forces for two or more areas if he is satisfied that it is necessary for facilitating naval, military or air force operations', a sword of Damocles that did not fall.

Police forces of all sizes were bolstered in times of emergency or special circumstance by a national system of mutual aid, demonstrated on more than one occasion during national coal strikes when Norwich officers travelled to the coalfields of the Midlands. On a more local level mutual aid could be found with Norwich officers assisting Great Yarmouth officers at the races, dealing with mods and rockers on the seafront, and in February 1953 assisting the Yarmouth and Norfolk forces after severe East Coast flooding. Ten Norwich officers were stationed at Yarmouth for three weeks to assist in flooding relief work. Mutual aid was donor aid rather than amalgamation, but it was a step over boundaries.

In 1952 Norwich officers joined Norfolk officers in a uniformed tribute at Sandringham House as King George VI's coffin was slowly taken to Wolfenden Station and in 1953 they travelled together to London to line the coronation route.

Norwich City and Norfolk County officers working at Great Yarmouth are thanked by Mrs Churchill, wife of the Prime Minister, for their work in combating the severe East Coast flooding of February 1953. The Chief Constable of Great Yarmouth, Charles Jelliff, accompanies her. Norwich officers in the picture are, left to right: Robert Chellis, Peter Everest, John 'Jock' Lester (shaking hands) and Johnnie Johnson.

(J.Johnson)

Off to see the Queen. Norwich and Norfolk policemen prepare to travel to London for the coronation of Queen Elizabeth II in 1953. The Chief Constable of Norwich, Alan Plume (right), and the Deputy Chief Constable of Norfolk, Leonard 'Jumbo' King, run their eyes over the city contingent which comprises, left to right, Sergeant Dudley Brook, Special Constable Jeff Bostock, Constables Philip Hemmings, Brian Rowett, Jimmy Downes, Bill Nicholson, Stanley Nunn, Herbert Burton, Don Hooper, Ted Bloomfield, Johnnie Johnson and Ronnie Lingwood. (ECN)

Contact was regularly made between the constituent forces of the county for operational and ceremonial purposes (four Norfolk forces became three in 1947 when Kings Lynn was absorbed into the county force). Not infrequently it was the satisfied announcement that a problem experienced in one force area was the territorial responsibility of the neighbour, and would they like to deal with it. Apocryphal stories are told of bodies found in the River Yare floating inconveniently on the side of the discovering force, then prodded over to the far side, and another jurisdiction, followed by an appropriate telephone call.

The county force had a lot of space and thinly-spread manpower and not uncommonly asked Norwich officers to 'pop over' the border and deal with an incident because the county officer was too far away. Great Yarmouth officers will similarly testify to these requests, especially to the number of accidents they dealt with on the Acle straight – in the county.

A pointer to future co-operation and amalgamation came in 1964. Regional Crime Squads were formed to combat wider ranging criminals. Nine regions were established within the country, forces in each region contributing officers and finance. These detective officers moved freely across force boundaries, sometimes disconcerting forces slow to appreciate a new age of authorised and unannounced intrusion.

The Norwich office of No 5 Regional Crime Squad was set up in portakabins at the rear of County Police Headquarters in Thorpe Road headed by Detective Inspector Ronnie Farman, a Norwich officer. The county force supplied two Detective Sergeants, Great Yarmouth a Detective Constable and the Suffolk Constabulary a Detective Constable.

In 1965 the city force recognised the value of the new squad, a stated view that had much to do with Norwich CID unearthing a complicated and time-consuming case of car ringing. The anticipated over employment of the Norwich CID on one case and the perceived under employment of the new Regional Crime Squad, particularly, it was thought, on behalf of the Norwich force, was noted. A telephone call was made.

It was true the Regional Crime Squad spent its early days looking for work and selling itself to the constituent forces, carrying out surveillance on haystacks hoping that the one being watched that night was the target for those who liked to light up the countryside. The first squad men (women were drafted in later – history repeating itself) were underused and misapplied in comparison with the better equipped and more strongly staffed squads that were to follow, yet they were capable and effective within their early scope of operations. They sold themselves by helping forces inhibited by custom and tradition. And Norwich, as inhibited as any, needed help: according to the telephone call.

A car stolen from Norwich had been recovered from Bury St Edmunds with a new identity and was clearly the first of many stolen in a pattern of such losses in Norwich. Thieves were waiting to be arrested and a large number of doctored cars recovered, from all over the county, maybe the country. The case was transferred to the new Regional Crime Squad with alacrity.

The Chairman of the Watch Committee, Alfred Nicholls, apprised of the car ringing case, drily commented that the only ringing he was aware of involved pigeons. But the Watch Committee, nearing the end of its life in 1966, found time to issue another certificate of commendation, to Detective Constable Maurice Morson – loaned to the Regional Crime Squad with the car ringing case to preserve the equilibrium of the city CID.

The city police may have moved a daunting, time-consuming investigation but it still had to pick up the bill, and the responsibility, for the safe custody of 16 cars containing false identities and the subject of disputed ownership, required as evidence in criminal and civil proceedings. The force hired a corporation building at the Westwick depot and Detective Constable Morson is seen reflecting upon the security of the non-police premises. The 19 Beat man found he had more door handles and windows to examine on his already exhausting round of scheduled property checks. Today, such a case would not cause any internal consternation, or warrant an historic reference. (R.Bass)

In 1966 the Government had not only declared its hand it was intent upon enforcing it. The Home Secretary was not going to tolerate delaying tactics. He hoped that the voluntary amalgamation schemes would be in operation by April 1967. He made this very plain.

The Norwich Watch Committee complained that they had been given insufficient time to enter into talks. They were given an extension of time but the Home Secretary told the Association of Municipal Corporations that if its members did not begin the process of amalgamation to achieve a union by April 1967 it would be imposed upon them by April 1968. The Vice-Chairman of the Norwich Watch Committee, Mrs Jesse Griffiths, thought this was a 'short step to a police state'.

The mood in Norwich, police and public, was not rapturous. Some of its serving officers continued to speak of a takeover and were only slightly mollified by the promise that they would not be posted outside the new city division into the awesome world where, according to stories, pig licences and diseases of animals abounded; and the streetlights, where they existed, went out at midnight! Those who wanted promotion would find that travel broadened the mind and fuelled ambition.

The Norfolk Constabulary was already established within the city, geographically. At the turn of the century they occupied a building in Castle Meadow adjacent to the Shirehall, moving to Thorpe Road in 1926 and locating their force headquarters on one side of the road and their divisional headquarters on the opposite side. County officers policing the Norwich dormitory areas were compelled to visit Thorpe Road on various occasions, notably pay-day, when they could be seen ponderously riding their monster like cycles through the city. They were known to maintain

a serious decorum while riding through city territory, solemnly exchanging greetings with city beat men in a regular formulaic manner. The tone was measured, without humour, on both sides.

'Morning, city!'

'Morning, county!'

So they passed, guardians of the law with nothing more to say.

Other changes were afoot in 1966, an unpopular year all round. Traffic Wardens appeared on the streets of Norwich and they found a new use for car windscreen wipers.

Traffic Wardens were supposed to save, restore or enhance the police image, depending on where you viewed it presently to be, hopefully returning the man on the beat to the 'aren't our police wonderful' era. It

Brothers-in-law. The city's image of the county force. These stalwarts of the rural scene are photographed in 1927 at Castle Acre during the farm strike, protecting a strikebreaking farmer. (ECN)

The railway police operated within the city at Thorpe, Victoria and City Stations and at related splinter holdings. Thorpe Station was opened in 1844 and originally policed by four Norwich Constables on behalf of the Norfolk Railway Company, with the Watch Committee unsuccessfully trying to get the company to foot the bill. In 1846 four men were sworn in as railway Constables for Thorpe Station plus one for the Wensum Swing Bridge, but the city force remained committed to the station for a long time. Norwich Police Orders of 1894 state, 'When on duty on Rose Lane beat to attend at Thorpe Railway Station on the arrival and departure of all trains'. This order must have lapsed with increasing trains, other commitments for the beat Constable, and the appearance of the railway company's own police. The British Transport Police appeared in 1947 following nationalisation of public transport. In the above photograph railway Constable William Hughes guides the VIP car past a cheering crowd at Thorpe Station. This photograph is attributed to the visit of Prime Minister Stanley Baldwin and his wife in May 1929, during the General Election campaign.
(C.Roe)

was said that the enforcement of parking regulations prevented the police investigating crime, antagonised the public and made police officers unpopular. It was believed that a new community liaison would be fostered by giving this task to a body of people everyone could dislike from the outset.

A new age of policing was arriving, irrespective of any amalgamations. More vehicles, better communications. Pillarphones and that beckoning scintillating light were doomed by the gradual introduction of personal radio sets, adding to the weaponry of the man

Proud memories! A pride of city police at the Great West Door of the Cathedral c.1929. Left to right Constables Ernest Spalding, George Tubby, Sergeant Jesse Mayes and Constable John Burton.
(A.Brown)

An amalgamation of men and machines. Another shot of the city and county forces joining together at the 1947 Royal Norfolk Agricultural Show at Keswick, integration proved by the display of five motor cycles when the city force did not possess that number. Norwich Constables in the picture are, first left, Wolseley driver, Lennie Coadwell; fourth from left, with helmet, Frank North; fifth from left, motor cyclist, Thomas 'Paddy' Mulrenhan; sixth from left, with helmet, George Piercy; seventh from left, motor cyclist, John Burton. The Inspector, far right, is Alec Doe. (C.Fisk)

The common denominator in this photograph is the Police Federation, an organisation, begun in 1919, representing the welfare of all ranks up to Inspector. An early failure was their attempt to persuade the Chief Constable to rescind split (four-hour) shifts. An early success was obtaining the right for an off-duty officer to leave the city without first obtaining permission. The federation viewed amalgamation with a wary resignation arising from their ineffective voice in the higher politics involved. Each of the three ranks of Constable, Sergeant and Inspector had a branch board, to collectively meet and represent all members. But they did not always agree. There was a period when the Constables and Sergeants were at odds with the Inspector's board and consequently found themselves ignored. This c.1944 photograph of federation representatives probably denotes a united front greeting to assess the new Chief Constable and let him know the state of the force, from the federation's viewpoint. Left to right, standing: Sergeants Alfred Wheatley and Francis 'Jimmy' James, Constables Raymond Blowers and John 'Blondie' Williams, Inspector Herbert Docwra, Sergeants Edward 'Shots' Foulger and Harry Rix and Constable John Calver (died in service in 1945). Seated: Sergeant Arthur 'Tishy' Collins, Detective Inspector John Watling, Chief Constable Alan Plume, Inspector Alec Doe (Chairman of the Board), Frank Price representing the Special Constabulary, Detective Constable Ronnie Farman, Inspector Hugh Murray and Constable George 'Jocky' Moll. It is of interest that the first Norwich Joint Branch Board Chairman in 1919 was Inspector Edward Doe, father of Alec Doe. (A.Rix)

1966 and Traffic Wardens prepare to take to the streets for the first time. Inspector Albert Turner briefs them outside Bethel Street Station. (ECN)

And women came too. Women were accepted as wardens almost from the start, unlike the beginning of police and specials. Seen being briefed in 1966 by Constable Basil Kybird are the first women wardens, left to right: Mildred Hayward, Joy Barnard and Betty Mann.The location is the Civil Defence training centre in Cattlemarket Street – Civil Defence ambulances in the background. (B.Kybird)

on the beat; but nothing compared to the ironmongery carried by the fluorescent yellow officer of the modern day. Old sweats looked suspiciously upon the issue of metal contraptions that represented the latest thing in 'walkie-talkie' radios, recalling the solitude of a bygone age on the beat, the old time exposure to bad weather, the use of cycle clips and the value of clips round lug'oles.

Amidst this period of change the Norwich Watch Committee met with the Great Yarmouth Watch Committee and the Norfolk Constabulary Police Authority to discuss the constitution and details of the new force, as indigestible as they were to most if not all the parties concerned. On 5 August 1966 they announced they were unable to agree on a title. Norfolk Constabulary was definitely out because it would project the message of a takeover by the county force, something that particularly irked Norwich. (In 1974, after injured feelings had time healed, the new force became the Norfolk Constabulary.)

On 10 October the Watch Committee suggested the title of Norfolk and Norwich Police Force. This fell on stony ground and on 18 November 1966 they met and formally accepted the name of Norfolk Joint Police, thoroughly disliked by nearly everyone who had to become a part of it. The Watch Committee then resignedly went on to debate Frank Brown's complaint of the inadequacy of the new pocket radios – too few and of poor quality. The pillarphone was not done for yet.

Some city officers anticipated amalgamation and moved over to the county force ahead of time. Some moved the other way, into the city. Promotion was the spur. And it was all going to happen anyway. Vacancies within the adjoining force offered opportunity to the ambitious, and the powers-that-be were anxious to achieve some early integration.

Detective Chief Inspector Reg Lester transferred to Norwich from Walsall in 1965, went to the Norfolk Constabulary in 1967 on promotion to Detective Superintendent and Head of the Force CID and, upon amalgamation, was promoted to Detective Chief Superintendent.

Woman Police Sergeant Claire Petty transferred to Norwich from Yorkshire, taking over from Eileen Craik in 1966, and went to the Norfolk Constabulary as an Inspector on 31 March 1967.

1967 was the year of anticipation, of knowing for certain, of regret and longing for what had gone – and in some cases had no right to come back. The greatest loss was undeniably going to be the pride of a force attached to a city, a force in which every member knew every brick and building and raised the flag of local knowledge in every case that came its way. In 1967 that view was regularly expressed.

Preparations for the declared day of 1 January 1968

included the winding up of the Sports and Social Club Fund. The proceeds were distributed to members with at least one city officer muttering darkly that they would not fall into the hands of the county. This action conjures up visions of the army commander destroying ciphers and documents before surrendering to an advancing enemy.

The new Norwich police (division instead of force) were destined to operate from an extended police station. In 1960 HM Inspector of Constabulary, Commander Willis, commented on the insufficiency of police accommodation. This caused the City Architect to produce plans for extending the Bethel Street frontage. The Council deferred the plans but promised to consider the possibility of utilising space in the Guildhall: progress in a circle – the police coming back to where they started, except that it did not happen. The force had already been allowed the use of disused buildings in Bethel Street and St Peter's Street, employed as inadequate stores for found (or lost depending on viewpoint) property, mostly cycles, and

which, through dust and creaking woodwork, threatened the welfare of every officer who ventured inside. To HM Inspector of Constabulary this did not count as measurable progress.

Commander Willis said at his 1961 inspection that he was concerned. When HM Inspector of Constabulary is concerned on the same point two years running it is serious. The Government grant to the Council of the proportional cost of the police force was dependent upon the Inspector's report.

In December 1961 plans for the station extension and an underground garage were approved, to start early in 1963; but the contract was not awarded until 1965. Colonel Sir Eric St Johnston, HM Chief Inspector of Constabulary, officially opened the new building on 11 October 1967, catching the tail-end of the force. At the official opening the departing Chief Constable, Frank Brown, said, 'You may find that policing in this city in the near future may be completely different. But it is not the fault of amalgamation or the new Chief Constable or anyone'.

And so the end. 1 November 1967 and Chief Constable Frank Brown (left) on his last working day in the force is accompanied by HM Inspector of Constabulary, Mr S.E.Peck, on the last inspection of the force. They are seen visiting the Crime Prevention Department in the new extension and speaking to Sergeant Basil Kybird. (B.Kybird)

The approaching end of this force chronology provokes thoughts of what has been pertinent and yet been missed from this account. Some detail is inevitably missing, but overall the picture is there. Hopefully it is a fair and unbiased picture. Looking over nearly 132 years of the Norwich City Police it is easy to see the credits and report on success and triumph, to congratulate and enthuse or just comment and commend, despite what may be described as a shaky start. The early force can be described as unruly, unreliable, untrained and ill-disciplined, which is unfair to the disciplined, honest and zealous men that did exist, many of whom remain anonymous within this history of the force. And is it fair to comparatively judge standards centuries apart?

The 19th-century picture of early police is perhaps unsurprising in a socially deprived society where corruption and class distinction were easily found, in some cases glaringly evident. Watch Committees and Magistrates of those times do not always stand out as paragons of honesty and beacons of public service. There are pointers to self-interest, nepotism and a sense of the passive when the positive was required. To those who served as police, Magistrates or members of the Watch Committee, and railed against the apathy and self-interest of colleagues goes the praise and credit for the integrity of the system that did evolve.

Irregularity, or alleged irregularity, has the greater impact as the force is the smaller – a theory of inverse ratio difficult to dispute. Edgar Dain was another scandalised Deputy Chief Constable and he was in a difficult position. He had arrived from Brighton on promotion to Inspector and Chief Clerk (having not long been promoted to Sergeant) on the express recommendation of his father, the Chief Constable. The Watch Committee minutes noted that, in the opinion of the Chief Constable, there was nobody already within the force capable of doing that job: hardly a passport to popularity for the new man or a declaration of confidence in the force. And he became a talking point when he crashed his car in an area policed by the county force, following which, according to those with an interest, no record was to be found of the accident, despite he and his passenger, Constable Bellamy, being hospitalised, the latter with serious injuries.

Deputy Chief Constable Edgar Dain might therefore have expected little support when he was the subject of inquiry in 1957 over his private life, a chapter of events that led him to divorce and remarriage, matters that would not attract the same attention today. The Chief Constable, Alan Plume, took it upon himself to speak to the force, or a fair number of them, personally, in the parade room, on the subject of morality. This went down very badly, thought to be pompous and unnecessary by those listening.

The force, or again a fair number, mounted a petition supporting Edgar Dain, believing him to have been hounded. It was presented to the Chief Constable and had as much success as the one presented to Robert Hitchman over 60 years previously. In fact it recoiled when the signatories were paraded through the Chief Constable's office and admonished for daring to present such a document. There is some evidence that the Home Office was not pleased at a petition in the force and contacted the Chief Constable to discuss the subject.

Edgar Dain, originally suspended, was reinstated without disciplinary proceedings, but he was fated. He found enduring unpopularity through his legacy of what became known as the 30-year rule, created when he sought permission to serve beyond this term, normally granted: refused in his case. The Watch Committee may have obtained some Hodges' type satisfaction from this decision but they had set a precedent and Superintendent Bernard Tester, and others following him, who would have expected by earlier precedent to be allowed to continue serving, found, after much publicity and appeal, that they were compulsorily retired.

Edgar Dain, like his father, made his mark on the force, though not quite in the same way; but he was handicapped, as others have been, by having a famous father. He, unlike Superintendent Hodges, did have some supporters.

Credit has been given to the magnificent achievement of John Henry Dain in setting up and running the Norwich Lads' Club, applauded on an international front yet unrecognised by appropriate honour within his own country. A view has been expressed from people of that time that his dedication to the club and his allocation of on-duty policemen to its daily working counted against him and explained the absence of a knighthood. An early example of police dedicated to community relations or a misapplication of police resources? Today the answer would be clearer.

There are others who are deserving and should not escape this historical account.

Inspector Alec Doe served from just after World War One to several years after World War Two and his father and grandfather served in the force before him, taking the family police line back to 1863. Alec Doe was the instigator and champion of the Sports and Social Club, a prime mover in the Police Federation and a volunteer historian for the force. His records and attention to detail and his pride in the force have contributed to the contents of this book.

Sam Bussey was part of another police family. He was a Sergeant when the police and fire brigade went their separate ways and he elected to become a member of the new National Fire Service. He was a Senior Company Officer in the brigade when he was killed in the German bombing raid in April 1942, leaving a wife and two young sons. His wife, Norah, joined the police auxiliaries (pictured chapter six) and his son Eric, six years old at the time of his father's death, grew up to join the Norwich City Police, retiring from the newly-constituted Norfolk Constabulary with the rank of Chief Inspector.

Sergeant William (Billy) Kemp was the popular Road Safety Officer of the 1940s and 1950s, internationally known and respected. His tireless and selfless work establishing and pioneering a new and desperately necessary post within the force made him a model of good public relations. Tragically he lost his own son to a road accident yet went on with inexhaustible energy to promote the cause of road safety throughout Norwich, becoming a father figure to schoolchildren as he lectured, demonstrated and filmed to reveal the dangers of modern traffic. How many lives did Billy Kemp save?

Memorable people in the life of the city police were not all police. Others unglamorously impinged and are remembered with less than affection, though time gives a more tolerant view. Others are more fondly recalled through the rosy mist of nostalgia.

The visiting Rector was an example of what you see is not what you get. Originally setting foot in Bethel

Street Police Station on the basis of a professed friendship with Inspector Edgar Dain, he gravitated to the canteen and there regaled astonished officers with a series of vulgar anecdotes and jokes. This was only the start. He found reasons for a number of return visits, usually homing straight into a group of policemen to expound his latest repertoire of foul stories the content of which would have shamed any Army barracks. An early warning system and avoidance policy reduced his audiences.

The CID practised a similar policy in the 1960s on behalf of an elderly lady of sweet and gushing disposition who, while casting conversational pleasantries around the police station, had a particular affection for detectives. News from the front enquiry office that she was in the building was guaranteed to empty the CID office. Two particular members of the CID were exceptions to the general exodus and would conversationally accommodate the lady. Her visits stopped suddenly, the reason for which became obvious when two CID men found themselves named in a will.

Jack Grigglestone was another visitor, a name known to the police and many others throughout the city in the 1950s and 1960s. Jack frequently attended the station in the clutches of the beat Constable as a drunk and disorderly prisoner, though he was never violent, just lively. His late night middle of the road dancing performances were for the benefit of the beat Constable and were often supported by malicious damage, depending upon where the empty bottle landed – only thrown when he was sure the policeman was looking. If there was no policeman available Jack found one by going to the police station. His request for a bed for the night was a formality. He would be refused and told to go away, which he did, across Bethel Street to throw his shoe through a shop window. He would then cheerfully return to the desk and repeat his request. The shoe throwing ritual reached a point where a suffering shopkeeper approached the police to ask if Jack could be steered towards a different shop.

Some of those who regularly came into contact with the city force are memorable for more commendable reasons. Such was Captain William Green, a man not easily missed and a familiar sight in the city, well-known to the beat Constables most of whom knew only vaguely of his distinguished military and police history.

The impeccably uniformed, bemedalled Captain could be seen striding through the city, his body held erect in military bearing, as if on a parade ground, a wide brimmed Mounties type Stetson set above dark glasses on a firmly set face. The unfamiliar uniform would be spotless, sharply creased, drawing the eyes of passers-by. With firm step and sharp voice he would acknowledge the presence of the beat Constable with the greetings of the day. At a pedestrian crossing covered by a traffic supervising Constable he would stand to attention on the pavement, waiting, then, in obedience to the crossover signal, march across and salute the Constable, offering at the same time a brisk 'Thank you, officer'. For those who wondered, the uniform was that of a Captain in the Legion of Frontiersmen. And the medals? How many recognised the George Medal?

William Green was born in Great Yarmouth in 1894. In World War One he served in the 7th Queen's Own Hussars following which he tried to join the police force. His lack of height caused him to be rejected. He then joined a police force that was unconcerned over height – the City of Bombay Police. He served in the mounted branch and had a successful career, which ended in Bombay harbour on 14 April 1944 – the day the SS *Fort Stikine*, laden with explosives, caught fire. The first explosion caused him to mount a rescue operation in the harbour and when the second, mighty, explosion occurred he received severe injuries which included being blinded in one eye, deafened in one ear and the fingers of one hand shattered. Undeterred, he continued his rescue operation, organising and swimming to the aid of many of the injured. Five hundred people were killed in the explosions and a square mile of Bombay was flattened. William Green was awarded the George Medal for outstanding policemanship, courage and devotion to duty.

Captain William Green returned to the United Kingdom in 1948 and served as a Special Constable and with the Civil Defence. He remained unwavering in his support and appreciation of Norwich police officers until the day he died, aged 99 years.

December 1967 was a harsh month with blizzards arriving and the Norwich City Police going. There was no official farewell; no parades or blazing publicity aroused by Watch Committee speeches of the captain going down with the ship. Like the beginning it was seemingly no big deal, except in the canteen, where city officers crouched over sandwiches forecasting a future of rurally influenced disaster.

There was one ceremony to mark the passing, held at St Peter Mancroft on Sunday, 17 December. The force padre, the Vicar of St Peter Mancroft, the Reverend Bill Westwood, officiated. At this service of commemoration, extended by public invitation to the citizens of Norwich, the Vice-Chairman of the Watch Committee, Mrs Jesse Griffiths, read the lesson.

Everything was cut and dried. Appointments in the new force had been made, formally announced and publicised. It was now a case of looking forward. In January 1968 keen observers would notice, among more blizzards, new badges on police helmets and the less keen could not fail to notice blue and white Hillman Imps zipping around the streets; but otherwise it was going to be business as usual. Anticipation was muted, dulled by the inevitable. Officers about to change from Norwich City into Norfolk Joint talked of history and, with the pessimism peculiar to the police service, spoke gloomily of the future. Some of them would find their careers prospering very nicely in the new force.

Among the new appointments was the chairman of the new combined police authority. Alfred Nicholls was not going down with any ship, or Watch Committee, because he was appointed to this post. If it was intended as a shrewd move to dilute his criticism of amalgamation it failed. He continued to voice his doubts from his new position and remained a staunch opponent to the end of his political career.

The last weekend of the force was testing. After a period of many years without a murder to investigate, since Dennis Moore's telephone call in 1950, a murder was reported at the very end, in the early hours of the last day, Sunday 31 December 1967. City officers went to Stevenson Road where Manual Gonzalez, a Spanish national who kept a watch and clock stall on Norwich Market, had been battered to death after a card game dispute. Donald MacLennan was arrested and charged with his murder. In terms of crime the Norwich City Police went out with style.

Officers assembled at Bethel Street Police Station, in the recently completed extension, on 19 September 1967. This was not a normal shift parade, evidenced by the caps outnumbering helmets. It is possibly the last picture of the Norwich City Police on parade. An eight-year-old girl had been reported missing from Shorncliffe Avenue and the force feared the worst. Leave was cancelled, officers were recalled to duty and search and house to house enquiry teams were formed, and briefed. The briefing officer is Chief Inspector John 'Jakey' Southgate (later Chief Superintendent and no relation to the Southgates of earlier chapters though his father, Cecil, did serve in the city force from 1915 until 1945, retiring with Sergeant rank). The Constables in this picture were to experience mixed fortunes within the new force, just over three months away. They include, in front, left to right: Peter King and Stan Wilson wearing caps; John Oliver with helmet (to tragically die in service in 1978); Ken Greer, with cap (not long after to be dismissed from the new force); Robin Brooks, with cap; Brian Butcher, with helmet (to become Superintendent in the new force and author of the history of the Norfolk police) and Peter Robinson and Brian 'Passey' Huckle, wearing caps. In the back row, wearing caps, are Harry Thompson (between Brooks and Butcher), and, framed by the window, Bob McLaren who became a member of the Traffic Department of the new force and was tragically killed when his police car crashed in Martineau Lane. The missing girl was found safe and well.

(ECN)

Sensitivity and sensibility rivalled each other in the prelude to change. But was there truly a case for one force? Had the world, and more particularly traffic and the criminal, moved on to leave the smaller police forces operating at a disadvantage, working with limited resources in a narrow perspective? The United States has a myriad of small police forces, many of which are minuscule, strange in a country that boasts of everything being so big.

The author cannot presume to quarrel with an exhaustive Royal Commission or the increasing demands upon the police apparent in the 1960s, more so later, neither does this historical narrative seek to impose an opinion. If one is detected through the many shades of grey surrounding this contentious issue then so be it. It was not deliberately projected. The purpose of this book was to dwell upon history and present the facts as they have been recorded and discovered. Irony can be found in another Royal Commission, that of 1835 which looked into rural policing and led to the formation of the Norfolk Constabulary in 1839.

At the last Watch Committee meeting in December 1967 Alfred Nicholls said that he regretted amalgamation. He thanked all city police officers for their past service and wished them well in their new force. On 1 January 1968 the Norwich City Police was no more.

New car; new system; new force! The emblem of the end. The story of the Norwich City Police goes no further. (ECN)